90 0600706 1

GW00383989

DVD Authoring with Adobe Encore DVD

Charles Seale-Hayne Library

University of Plymouth

(01752) 588 588

LibraryandITenquiries@plymouth.ac.uk

Computer software to accompany this item can be found inside the back cover. Please check contents on issue and return

DVD Authoring with Adobe Encore DVD: A Professional Guide to Creative DVD Production and Adobe Integration

Wes Howell

ELSEVIER

AMSTERDAM • BOSTON • HEIDELBERG • LONDON
NEW YORK • OXFORD • PARIS • SAN DIEGO
SAN FRANCISCO • SINGAPORE • SYDNEY • TOKYO

Focal Press is an imprint of Elsevier

Focal
Press

Focal Press is an imprint of Elsevier
200 Wheeler Road, Burlington, MA 01803, USA
Linacre House, Jordan Hill, Oxford OX2 8DP, UK

Copyright © 2004, Elsevier Inc. All rights reserved.

No part of this publication may be reproduced, stored in a retrieval system, or transmitted in any form or by any means, electronic, mechanical, photocopying, recording, or otherwise, without the prior written permission of the publisher.

Permissions may be sought directly from Elsevier's Science & Technology Rights Department in Oxford, UK: phone: (+44) 1865 843830, fax: (+44) 1865 853333, e-mail: permissions @elsevier.com.uk. You may also complete your request on-line via the Elsevier homepage (http://elsevier.com), by selecting "Customer Support" and then "Obtaining Permissions."

∞ Recognizing the importance of preserving what has been written, Elsevier prints its books on acid-free paper whenever possible.

Library of Congress Cataloging-in-Publication Data
Application submitted.

British Library Cataloguing-in-Publication Data
A catalogue record for this book is available from the British Library.

ISBN: 0-240-80563-1

For information on all Focal Press publications
visit our website at www.focalpress.com

04   05   06   07   08   09   10   9   8   7   6   5   4   3   2   1

Printed in the United States of America

University of Plymouth Library

Item No. 9006007061

Shelfmark 006·696 HOW

Contents at a Glance

Introduction

The Information Age is about more than just new technology. It's about empowering individuals with the tools to bring their ideas to the world. For years, money has decided who gets heard and who doesn't. Now that tide is turning. We are beginning to see that the common man isn't so common after all.

The advent of the compact disc ushered in a new era for music. New artists could create their own CDs without a recording contract. Now it's the filmmaker's and even the hobbyists' turn to enjoy the benefits of digital technology. DVD offers a new experience to the audience, with special features, increased quality and navigation not offered by VHS. DVD, however, had one major stumbling block—the elaborate DVD spec. In its initial stages DVD authoring was both complicated *and* expensive. Fortunately, new DVD authoring applications such as Encore have made DVD authoring intuitive and inexpensive, bridging the gap between thought and execution.

Whether you are just putting your home movies together, or creating an unparalleled multimedia experience for your customers, Encore provides the means to unleash your imagination without wasting too much time on tedious technical concerns.

Book Overview

The intent of the book is not only to provide valuable reference material, but also to introduce Encore using a project-based workflow. If you're a beginning author using Encore for the first time, it's recommended that you start at the beginning and work your way from cover to cover.

If you're an experienced DVD author and you wish to dive right into the intricacies of Encore, feel free to start with Chapter 4, Building the Project. This project will provide solid fundamentals and will get you comfortable with the application very quickly. You can always peruse the first three chapters as needed.

You'll find tons of screenshots, reference information, and tips and tricks to help you get the most out of Encore. If you're looking for specific information, the index provides quick access to topics of interest.

This book would not be complete if it didn't cover integration between Adobe applications, especially Photoshop. Photoshop has long been the graphics program of choice for the majority of DVD authors. In Chapter 5, you'll see how the new integration and interactivity can save you time and money and empower you creatively.

Many users will also be using Adobe Premiere and After Effects. Premiere is a perfect application for managing assets and preparing content, while After Effects excels at creating motion graphics. We'll cover these issues in Chapters 6.

If you're a seasoned Adobe user, you'll certainly appreciate and benefit from the familiarity between applications. If you're using other software, don't worry, many of the concepts will remain the same and you'll be able to develop an efficient workflow regardless of the tools you choose.

The final two chapters, 7 and 8, focus on finishing touches, advanced features and output considerations.

Projects

This book includes several projects that illustrate the various features of Encore.

Project 1 starts in Chapter 4. It's nothing fancy, but it will illustrate some key concepts in a quick and concise manner. We'll import assets, run through several of the main windows inside Encore, and build our first working project. This project will cover the interface and basic behaviors of working with imported graphics, creating text, buttons, and a menu. It will also provide the first peek into the layer structures and conventions used to create menus and buttons.

This project does not simply show you how to modify existing menus and button templates. This subject is already covered quite well in the Encore *Users Manual* and help files. The intention was to go one step beyond templates, to show more of what can and can't be done inside Encore. Once you complete the project, you will have a better understanding of Encore from a nuts and bolts perspective, and you will feel more confident about making your own menus and buttons. (We're doing this for your own good!) At this point, you'll understand templates better and you'll be able to start adding your own to the Library palette.

Several smaller projects are scattered throughout the later chapters. Most of these projects include complete projects with files used to illustrate key concepts. Feel free to reverse engineer any project in order to gain a complete understanding of the concepts being covered. Think of them as rest areas on a highway. If you want, stop and take a look for yourself. If not, just keep driving. You can always come back to them later.

NOTE: While there are typically several ways to access different functions in Encore, keyboard shortcuts offer instant access, save tons of time, and help to refine a speedy workflow within the application. The most common keyboard shortcuts will be listed where relevant throughout the book. An inclusive list is also provided in Appendix A ("Keyboard Shortcuts").

Sample Files DVD-ROM

All sample files (PC content) are included in a folder on the accompanying DVD. These files can be accessed by inserting the DVD-ROM into a computer, browsing the drive and accessing the Sample Files folder. We will be using these files throughout the book as they are incorporated into different projects.

FREE VIDEO TUTORIALS!!!

You can also play this disc on a set top player, or with your favorite DVD software player. Several tutorials are included that will help illustrate some of the more "sophisticated" aspects of Encore. It's not recommended to start with these tutorials. Please make sure to read through the book first. These tutorials are designed for someone who has spent some time with the program, not the total beginner.

At this point, it's recommended that you transfer the sample files project folder to a readily accessible directory such as your desktop. Accessing from the DVD-ROM is not recommended, and can cause technical problems. You'll get much better results by transferring to a local drive. You can always delete the folder after you've finished.

Chapter 1

DVD Basics

In this chapter, we are going to go over the elementary considerations of a DVD author. If you are new to DVD authoring, then this is a great starter. If you are a seasoned pro, we are optimistic that there are a few new tricks you can pick up along the way. We'll talk about the different types of DVD media, DVD formats, and what to think about while you are planning your project.

Many books go into extreme detail, covering the most technical and complicated aspects of DVD. There's even a big, thick book that costs $5,000.00 and is guaranteed to suck at least a good year from your life. (This is the DVD specification, or DVD spec.) This rigid standard is what keeps everyone on the same page. It also covers every technical detail you could imagine.

Encore is about making DVD authoring simple, incorporating many of the most complicated aspects of authoring "under the hood." Encore doesn't require you to be a programmer or a full time author; instead it sticks with a graphical concept that makes advanced functions simple and accessible. Likewise, the goal of this book is to present some of this information, helping you become productive without bogging you down with too many details. We'll refer to the DVD spec from time to time, but our goal is to offer the most clear, concise, and pertinent information that will help you become proficient and productive with Encore.

If you are truly interested in the most technical aspects of DVD production, or if you want to expand your knowledge of the DVD standard, there are several good books on the market. We'll include these and some other good resources in Appendix B.

Now let's get down to business.

- Encore overview
- Disc capacity and data rate
- DVD formats
- Compatibility considerations
- Organizing and planning your project

Encore Overview

With the introduction of Encore, Adobe finally brings affordable and professional DVD authoring to the PC. Many of Encore's features are offered at a small fraction of what they would have cost a few years ago. DLT support, copy protection, and "under the hood" scripting capabilities establish Encore as a serious player in the world of DVD software.

> TIP: Scripting is the process of using a basic assembly type of computer language to enhance navigation, web access, and other more advanced functions of the DVD spec. Encore does not fully support scripting at this time. However, some scripting functions are accommodated within the application itself.

Encore is an even better value for those of you who already use Adobe applications. Taking advantage of the natural synergy between applications, Encore bridges the gap between Photoshop, After Effects, and Premiere, opening up new creative opportunities and workflows not available on any other platform.

It's an exciting time to be a DVD author. Modern tools, such as Encore, have brought the power of desktop DVD authoring to anyone with a PC and a desire to master the technology. It's getting cheaper, faster, and easier too! Can't complain about that.

Disc Capacity and Data Rate

Capacity and data rate are two of the most important concepts in DVD authoring. It's only fitting that we cut right to the chase and address these right from the start.

By default, Encore automatically sets compression parameters according to the size and quantity of assets used in the project. These automatic transcoding features will automatically compress non-DVD compliant content, preparing them for use on the finished disc. This takes a lot of the guesswork out of producing a DVD and is a good starting point for beginning authors.

Encore also provides access to all compression settings, allowing authors direct control over bitrate and other important details.

There are many advantages to specifying your own settings. Taking control over the encoding process can aid project management, provide more control over bit allocation, and improve the quality of video content. Although Encore is a very intuitive program, it cannot read minds to determine which assets require more attention than others.

Capacity

The capacity is the maximum amount of data that can be stored on the DVD. Total available capacity will vary by project and is also dependent on the delivery medium. Encore provides several templates including options for Single-Layer or Dual-Layer DVDs as well as options for general and authoring media.

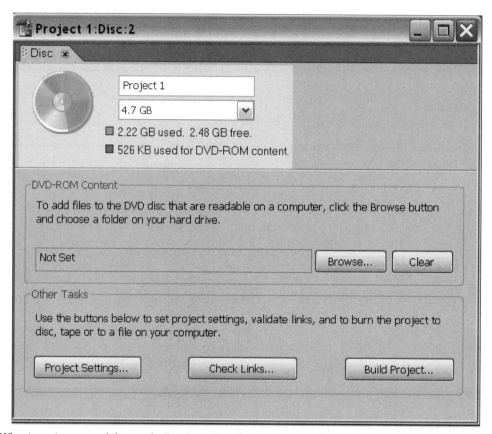

When importing pre-encoded assets, the Disc Properties palette provides a graphical view of remaining disc capacity.

TIP: Encore also provides presets for burning small DVD projects directly to CD, 650 MB and 700 MB. This is a great option for those times when you may want to burn a smaller project to a CD while avoiding the expense of a DVD-R/+R. In this case, the DVD would be burned to a CD; however, do not mistake these for video CDs. Video CD is not a format supported by Encore. Also, remember that these CD-DVDs do not play in set top players. They will only play in computers with a software DVD player.

Most readers will be using general purpose DVD-R / DVD+R media, which have a capacity of 4.7 GB. This is the most popular consumer format. Another popular format offering increased capacity, DVD-9, is available from professional replication houses and is typically used for most

DVD-ROM Disc capacity

MEDIA	CAPACITY (DVD)	CAPACITY (COMPUTER)	LAYERS	SIDES
DVD-5	4.7 GB	4.37 GB	1	1
DVD-9	8.54 GB	7.95 GB	2	1
DVD-10	9.4 GB	8.75 GB	1	2
DVD-18	17.08 GB	15.9 GB	2	2

Figure 1.1 *The maximum capacity of popular DVD formats.*

commercial movies. DVD-9 can store up to 8.54 billion bytes or 7.95 (computer) gigabytes. There are many other formats that offer multiple layers (on one side of the disc) as well as dual layer, dual sided discs with a maximum capacity of 15.9 gigabytes. These capacities will only continue to increase as new technologies are introduced.

If you analyze the capacity of a DVD-5 disc on a computer, you'll find that a standard DVD-R/+R capacity is listed as 4.37 gigabytes. However, the label on the disc clearly advertises 4.7 GB, right? So what gives?

The real issue here is the way the math is done, and more specifically, who is doing the math. Using powers of 10 (think of this as regular, simple math), 4.7 GB is used to describe 4.7 billion bytes. This powers of 10 standard is typically used in the communications industry. This is not the same as 4.7 (computer) gigabytes. Computers think in binary terms, or in powers of 2. In this case, a gigabyte is actually 1024 megabytes. Each megabyte is 1024 kilobytes and so on. **To a computer, 4.7 billion bytes equates to 4.37 gigabytes.**

For the purposes of this book, we will use the powers of 10 technique (as does the Disc Properties palette in Encore).

TIP: When working with DVD-R/+R media, many authors have found that bitrates in excess of 7 Mbps can actually hinder compatibility. Certain set top players can struggle with these high bitrates. Older, slower computers may also experience difficulty playing extremely high bitrates. In general, I would recommend staying below 7.5 Mbps whenever possible.

Data Rate

The data rate, or bitrate, refers to how many bits are utilized, measured in **bits** per second, to playback or encode streams for the DVD. This figure can represent individual streams, such as audio or video, or the final multiplexed DVD-video stream that includes all audio, video, and subpicture content.

According to the DVD specifications, the maximum combined bitrate for DVD is 10.08 Mbps. This includes all video, audio, subtitles, subpictures, etc. The maximum bitrate for video alone is 9.8 Mbps.

Most authors will find themselves working with average combined bitrates between 5 and 7 Mbps.

Bitrate is specified by the author when encoding assets. Higher bitrates produce higher quality content, so most authors strive to set the bitrate as high as they can. Unfortunately, higher bitrates take up more disc space. The goal is to find the perfect balance between quality and file size. To find the target bitrate when encoding video streams, we simply take the *available* capacity and divide by time. (See section on non-video assets.)

> TIP: Make sure to experiment with your own compression settings. Start by compressing small sample clips to determine which settings provide the perfect balance of quality and compression.

In order to determine data rate, first we need to know the maximum capacity of the disc. For example, is the project destined for a single or dual layer, single- or dual-sided disc? DVD-5, DVD-9, DVD-18?

Once disc capacity is established, we need to determine how many bits all the different assets in the project will require. The amount of space that non-video assets require also needs to be taken into consideration before the video encoding rate (bitrate) can be determined.

Non-Video Assets

Here are a few questions to help insure that non-video assets are accounted for:

- How much space will is needed for DVD-ROM content (i.e., screensavers, PC files)?
- How much space is required for menus? Will there be motion menus?
- How many audio tracks will be used? How many languages will be used on the disc?
- Will the disc require subtitles? If so, How many?

After these factors are taken into account an additional reserve of 5% to 7% should be deducted to compensate for overflow and disc file structure.

Finally, the remaining bits can be used to encode the main video streams for the project.

If all of this seems a bit overwhelming at this point, don't worry. We'll cover these topics in greater detail in Chapter 3.

Determining the perfect bitrate is somewhat of a balancing act. A small project that doesn't utilize all of the available space on a disc might not be living up to its potential in terms of picture quality. In many cases, a higher bitrate could increase video quality substantially. On the flip side, a project that is too big won't fit on the disc and could require re-encoding and re-authoring. Not only can a few minutes of planning improve the quality and flow of your production, it can also eliminate hours of wasted time, money, and frustration. To learn more about calculating the perfect bitrate, see Determining Bitrates in Chapter 3.

DVD Formats

DVD formats can be divided into two separate categories: physical and logical formats.

Physical Formats

The physical format refers mainly to how the disc is physically configured. Every DVD will have a specific format. Some of the most common physical formats are: DVD-ROM, DVD-R, DVD+R, and DVD-RAM.

The physical format also refers to how the disc is constructed. The main consideration for most authors will be what type of discs are supported by their DVD burner. Some burners were designed to burn DVD-R media, while others support a rival format, DVD+R. This is becoming less of an issue as modern burners begin to support multiple formats. Below, several common physical formats are listed.

DVD-ROM

DVD-ROM refers to both the physical structure as well as the file system used on the disc. In other words, DVD-ROM can be considered both a physical and logical format. DVD-ROM is the foundation of DVD and includes several variants listed in this section. Although DVD-ROM can hold virtually any kind of digital information, variants such as DVD-Video and DVD-Audio are logical formats limited to specific data types that cater to video and audio playback.

DVD-R

DVD-R is a write once, read many times format adopted by the DVD consortium that allows consumers and professionals alike practical access to the DVD spec. Two types of media are available—General and Authoring. 4.7 GB general media discs are the most common. These are the discs supported by devices such as the Pioneer DVR-A04, A05, and A06 burners. Authoring media, designed as more of a professional format, requires specific hardware that supports it, such as the Pioneer DVR-S201. The authoring format has become less relevant as most authors will find DLT to be a superior format for delivery to a duplication facility. DLT is less expensive, supports copyright protection, and is also more reliable as a master.

DVD-RW

DVD-RW allows the author to rewrite (overwrite) content to the same disc up to 1,000 times. This format is often used to test projects while eliminating the expense of "wasting" write once, DVD-R media. Most new set top players can read DVD-RW; however, the discs are less compatible than regular DVD-R media. So keep this in mind when doing final compatibility tests.

DVD-RAM

Panasonic and Hitachi have championed DVD-RAM, another DVD format. DVD-RAM allows for multiple session recording and is recognized as a great format for tasks such as data backup and archiving. Unfortunately, it has never enjoyed the same compatibility and acceptance as the DVD-R and DVD+R formats.

DVD+R

Sony and Phillips, promising better compatibility than the existing DVD-R format, introduced DVD+R. This format is similar in many ways to DVD-R, offering write once capability and a 4.37 GB maximum capacity. While many people swear by this new format, the same can be said for die-hard proponents of the DVD-R format. It's not readily apparent which format is superior. Most users find the two formats very comparable. Realistically, other factors such as media quality and player performance are more important. In addition, most newer burners such as the DVR-A06 and the Sony DRU-510 support both DVD-R and DVD+R formats.

DVD+RW

Comparable to DVD-RW, the DVD+RW is in accordance with the DVD+R format, adding the ability to write multiple times to the same disc.

Logical formats

Logical format refers to the type of data that a DVD contains.

DVD-ROM

The DVD-ROM file structure can hold just about any type of digital information. This includes files that are created by and intended for use on a computer. DVD-ROM discs can hold many different types of data including audio and video content. This format is quickly replacing CD-ROM in the computer industry.

DVD-Video

This variant holds video that is formatted for use with a set top player or a computer with a DVD-ROM drive and a software player. DVD-Video can deliver full screen 720×480 pixel frames at 23.97 or 29.97 frames per second in NTSC, or 720×576 pixel frames at 25 fps in PAL. Progressive NTSC sources can be displayed on progressive displays or can be converted inside the player to a 29.97 fps interlaced signal for playback on interlaced sets. NTSC players also support a process known as 3:2 pulldown that converts 23.976 progressive content into 29.97 interlaced video. This process is commonly used to transfer film to video for NTSC playback. DVD-Video discs contain a Video_TS folder, and some may also include an Audio_TS folder; however, this is not required.

Hybrid DVDs

As the name implies, Hybrid DVDs contain a mix of information. A Hybrid disc contains DVD-Video files and a file structure that accommodates playback on a set top player. Hybrid discs also contain content that is intended for use on a PC, such as supplemental information, HTML pages, or screen savers.

DVD-Audio

DVD-Audio was introduced as a replacement for the audio CD. Taking advantage of increased capacity, DVD-Audio offers much higher fidelity provided by higher sample rates and bit depths. Audio CDs offer 44.1 kHz, 16-bit audio while DVD-Audio can support 24-bit audio with sample rates as high as 192 kHz. Encore does not support DVD-Audio at this time.

Compatibility Considerations

There are several different factors that contribute to the overall compatibility and playback of burned DVD media.

First and foremost is media, the actual DVD-R/+R discs themselves. Many thorough tests have been performed that show wide variances among manufacturers. If compatibility is critical to your application (and it almost always is), it's always a good idea to start with a good brand name disc such as Verbatim, TDK, Maxell, Mitsui. Oftentimes, the brand name discs can be more expensive. If it's a critical audience, many authors will find the extra dollar or two a worthy investment when compared to the overall expense of a DVD project. Name brand discs have also proven to be far superior as an archival medium.

The next consideration is the player. It's generally accepted that older players are not as adept at playing burned media. Many first-generation DVD players did a fine job of playing replicated, stamped discs (Hollywood-style discs). Unfortunately, these players weren't designed with newer formats in mind (e.g., DVD-R/+R). Newer players have continually improved when it comes to

TIP: It's always a good idea to test your completed DVD in several different players. This is even more critical if you are planning to deliver your final project on burned media (DVD-R/+R). Make sure to test your DVD on several different types and brands of set top players. Also, don't forget to test the project on computer DVD-ROM drives to complete the process.

compatibility and reading consumer grade burned DVDs. Once again, keep in mind that media can affect player performance. Cheap media are even less likely to playback in an older unit.

Inexpensive DVD players on the market today (even those in the sub-100-dollar price range) can outperform players that sold for $500 to $600 just a few years ago.

Another compatibility consideration is the authoring software itself. Fortunately, Encore is a very capable piece of software and is provided with a great authoring engine licensed from Sonic. Sonic has been a leader in the DVD field for years, and much of their experience and leading-edge technology has been incorporated into Encore DVD.

Organizing and Planning Your Project

In order to optimize quality, compatibility, layout, and duration, it's best to do some planning in advance. Most seasoned authors have gained an appreciation for the process of using a flowchart. Flowcharts can be used to organize all of the project elements in advance, arranging all assets according to size, relation, and layout. Organizing the different elements will help utilize disc space efficiently and will help the author plan for important aesthetic design and layout considerations. Flowcharts are also great tools for enhancing the flow and intuitiveness of menu structures. If it's a complex project, a flowchart can save you a great deal of time.

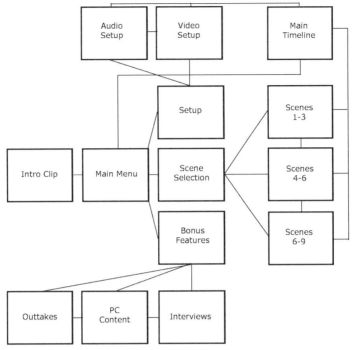

Figure 1.2 *A simple flowchart.*

TIP: After layout and aesthetics have been designed, the same flowchart can also be used as a worksheet for determining bitrates. Simply use the same diagram to list durations and file sizes for the different elements.

The Authoring Cycle

A chart illustrating a typical authoring cycle is shown on page 13. Although it may seem a bit simplified to a professional author or replication house, it should give a good overview of the software required and general process.

The first step is the planning and content acquisition. Organize and list the content that will be included in the finished DVD. If you're authoring for a client, you may want to get an approval on the flowchart before work begins. This way you don't have to create five or six different projects to satisfy the client. It's good to finalize menu design and contents, as this will help keep the project on budget and on time.

Next, a non-linear editor is used to import, create, prepare, and edit assets. We'll look at using Adobe Premiere Pro alongside Photoshop to help create graphics and menus. Most DVD authoring applications rely heavily on Photoshop for menu creation and graphics. Although basic menus can be created totally inside Encore, to truly appreciate the full power of the application, Photoshop is a prerequisite.

After the assets are edited and the menus are ready to be encoded, the next step will be to encode the video and audio to DVD-compliant files. This process simply converts your source material to files that DVD set top players expect and understand (i.e., MPEG-2, AC-3). Encore provides several presets that make this process extremely easy, even for those who are authoring a disc for the first time.

For video, Encore comes with the MainConcept MPEG encoder. This is the same encoder that ships with Premiere. Later, we will look at the pros and cons of encoding with both applications. For audio, Encore comes with a built-in two-channel AC-3 encoder. Encore also supports PCM and MPEG Layer II audio.

Figure 1.3 *Typical authoring cycle.*

After the content is encoded, the next step is authoring. In this stage, menus are assembled, layout is finalized, and content is organized inside Encore. The DVD is assembled and simulated directly on the hard drive. In this stage, final decisions on copyright protection are also determined.

After the disc has been assembled inside Encore, it's time to do some quality control. This stage involves compatibility testing and simulation. One effective way to test your work is to burn directly to DVD and preview the results in a set top box.

The final step is export and delivery. How will the disc be delivered to the audience? Will it be provided on burned media, or will it be output via DLT and sent to a replication house for stamping? Chapter 9 covers these and other important delivery considerations.

Now that we've gone through the basics of DVD, we can finally take a look at our tool of choice, Adobe Encore DVD.

Chapter 2

Inside Encore

I know some of you are probably thinking, "Yeah, yeah, that's great, but let's get to Encore." Fair enough, we'll cover the basics of the interface in this chapter, getting you ready for Project 1 in Chapter 4.

If you're dying to get your hands dirty, you can head straight to Chapter 4, but keep this chapter bookmarked. Chances are, you will refer back to it several times as you work through the project.

When it comes to authoring apps, many different conventions and paradigms are used to make the process more accessible to authors. Most applications, including Encore, are abstract layer applications. This means that Encore supplies its own paradigm, its own methodology, to make the complex features of the DVD spec more accessible to authors. This can be compared to the way that Microsoft Windows uses icons and pull-down menus to simplify complex operations. The goal is to afford users who may not be programming experts, or full-time authors, more time to focus on creative possibilities.

We'll start by going over the main windows, progressing to importing assets and setting preferences. In other words, getting to know Encore, and making sure it knows how we like to get the job done.

- Creating a new project
- Importing assets and menus
- Supported file types
- Setting preferences
- Organizing clips with the Project window
- Locating and replacing assets
- The menus tab
- The timelines tab
- Previewing with the Monitor window
- Safe zones
- The Menu Editor
- The Toolbar
- The Properties palette
- The Library palette
- The Layers palette

Creating a New Project

When opening Encore for the first time, you'll find the screen to be relatively blank. The first step is to either open an existing project, or, in our case, start a new one.

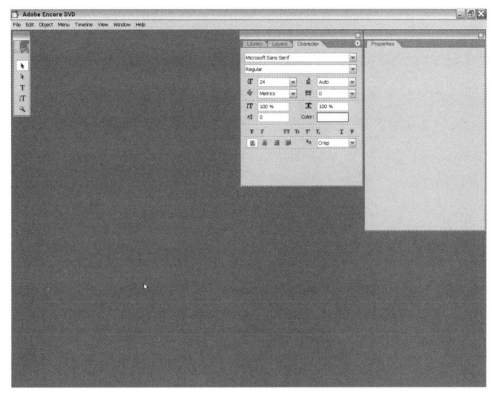

Our first look at Encore.

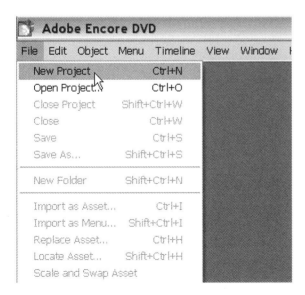

To open a new project, choose: File>New Project or use the keyboard shortcut CTRL+N.

Next, Encore will prompt you to choose a television standard. NTSC is predominately used in North America and Japan, while PAL is used exclusively in Europe. Select the option that best suits your needs. If you plan on doing NTSC or PAL DVDs exclusively, check the "Don't Prompt for Setting; Always Use Default Setting" checkbox.

The television standard dialog. Checking "Don't prompt for setting" will let you skip this step on your next project.

After the TV standard has been selected, the Project window will open. Encore is ready to import assets.

Encore is ready to go.

Importing Assets and Menus

Most of the files you will be working with in Encore will fall under the definition of assets. Assets include MPEG-2 files, AVI files, audio files, and graphics. In the File menu, you'll notice there are two options for importing elements into Encore. You can choose between importing as an asset or importing as a menu.

So, what's the difference?

Menus are specialized Photoshop files that Encore uses to create a menu. Photoshop files can also be used for graphics that are imported as assets. One project may have several different Photoshop files—some used as assets, others as menus. If a Photoshop file is imported as an asset, it will flatten the layers. If you import it as a menu, it will preserve the layers. These layers will then be used to differentiate the different elements that create the menu. These two import options help Encore differentiate between assets and menus. We will talk more about this in Chapter 5.

There are many different ways to import assets into Encore. The most obvious way is to use the file drop-down menu in the menu bar at the top of the application.

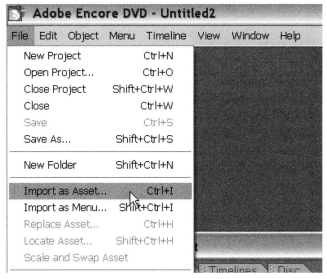

Use the file menu to import assets.

To import assets, use the keyboard shortcut CTRL + I, or you can double click on an empty area in the Project window to open the Import as Asset dialog directly. Files can also be imported as assets by dragging directly into the Project window from Windows Explorer or other folders that contain the desired files.

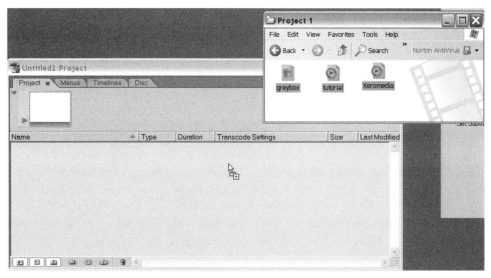

You can drag files directly from Windows Explorer.

To import a Photoshop file as a menu, you can use the file drop-down menu, or the keyboard shortcut CTRL + Shift + I. You can also switch to the Menus tab and double click in the upper pane to import as a menu. If you prefer the drag and drop method, hold down the Alt key while dragging Photoshop files into the Project window.. This will cause the files to be imported as menus rather than assets.

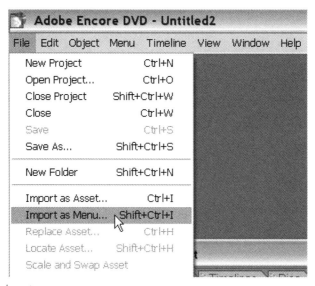

Use the File Menu to import as menu.

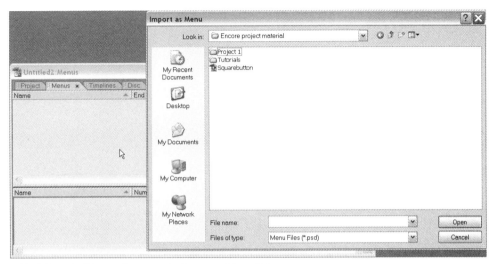

Double click in the Menus tab to open the Import as Menu dialog.

Supported File Types

Encore supports a wide variety of file types.

Supported Video*

Any AVI or MPEG-2 file that can be played back in Windows Media Player (Direct Show), with the following restrictions:

- File cannot have an extension of .qt or .mov
- NTSC projects require a resolution of 720 × 480, 720 × 486, or 704 × 480
- NTSC projects require a frame rate of 23.976, 23.98, 24, or 29.97 fps
- PAL projects require a resolution of 720 × 576 or 704 × 576
- PAL projects require a frame rate of 25
- Half-resolution MPEG1 and Quicktime are not supported in this release

*These file types apply to Encore 1.0 and will change when 1.5 is released.

Supported Audio

Any WAV, AC-3, AIF, WMA, MP3 file that can be played back in Windows Media Player, with the following restrictions:

- File cannot have an extension of .qt or .mov
- Must be mono, stereo, or multichannel
- Variable bit rate MPEG audio is not supported

2-channel as well as 5.1-channel AC-3 audio is also supported.

Still Graphics

- PSD – Photoshop files
- BMP – Bitmaps
- GIF – Popular Web format
- JPEG – Format often used for photographs
- PNG – Popular Web format
- TIFF – High-quality, uncompressed format

Quicktime graphic files are not supported.

Other Considerations

Encore 1.0 supports a subset of streams that are legal for DVD without having to transcode them. This allows authors to use their choice of tools, opening more workflow options and creative choices. If you plan to prepare assets in external applications, these formats can be imported directly into Encore and will not require additional transcoding.

If a file does not fit into this set, or if certain parameters are not DVD compliant, Encore will automatically transcode the file.

The following files can be imported without requiring recompression inside Encore.

- Elementary MPEG-2 video (according to the frame sizes listed previously)
- PCM in the form of a .wav file. Only mono/stereo, 48 kHz, 16/24 bits per sample are supported.
- AIFF (not AIFF-C)
- Elementary MPEG audio, layers I and II, constant bit rate
- AC3—Both 2-channel and 5.1 can be imported
- Program streams that contain DVD legal audio and video streams.

Setting Preferences

The Preferences dialog will offer options to cater your project to your individual needs. Most of these setting are relatively straightforward.

To access project settings, choose: Edit > Preferences

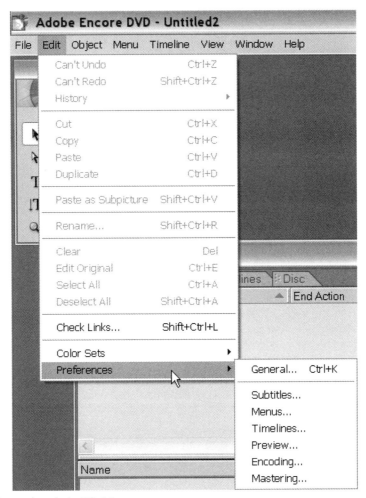

Access the Preferences through the Edit Menu.

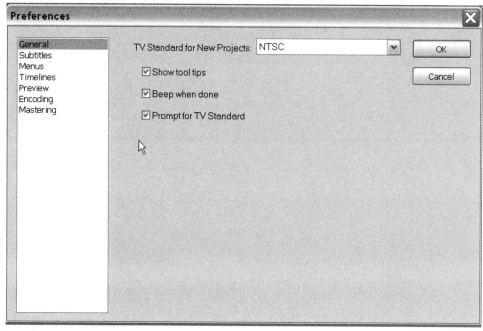

The Preferences settings begin with the General Preferences dialog.

General. This setting allows you to specify the default TV standard, toggle the TV standard prompt and turn tool tips on and off.

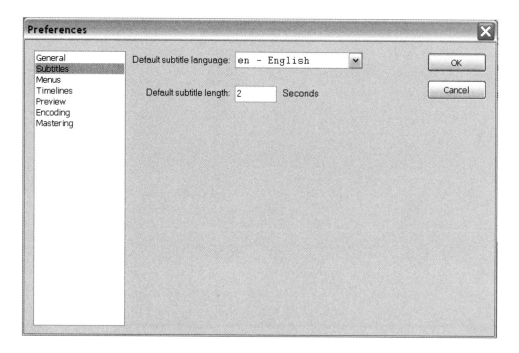

Subtitle. All subtitles are created at a default length. These preferences allow you to specify this length and also the default subtitle language.

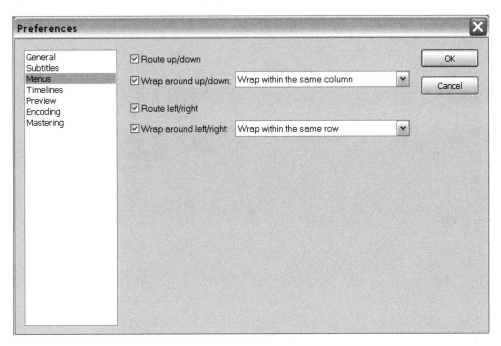

Menus. The menu options pertain to button routing. Button routing parameters determine how viewers will navigate from one button to the next when navigating within a DVD project (more in Chapter 8). Think of these as a few extra settings that will help you control how the automatic button routing occurs.

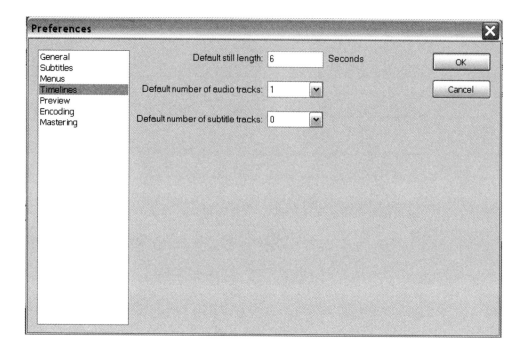

Timelines. This setting determines the default duration of stills added to your timelines as well as the number of audio and subtitle tracks in your timelines.

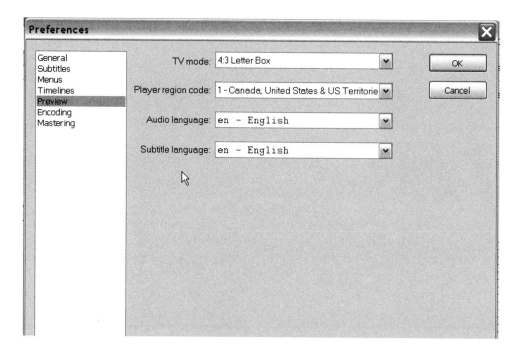

Preview. 4:3 and 16:9 preview modes can be specified as well as default audio and subtitle languages. These settings apply to the disc simulation window.

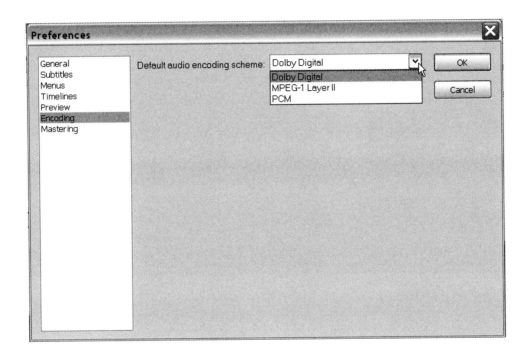

Encoding. This setting determines how audio assets will be transcoded inside of Encore. By default, Encore will encode all audio files to 2-channel AC-3. AC-3 is the most popular audio format for DVD and is typically the best choice for most projects. PCM, an uncompressed format, requires much more space than AC-3 or MPEG layer 2 audio. MPEG layer 2 requires less space than PCM; however, not all players support this format. Dolby Digital (AC-3) or PCM are required for NTSC projects. MPEG1 audio files are not recommended for NTSC projects due to the possibility of player incompatibility. PAL discs do not have this restriction as MPEG1 audio is more widely supported in PAL players. AC-3 is the most popular and efficient choice for both standards.

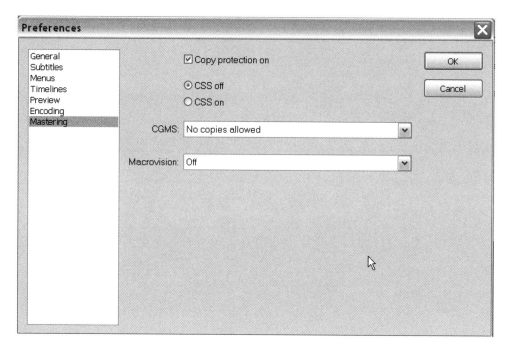

Mastering. Allows you to set the copy protection scheme for DLT export. You can determine whether your audience will have the ability to make copies of your stamped disc. This is strictly a DLT, replication-house consideration. These copy protection and region code settings will not be present on burned media. See Chapter 8 for more information.

Organizing Clips with the Project Window

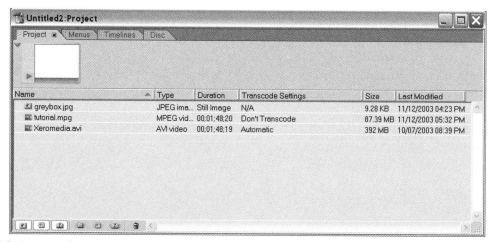

The Project window showing the Project tab.

The Project window provides several tabs that support different functions. The first tab, the Project tab, contains all the audio, video, and still image assets. It also lists the timelines and menus that have been added to your project. The Project tab also has several different columns that provide additional information on the different elements of your DVD project.

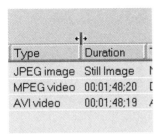

These columns can be resized and arranged in any order. Feel free to drag and drop them wherever you wish. You can also click directly on properties in these columns to sort by the individual categories. Click again to toggle sorting in ascending and descending order.

Resize your columns by clicking and dragging on the sides of the headings.

Tip: Right click on the headers to customize the fields displayed in the Project window.

Name	Type	Duration	Transcode Settings	Size	Last Modified
greybox.jpg	JPEG image	Still Image	N/A	9.28 KB	11/12/2003 04:23 PM
tutorial.mpg	MPEG video	00;01;48;20	Don't Transcode	87.39 MB	11/12/2003 05:32 PM
Xeromedia.avi	AVI video	00;01;48;19	Automatic	392 MB	10/07/2003 08:39 PM

Clicking on the column header sorts the files by that attribute. Clicking again reverses the order according to that attribute.

Folders can be created and used in the Project Window to categorize different elements of your DVD.

To create your own folders, simply choose File> New Folder.

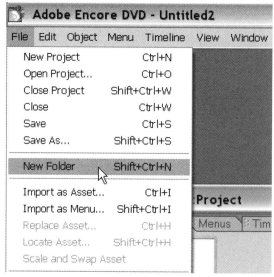

You can use the file menu to create a new folder.

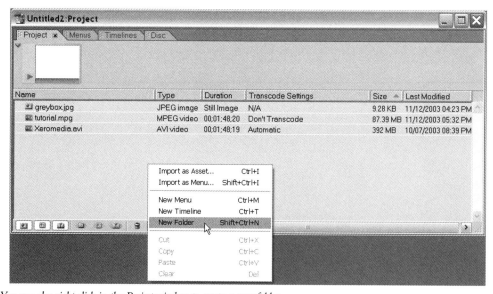

You can also right click in the Project window to create a new folder.

You can drag and drop assets, menus, and timelines into a folder, or even nest other folders within folders.

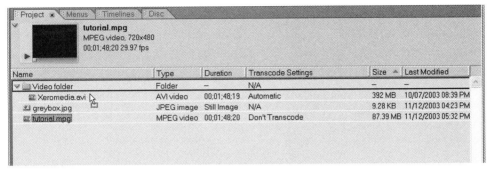

Any item in the Project tab can be dragged and dropped into a folder.

Locating and Replacing Assets

Over the course of a project, some assets might get relocated or deleted altogether. You will notice that missing media is in *italics*. This informs you that the original asset or menu is no longer available and should be found before the DVD disc is burned.

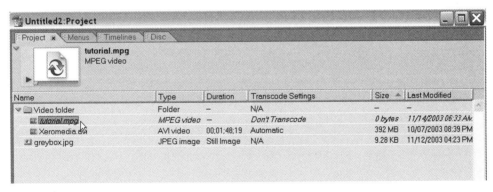

Assets in italics are missing.

To locate a missing asset: Right click the italicized asset and select Locate Asset. This opens a file browser. Locate the asset and select Open. This makes re-linking lost files simple and easy.

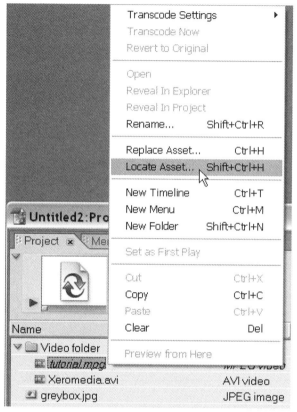

Right clicking on a missing asset makes the Locate Asset option available.

The Replace Asset feature can also be used to swap files in a project. This feature is especially handy when you want to replace minor graphics and assets. If you make several DVDs with a similar format but different content, you can replace assets without having to create a whole new project. If you replace your main video assets, remember to adjust the chapter points in the associated timeline.

To replace an asset: Right click the asset and select Replace Asset.

This will open a file browser. Locate your desired asset and select Open.

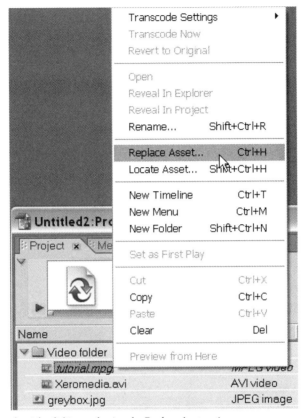

You can replace any asset by right clicking and using the Replace Asset option.

TIP: The Replace Asset feature is available at all times and will allow you to select a different file. Once replaced, the file name will change in the Project window. The Locate Asset feature is only available when an asset is missing, and it will keep the name the same in the Project window regardless of the file you locate, *even if it is different from the original file used in the project.*

Filtering Views

The Project window offers several different methods of sorting and previewing the elements of your DVD project. At the top of the Project window, several tabs can be used to display timelines or menus. These tabs can be used to help toggle between and link different elements of your DVD.

You can also sort directly inside the Project tab to isolate file types. On the bottom left are three icons. Use these icons to toggle the view of the timelines, assets, and menus.

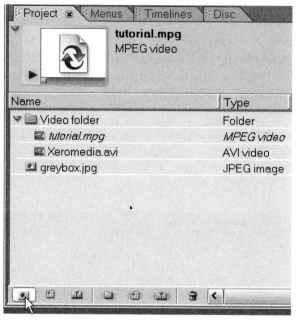

The Display Assets icon allows you to hide or view assets.

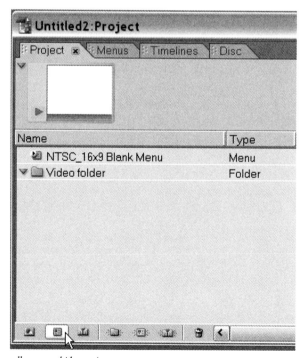

The Display Menus icon allows you hide or view menus.

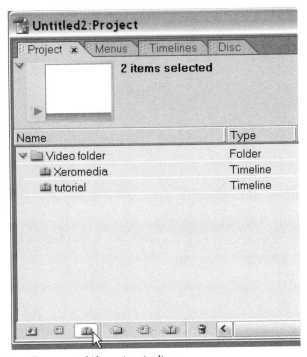

The Display Timelines icon allows you to hide or view timelines.

TIP: You can sort by column headers, and you can show or hide different attributes. This is pretty powerful stuff. Essentially it's a spreadsheet view of your project. It also allows you use to use several different windows to link the different elements of your DVD project.

The Menus Tab

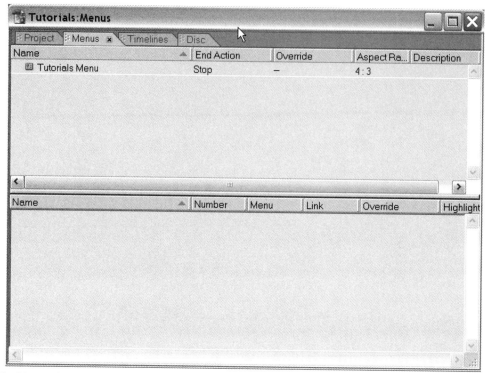

The Menus tab.

The Menus tab displays all of your menus and the aspects of those menus such as End Action, First Play, Aspect Ratio, and the Override. You can drag and drop Photoshop files as menus from the Library palette or Windows Explorer into the upper pane.

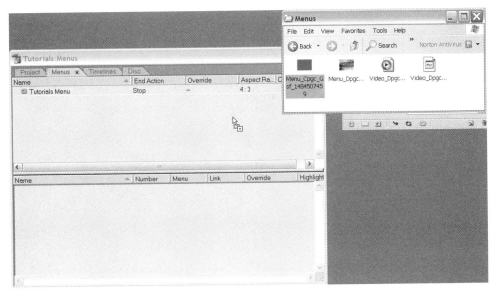

You can drag and drop Photoshop files from Windows Explorer.

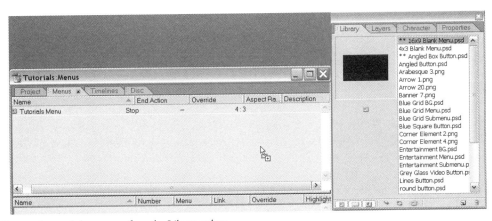

You can drag and drop menus from the Library palette.

By selecting a menu, all of its buttons are displayed in the bottom pane of the Project window. At a glance, you can see many properties of the buttons. You can see if they have a subpicture highlight, what menus they are associated with, and their corresponding button number.

The Timelines Tab

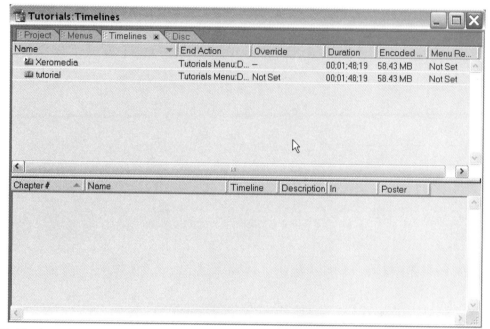

The Timelines tab.

Timelines are home to video clips, audio clips, subtitles, graphics, and still images. Think of the timelines as building blocks that can be linked together to form the structure for the DVD. Direct access (navigation) to specific sections of a timeline is provided through the use of chapter points. An end action can also be specified for each timeline to determine what happens when it reaches the end.

The Timeline tab in the Project window lists all timelines in a spreadsheet view. Instantly you can see what those timelines are linked to, what their end action is, their duration, and if there are any overrides set.

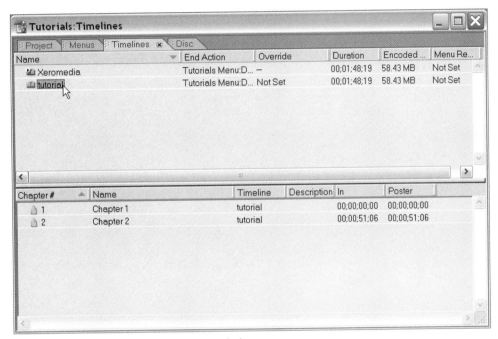

Clicking on a timeline displays its chapter points in the bottom pane.

By clicking on a timeline, its chapters are displayed in the bottom pane, providing information about each chapter point. This also provides another method to select and link these chapter points to other elements in the project.

Next, let's take a look at the Timeline window.

Timeline Window

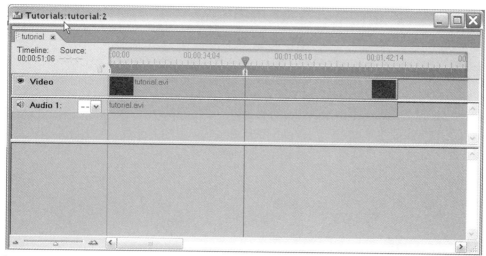

The Timeline window.

TIP: Encore groups multiple time-lines as separate tabs in a single window. Tabs can be selected to bring individual timelines into view. You can also tear off these tabs to create a new window at any time. This same concept applies to many other palettes inside Encore as well. Click on a tab and drag to isolate a palette or to position inside a different window.

Subtitle placement and duration is determined on the Timeline window. Audio tracks, still graphics, duration, even the length of video streams can be adjusted directly in the Timeline window as well.

Once clips are added to the timeline, it's good to know some basic keyboard shortcuts that will aid navigation. To view different events in the timeline, simply drag the CTI (current time indicator) to the section you wish to view in the Monitor window. You can also specify timecode values directly by clicking on the timecode and typing in the value. This technique will position the CTI at the specified timecode.

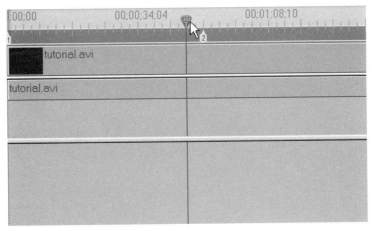

The CTI can be dragged to the desired position.

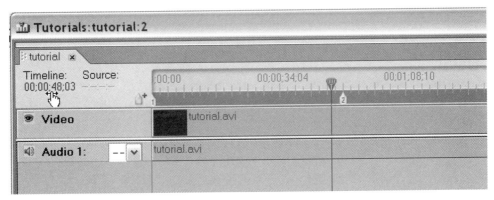

Click and drag to adjust timecode.

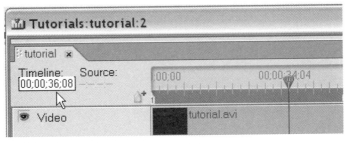

The timecode value can be entered directly.

If MPEG-2 clips are present in the Timeline, you may notice some smaller white lines or tick marks. These marks represent GOP headers. Think of GOPs as small clusters that MPEG-2 uses to create a video stream. If MPEG-2 clips are imported, these clips will have GOP headers that represent the first frame of all Group of Pictures (G-O-P). These are important because it is the only place that you can add a chapter point to pre-encoded clips.

TIP: For more on GOPs and MPEG-2 structure, see Appendix C.

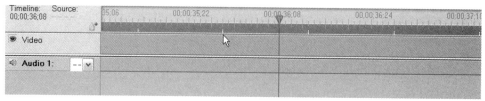

At this zoom level we can see the GOP headers as white ticks.

TIP: If you're working with AVI files, there are no GOP headers and the chapter point limitations do not apply. This is good to know because chapter points can be set almost anywhere (at least 12 to 15 frames apart). Encore will automatically create GOP headers that correspond perfectly to the chapter point when the AVI is transcoded to MPEG-2.

Basic trimming can also be performed once a clip has been added to the timeline. Subtitles, audio, and video tracks can be lengthened or shortened by hovering over the edge of the clip. Use the selection tool and hover over the head or tail of the asset. You'll notice a red, bracket-shaped trimming icon will be displayed. You can then drag the in and out points to determine durations.

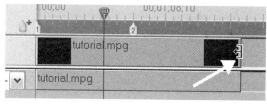

Hovering over the head or tail of a timeline brings the red bracket into view. You can increase or decrease duration by dragging it out or in.

TIP: You can add up to 99 different timelines to one project and up to 99 chapter points for each timeline.

TIP: There is no way to ensure smooth playback between timelines. Certain limitations in Encore and the DVD spec apply. If seamless, uninterrupted playback is critical, it is best to prepare your assets as one large timeline in an external editor rather than trying to play several smaller timelines sequentially. (See video tutorial on accompanying DVD-ROM.)

Previewing with the Monitor Window

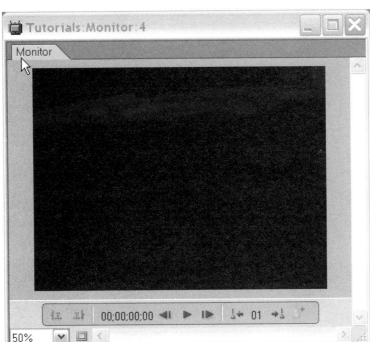

The Monitor window.

The Monitor window reflects what is occurring at the playhead down in the timeline. If you've used a non-linear editor before, you're probably already familiar with the concept.

You can specify the size of the Monitor window by using the drop-down menu that is located toward the bottom of the window, or you can simply use the keyboard shortcut CTRL + / − to modify the size directly. The Monitor window also allows you to navigate and set chapter points and provides controls to set subtitles. If there is a subtitle track present, the view can be turned on and off in the Monitor window. Like many other windows in Encore, timecode can be input directly, by clicking on the timecode field and specifying a value. Specifying timecode in the Monitor window moves the playhead to the specified frame in the timeline.

Safe Zones

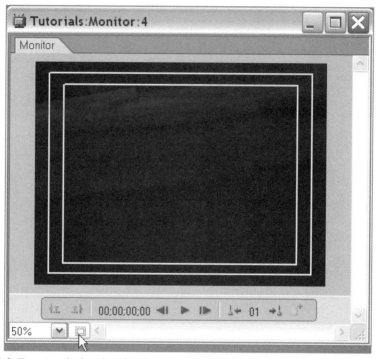

Clicking the Safe Zones icon displays the title safe and action safe zones.

Safe zones help authors preview how their content will be displayed on the end user's television. Not all televisions are capable of displaying the full frame, full resolution picture. The safe zones are simply small lines or guides that help the author position content and titles so they won't be cut off by displays that don't display the full picture. The action safe zone is the outermost box. Assume that anything outside of this zone probably won't be seen by viewers. The title safe zone is the innermost box. This is where all titles, buttons, and subtitles should be placed to ensure they will be seen on all televisions.

The keyboard shortcut CTRL+7 toggles the view for safe zones.

The Menu Editor

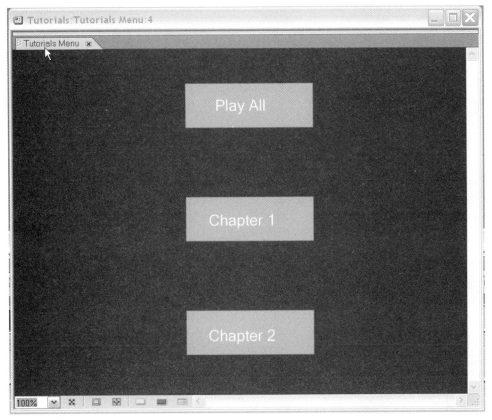

The Menu Editor.

The Menu Editor, as its name suggests, provides the ability to design and adjust menus inside of Encore. It also allows different views of subpicture highlights that will eventually be used to show button selection and activation. Button routing can also be adjusted to assure proper navigation in menus. For more on button routing, see Chapter 8.

This window opens automatically when a new menu is imported or created. One of the nicest aspects of the Menu Editor is the fact that it also allows direct adjustment of buttons and graphics. This is especially nice when working with menus designed and imported from Photoshop. In the past, a drawback of many DVD applications has been the rather clumsy integration with Photoshop. Fortunately, this is no longer the case for Encore users. We'll be working with this window extensively in Chapter 5.

TIP: Remember that all tools inside of the toolbar can be accessed directly using keyboard shortcuts. For more information, see Appendix A.

The Toolbar

The toolbar, as you might think, provides access to several useful tools inside of Encore.

The first two options are selection tools. In order to understand the difference between the tools, it's best to keep in mind that Encore stores all assets in the form of layers in the Layers palette. The two selection tools simply provide the ability to choose between affecting layer sets as a unit or the individual elements.

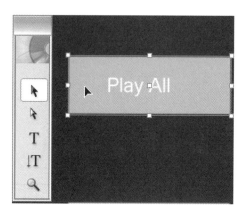

Selection Tool

The Selection tool can be used to select a layer set or an individual layer. This tool is typically used for selecting and manipulating an entire layer set or an individual layer that contains a graphic. This tool can be accessed directly using the keyboard shortcut V.

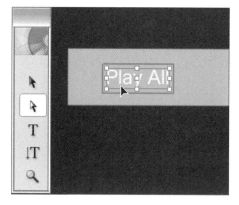

Direct Select Tool

The Direct Select tool is used to select individual layers, allowing the user to focus on individual elements such as text or a single graphic. Multiple layers can also be selected by holding down the SHIFT key. To select multiple layers, they must be all independent layers or all within the same layer set. This tool can be accessed directly using the keyboard shortcut A.

TIP: If stacking order presents a problem, layers can be selected and arranged directly inside Layer sets. However, Layers cannot be moved between layer sets. For full control, Photoshop is required.

TIP: Use the Layer palette to isolate and select elements of a menu. Clicking on a layer selects the corresponding graphic in the Menu Editor window.

Text Tool

This tool is used in conjunction with the Character palette to add text to a menu and can also be used to add subtitles directly inside the Monitor window. When adding text to a menu, two methods can be used. You can click and drag to create a bounding box. This will define boundaries and is used to contain text within a specified section. The other technique is simply to click once, then type directly into the window, using the return key to determine line breaks. This tool can be accessed directly using the keyboard shortcut T.

TIP: After creating text, it can be selected with the selection tool and scaled directly inside the Menu Editor.

Vertical Text Tool

Similar to the Text tool, use this tool with the Character palette to add vertical type to a menu. This tool can be accessed directly using the keyboard shortcut Y.

TIP: Press the T key to toggle between vertical and horizontal Text tools.

TIP: When using the Text tools, remember if you click inside the Menu Editor a text layer is automatically created, regardless of whether you type anything or not. Be very careful NOT to create unnecessary layers as this can cause problems with navigation and button routing. Use the Layers palette to check for unwanted text layers. A large capital T is visible to the left of each text layer.

Zoom Tool

The Zoom tool can be used to control the zoom level of the timeline and the Monitor window. Use the Zoom tool to determine how many frames are visible on the timeline. To zoom down to the frame level, simply click on the timeline. As you continue to click, individual frames will fill the timeline window. To zoom out, simply hold ALT while clicking with your mouse.

The Zoom tool can also be used to zoom into specific sections of the Menu Editor. While designing menus, simply hover over the area you wish to magnify and click with your mouse. To reverse this action, hold ALT while you click with your mouse. This tool can be accessed directly using the keyboard shortcut Z.

TIP: Once you practice the keyboard shortcuts a few times, you'll find selecting tools with the keyboard more efficient than using the mouse to select them from the tool palette.

The Properties Palette

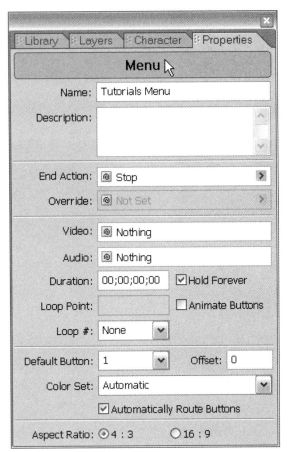

The Properties palette of a menu.

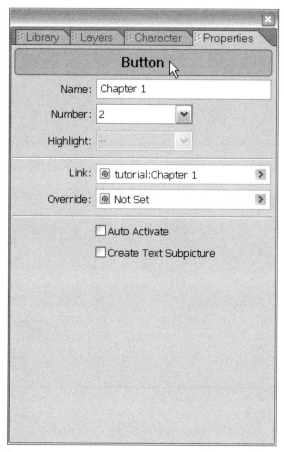

The Properties palette of a button.

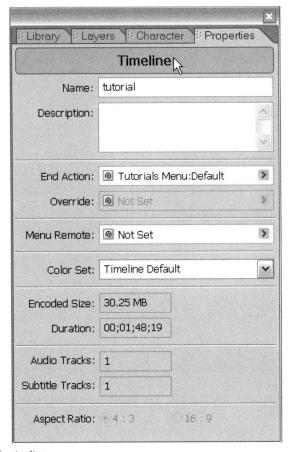

The Properties palette of a timeline.

The Properties palette provides information for all of the different assets and menus inside Encore. Do not confuse the Properties palette for a simple info palette; it is used extensively as part of your workflow. It's important to note that this window reflects the active selection. For example, if you select a menu, this palette will display functions and properties relating to that specific menu. Some properties of a menu include: Loop point, end actions, default button, color set, etc. If a button is selected, it will display the properties of that button, where it links to, if it's auto activated, etc. Similarly, if you select a timeline, it will allow you to specify timeline-specific parameters.

TIP: As you work you will find that you are referring back to the Properties palette often. I recommend keeping it in an accessible place in your workspace, so you don't have to dig through windows every time you need to use it.

The Library Palette

The Library palette.

The Library palette can be used to store, display, and access still image assets, menu templates, and button templates. This is particularly advantageous for projects that can be used multiple times with minimal changes. The Library palette also contains a good amount of predesigned templates that can be incorporated into your own projects.

Adding Items to the Library Palette

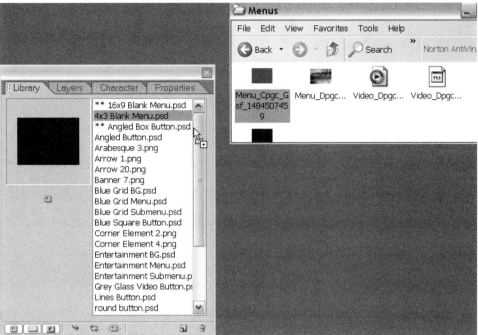

A Photoshop menu can be dragged from Windows Explorer.

Items can be added to the Library palette from either the Menu Editor or the Project tab. Simply activate the Library palette and drag the desired item directly into the window. You can also use the Add Item button in the Library palette itself, or drag and drop directly from Windows Explorer.

TIP: Extra templates are included in the Goodies folder on the Encore installation disc. Many different examples are included that make a welcome addition to the existing templates that are included with a basic installation (extra templates not included in educational version).

Library Defaults

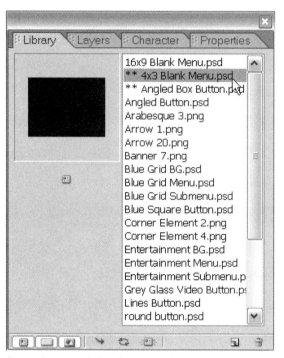

The default menu in the Library palette is marked with two asterisks.

The Library palette maintains a default menu as well as a default button.

Encore uses the default menu as a starting point for any new menu that is created. This may not be obvious at first, because the default template is set to a blank menu. Inside the library palette, the default template is always marked with two asterisks before the name. It's easy to specify other menus inside the Library palette as the default, if desired.

TIP: If you don't like the default menu that opens every time you create a new menu, feel free to create your own menu, import into the Library palette, and set as the default.

To change a default menu, simply select the menu that you wish to make the default, right click, and choose Set as Default Menu.

The Default Button

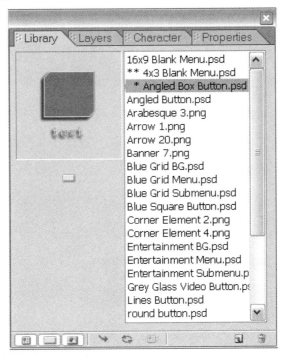

The default button is marked with one asterisk.

Encore uses the default button every time you drag a video, timeline, chapter point, or menu *from the project tab* directly to the Menu Editor window. While this feature is somewhat confusing to some beginning authors, it was designed as a shortcut. The idea was to offer a workflow that automatically creates a button with a link from the menu back to the original asset.

Of course, just like with the default menu behavior, you can set any button in the Library palette as the default. Simply select the button that you wish to make the default, right click, and choose Set as Button Default.

The Layers Palette

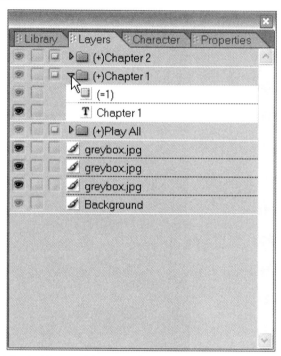

The Layers palette shows individual layers and layer sets of menus.

The Layers palette keeps track of the different elements in a menu, utilizing a specific layer structure similar to the Layers palette in Photoshop. The Layers palette can be used to rearrange the stacking order of layers in layer sets and can also be used to help select elements in the Menu Editor window. This is most useful when working with multilayered menus with several graphics and buttons. You can also hide layers, convert layers into buttons, and vice versa, all from the Layers palette.

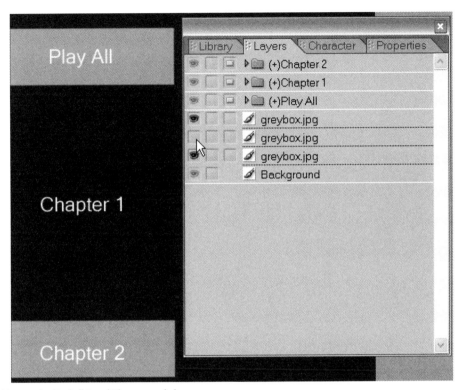

Clicking on the Eyeball icon hides or reveals layers.

Now that we've covered the interface, hopefully you're starting to feel comfortable finding your way around inside Encore. In the next chapter, we're going to dive into some of the more technical aspects of DVD production. It's time to start thinking about asset preparation and compression settings for our audio and video assets.

Chapter 3
Preparing Assets/Encoding

We live in a world where compression makes things happen; and when it comes to compression, it all boils down to quality and efficiency. The ultimate goal is to squeeze large amounts of information into a delivery mechanism. This mechanism could be a disc, a cable, a telephone line, or even a satellite.

With the Internet, one of the first challenges was to find ways to send large amounts of information over regular phone lines. Compression was incorporated to save bandwidth, transferring more information using fewer bits. Remember Napster? Its success was directly attributed to a new form of compression. With the introduction of the MP3 audio codec (COmpressor / DECompressor), Web surfers were able to enjoy CD-quality music at 10% to 15% of the size of a CD audio file.

Today, this is the same situation with DVD. Good compression makes everything possible. MPEG-2 is a very efficient and very capable codec. MPEG-2 compression provides broadcast quality, full motion video at a reasonable bitrate that allows consumers to enjoy much higher quality and convenience than VHS.

As a DVD author, your goal will be to fit high-quality audio and video content onto a limited capacity disc using compression. However, finding a way to store this information is only half of the story. Compression typically decreases quality, so a happy medium between compression and bitrate must be obtained.

Finding the perfect compromise between the two is the trick to successful authoring. In this section, we'll cover the process of preparing audio and video, then we'll move on to MPEG-2 compression and determining the bitrate. We'll also cover important issues that will help optimize the quality and efficiency of the encoding process.

- Preparing source material
- Optimizing video for broadcast
- MPEG-2 compression
- Specifying transcode settings
- Video compression settings
- Encoder quality settings
- Audio compression settings
- Multiplexing
- Choosing an audio format
- Encoding 2-channel AC-3 audio
- Importing 5.1 AC-3
- Determining bitrates

Preparing Source Material

Many things can affect the quality of a DVD project. First and foremost is the quality of the source. First rule of thumb: always make an effort to use the best-quality source material available.

TIP: When preparing video using a program such as Adobe Premiere, try to avoid exporting the entire timeline using the DV codec before importing into Encore. In this situation, it would be better to export the timeline directly to MPEG-2 using the Adobe Media Encoder. After rendering, the resulting MPEG-2 file is ready for use inside Encore and should not require additional transcoding. Using this technique, the text, titles and graphics will not be compressed to an intermediate codec (DV). They will be encoded directly to MPEG-2, thereby eliminating unnecessary transcoding. This will reduce compression artifacts by eliminating an unnecessary transcoding generation and will create better looking motion menus and graphics

When creating menus with complex motion, animation, or graphics, it's important to work with clips that are uncompressed or that have been prepared with a high-quality codec. For example, motion menus created and encoded from uncompressed AVIs will produce better results than 2nd generation material captured or compressed with the DV codec.

If you're using footage from a DV camcorder, the DV codec can also produce acceptable results. When creating custom graphics and text using Premiere or After Effects, you'll get better results if you avoid compressing your own custom graphics and text to the DV codec *before* conversion to MPEG-2. In this situation, encode high-quality graphics, animations and text directly to MPEG-2 when possible.

What is a codec? A codec, or COmpressor DECompressor, is a software or hardware module/algorithm responsible for compressing and/or decompressing an encoded media format (in our case, digital video). Codecs are used to compress the original information, allowing more information to be stored when compared to the original uncompressed data. The data is typically transported or delivered in its compressed form, then decompressed upon playback through the use of a software or hardware device. DVD set top players provide a decoder that is used to decompress and playback MPEG-2 streams. Computers also decompress these MPEG-2 streams upon playback using slightly different methods. Newer computers are able to perform this decompression utilizing software decoders while machines from 2 or 3 years ago often relied on a hardware decoder for smooth DVD playback.

Rule of thumb: Try to eliminate excess transcoding (from one codec to another), and use uncompressed or lossless codecs when creating your own custom motion menus.

The type of content that is being encoded will also have a direct effect on the quality of the encode. Some material is more difficult to encode than others. Video that consists of gradients, complex detail, or fast motion will always require more bits per second than video with slow moving simple shapes and consistent color. It's important to experiment with compression settings, especially when it comes to challenging content or projects requiring low bitrate encoding.

Once the best possible source material is obtained, the next step is to optimize the encoding process for best results. In addition to optimizing bitrate, which we will cover later in this chapter, there are a few other important considerations to keep in mind.

As mentioned, MPEG-2 compression has a hard time encoding images with intricate detail and complex motion. This is compounded by the fact that most MPEG-2 is displayed on interlaced displays that struggle with sharp lines, small text, and moiré patterns. These issues create noticeable artifact and flickering that should be recognized and minimized whenever possible.

The most effective and simplest method of remedying these issues is to minimize thin lines and complex miniature details when creating graphics and text. Experiment with blur filters in your NLE. Small horizontal lines can be smoothed using a vertical blur filter. For complex patterns, small text, or images with elaborate detail, try smoothing the entire image with a Gaussian blur filter.

When creating titles, buttons or other text-related objects, don't use small, thin fonts. Thicker fonts are easier for television to reproduce. Don't use fonts with serifs. Sans serif fonts will display best on interlaced monitors. Also, keep type size above 18 point whenever possible.

> TIP: Blur filters reduce the amount of detail in the image. This can *also* increase the efficiency of the compression and improve image quality.

If your DVD project is destined for broadcast, there are a few more issues that need to be addressed.

Optimizing Video for Broadcast

Today's computer monitor is more capable of displaying detailed, high-quality content when compared to most interlaced NTSC television sets. Not only can a computer monitor refresh faster and reproduce higher resolutions, it also displays more colors. This is especially noticeable when reproducing bright colors and deep blacks. For this reason, this must be considered when working with content produced on a computer. Whether it's a 3-D sequence or a custom animated motion menu, content originating on a computer needs to be modified and optimized for playback on a normal television set. If it isn't it, the colors will bleed together and the image will look overly saturated. Illegal colors can even cause pops and noises in the audio during playback. In addition, some clients will reject content that does not fall within broadcast legal specifications.

Fortunately, tempering these issues can be accomplished using tools provided by most NLEs by applying a broadcast safe, or broadcast legal, filter to your video.

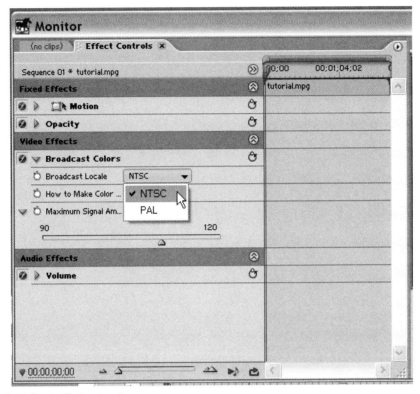

Broadcast legal filter inside Premiere Pro.

These filters will bring all colors within legal range and will also improve playback quality.

<table>
<tr><td>

TIP: It's generally best to stay away from extremely bright reds and yellows when designing content intended for NTSC broadcast.

</td><td>

MPEG-2 Compression

MPEG stands for the Motion Picture Experts Group, an international organization responsible for the development of the MPEG compression. Many different variants of MPEG are available today. MPEG-1 layer 3 audio, aka MP3, is a popular audio codec used for musical storage and playback. MPEG-1 video is another popular variant providing low bitrate video compression for VCD and DVD. Although the DVD spec does support MPEG-1 video, Encore does not. For this reason, our main focus will be MPEG-2.

</td></tr>
</table>

MPEG-2 is the most popular format for DVD-Video. MPEG-2 provides broadcast-quality video at extremely low bitrates. The efficiency of MPEG-2 can be attributed to its utilization of temporal as well as spatial compression.

Spatial compression is performed on a per frame basis. This can be compared with the DCT process utilized in JPEG compression. Spatial compression works within the frame to compress the image.

Temporal compression compares frames over time and focuses on changes between frames. The function of temporal compression is to recognize portions of the image that don't change over time, or between frames, and to eliminate this information during the encoding process. Temporal compression uses motion vectors, essentially recording where the action or color changes between frames, eliminating redundant data and improving the efficiency of the encode.

Specifying Transcode Settings

Transcoding is the process of converting from one file format to another. Converting an AVI to an MPEG-2 file is one example of transcoding. In Encore, all assigned transcode settings are listed next to the assets and can be directly modified inside the Project Window. It's important to note that Encore applies compression settings to individual assets by using presets; there are no global settings. Each asset can have its own unique setting. This is a good thing as most authors will be working with content, and choosing between presets is an easy way to work. If you want to modify an existing preset, or create a new one from scratch, you must go into the Edit Transcoding Presets dialog. We will go over that process shortly.

By default, Encore will automatically transcode files that are not DVD compliant. Encore determines ideal encoding settings by analyzing the number, length, and size of assets. Of course, the capacity of the media is also used to determine the ideal settings. This automatic transcode feature is not only useful to beginning authors, but it can also boost production and save time on quick and simple DVD projects.

If DVD compliant MPEG-2 files are imported into a project, Encore recognizes them as such and will not automatically re-transcode these files. These files will be marked "Don't Transcode" in the Project Window and are thereby deemed ready to burn to disc. The size of these files will also be factored into and reflected in the disc capacity graphic in the disc properties palette.

In the Project window, video files will be listed in one of the following categories.

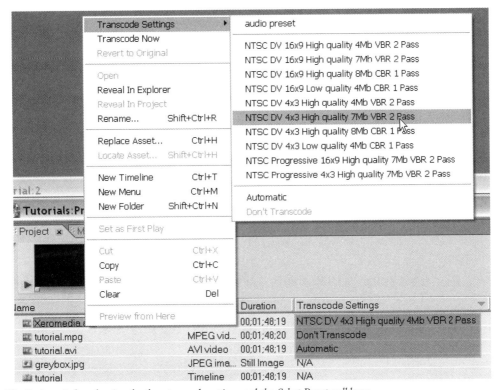

The Project window showing the three transcode settings and the Select Preset pulldown.

Automatic

This setting applies to non-compliant DVD video files as they are imported into Encore. This includes uncompressed and DV AVI files. All files set to Automatic will be automatically encoded. Encore will determine all encoding settings automatically by factoring in the size, quantity, and length of all assets in the project.

Don't Transcode

This setting is displayed when DVD compliant MPEG-2 files are imported into Encore. This setting indicates that the file will not require additional transcoding and is ready to be burned to disc. This setting can be changed to Automatic, or you can create or specify an existing transcode preset.

Other Templates

Encore provides the ability to save, load, and specify presets for future use. Many presets are offered allowing you to choose between variable and constant bitrates at different quality settings.

In addition to the standard templates that ship with the application, you can also create, save, and reuse your own custom templates that reflect personalized settings. This is a convenient way to save settings for use on future tasks and projects. Once a preset is named and saved, Encore allows you to assign these presets to individual assets in the Project Window.

To create your own custom presets that can be used in Encore:

Go to File>Transcode>Edit Transcode Presets

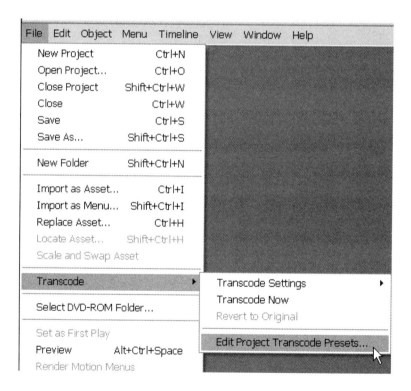

This will open the Edit Transcode Presets dialog.

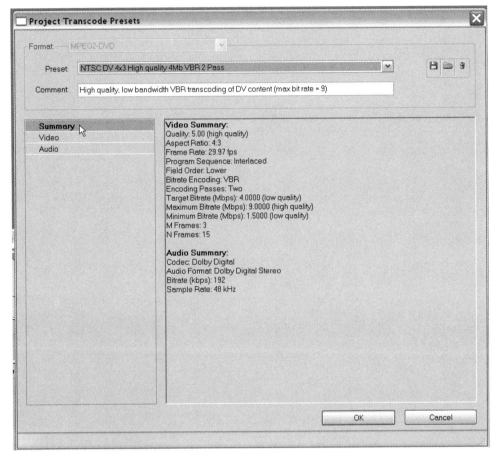

The Edit Transcode Presets dialog.

Select a preset that best matches your desired custom preset, then change the values per your requirements. If you change anything in a preset, it becomes a custom preset. When you're finished making changes, either click Save Preset icon (the small floppy disc icon toward the top) or press OK. Encore will then prompt you for a name for your new custom preset. After saving a preset, it will automatically be accessible from the Project window.

The three icons near the top allow you to manage settings. The Trash Can lets you throw away unneeded presets. The Disc is for saving a new preset, and the File Folder is for importing presets.

*Custom Preset
Management icons.*

Video Compression Settings

The MainConcept encoder, which Encore uses for transcoding, includes a simple, clean interface providing plenty of options. The MC encoder also offers the ability to save and load templates for future use. Below is a list of settings that can be adjusted.

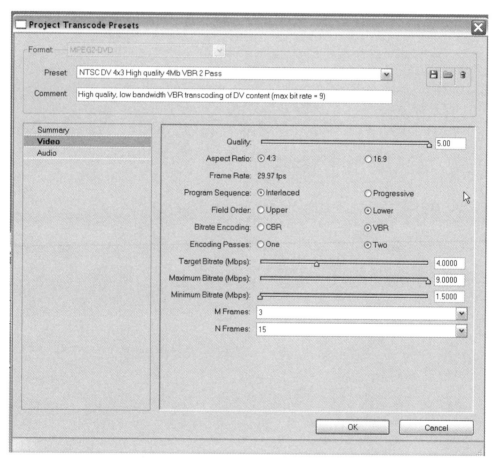

Video compression settings.

Quality

Quality determines the amount of time dedicated to encoding. Higher quality settings can improve picture quality and will increase render time.

Aspect Ratio

Use this setting to choose between 4:3 or 16:9 aspect ratios.

Frame Rate

This displays the frame rate. You can choose between 29.97 fps NTSC or 25 fps PAL.

Program Sequence

This setting determines whether the output is interlaced or progressive.

Interlaced content uses a frame comprised of two fields, even and odd. These fields alternate, displaying half of the frame each time the scanning beam moves down the screen. Most televisions in homes today display interlaced video.

Progressive is non-interlaced video displaying all the lines of a frame in a single pass as opposed to refreshing only half the display at a time. With progressive you do not see the line jitter in the display as you do with interlaced displays. High end widescreen monitors, computer monitors, plasma screens, and most HDTV displays display progressive video.

Field Order

Fields are only applicable when working with interlaced video. When interlaced is selected, it offers a choice between upper and lower field first.

Bitrate Encoding

This setting determines whether CBR or VBR encoding is used.

CBR vs. VBR

One of the biggest choices when specifying encoder settings is whether to encode using constant (CBR) or variable bitrate (VBR).

With constant bitrate encoding, picture quality may fluctuate according to content and motion. Quite simply, with a constant bitrate some scenes will look better than others. Of course, as its name implies, the data rate stays the same, while the content does not. While CBR is simpler and generally faster, it's not as efficient at allocating bits where needed. It can be used for a quick and easy approximation of encoding quality, or on a shorter project where capacity is less of an issue.

VBR is almost always a better choice when it comes to preparing assets. For example, using constant bitrate, the bitrate may be too high for low motion scenes and too low for action-packed, motion scenes. VBR will allocate bits where they are needed, utilizing your disc capacity more efficiently and improving overall quality.

VBR is often implemented with a multi-pass function. Using multiple passes gives the computer an extra opportunity to analyze the video stream before encoding. This helps the encoder determine and allocate bits where needed. Unfortunately, increasing the quality setting results in a slower encode. Encoding with two-pass selected can take twice as long when compared to a single-pass CBR setting.

Single-Pass vs. Two-Pass Encoding

This setting determines how many passes are used to perform compression. Two-pass encoding can be specified when encoding with variable bitrates. With two-pass encoding, the first pass strictly analyzes the content to determine where bits should be allocated. This first pass helps increase the efficiency and quality of the resulting encode.

M Frames

This setting specifies the number of B frames between I and P frames. *(See GOP structure, Appendix C.)*

N Frames

This setting determines the number of frames between I frames. An N frame must be a multiple of the M frames value.

Bitrate

This option only applies to CBR encoding. When encoding with CBR, use this value to determine a constant bitrate.

Encoding Passes

This option only applies to VBR encoding and determines how many passes the encoder will use to analyze the video content before encoding. Two-pass encoding produces better results at the same bitrate; however, it takes approximately twice as long.

Target Bitrate

This specifies the intended average bitrate, measured in megabits per second, for VBR encoding.

Maximum Bitrate

This setting determines the maximum possible bitrate that the encoder will allow. Although this setting allows a bitrate up to 9.0 Mbps, it's generally recommended to stay below 7.5 Mbps whenever possible.

Minimum Bitrate

This determines the minimum bitrate that will be used for low motion scenes, or content that is relatively easy to encode. The minimum bitrate must be at least 1.5 Mbps. (Determining bitrate is detailed towards the end of this chapter.)

Encoder Quality Settings

Many users are tempted to think that setting the quality slider to maximum will always produce better results. This is not always the case. On certain projects, setting the slider to full quality will achieve the same results as specifying a value between 2 and 3.

The lower quality settings in the encoder still produce excellent results in many cases, quite often indistinguishable from higher settings. *Of course, as discussed in a previous chapter, this is all heavily dependent on the character of the video being encoded.*

The quality setting works on a threshold basis. It tells the encoder how long and far to look for certain types of motion. In many cases, the necessary data can be gained from a relatively short search. The point here is that increasing the quality setting is not always necessary, and doesn't always produce better results.

The introduction of two-pass encoding only complicates this issue. If an extremely high-quality setting is chosen, in addition to two-pass, the result could be that it takes up to four times longer to encode than with single-pass encoding at a low- to midrange-quality level!

Don't shoot yourself in the foot by always assuming the two-pass, maximum-quality setting will always produce better results, because it won't. In some cases, it's simply a waste of time.

Make sure to create your own presets and experiment with your own footage.

Audio Compression Settings

Audio compression settings.

Codec

The setting specifies the codec or compression type for the audio. The choices are: Dolby Digital, MainConcept MPEG Audio, and PCM Audio.

Audio Format

This is not a setting. It simply displays the audio type of the selected codec.

> TIP: Dolby recommends a bitrate of 192 kbps for encoding 2-channel AC-3 and 384 kbps when working with 5.1 AC-3 files.

Bitrate

This is where bitrate can be specified for audio. PCM is uncompressed and therefore does not allow compression or bitrate adjustments. Bitrate can be specified for MPEG audio and AC-3.

> TIP: An elementary stream is an individual audio or video stream. A program stream typically consists of two elementary streams, or one audio and one video stream, that have been multiplexed together.

Multiplexing

DVD compliant video streams must eventually be multiplexed before they can be burned to disc. Multiplexing combines the audio, video, and subpicture streams into a single stream that can be read by the DVD player. Many applications also refer to multiplexed files that contain just the audio and/or video. These are referred to as program and elementary streams. In the past, some authoring applications have preferred to work with one or the other. Encore is happy to accept both.

Choosing an Audio Format

> TIP: MPEG audio is a format commonly used in conjunction with the PAL standard. Encore allows the use of MPEG audio on PAL projects. MPEG audio is not widely accepted and does not enjoy the same compatibility when it comes to NTSC players. For this reason, Encore requires either AC-3 or PCM for NTSC projects.

Encore supports several different audio formats. Encore can encode 2-channel AC-3 files, PCM audio, or MPEG-1 layer 2 audio. Encore can also import 5.1-channel AC-3 streams prepared in an external application such as Adobe Premiere.

Choosing an audio format should be fairly simple for most authors. In the past, most consumer / pro level DVD applications did not offer Dolby 5.1 / AC-3 support. Most pro-consumer tools in the sub $1000 price range forced authors to utilize PCM audio in their projects. While PCM audio is very high-quality format, it does not use an efficient compression scheme. PCM is an uncompressed standard that can take up 25% or more of your total disc capacity. For this reason, most authors will choose AC-3 (2-channel or 5.1). This frees up valuable space that can be used to increase bitrate and improve video quality.

> TIP: AC-3 can produce comparable quality at approximately 10% of the bitrate of PCM audio.

Audio Format	Typical Bitrate
2 Channel AC-3	192 Kbps
5.1 Channel AC-3	384 Kbps
MPEG1 Audio	224 Kbps
PCM Audio	1.5 Mbps

As mentioned, Encore allows authors to import 5.1-channel AC-3 files that have been prepared in an external application, such as the Surcode encoder that ships with Adobe Premiere Pro. As one would expect, Encore does not provide tools to mix surround sound internally; however, it does encode 2-channel AC-3s.

Figure 3.1 *Chart showing bitrate comparison between 2-channel AC-3, 5-channel AC-3, PCM, and MPEG-1.*

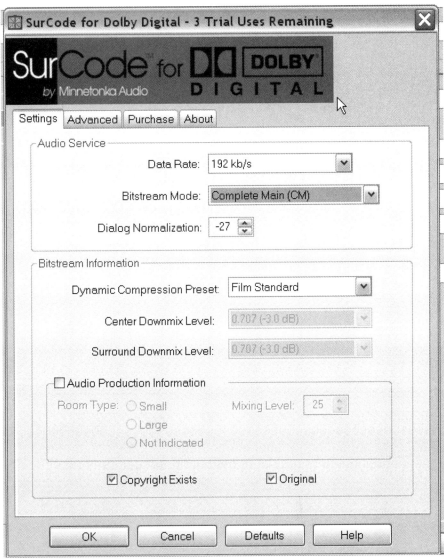

Surecode Encoder in Premiere Pro.

TIP: The DVD spec also supports DTS audio (Digital Theater Surround). However, Encore does not support DTS at this time.

AC-3 2-channel will suffice for most personal and corporate projects. More advanced users, or individuals with a background in audio, will appreciate the ability to import true 5.1 streams as well.

TIP: In the past, some have confused THX for an audio format. This is not the case. THX is a certification granted to products that meet stringent standards adhering to their own established specifications. For more information on THX, visit www.thx.com.

Encoding 2-Channel AC-3 Audio

In the preferences settings, Encore allows users to select the type of compression used to transcode imported audio. This is referred to as the default audio encoding scheme. By default, Encore will automatically transcode imported audio files to 192 kbps 2-channel AC-3 files. Files prepared externally as 2-channel AC-3, or 5.1, should not need to be re-encoded.

Most users will prefer to take advantage of the built-in 2-channel AC-3; however, this behavior can be easily altered by choosing Edit>Preferences>Encoding.

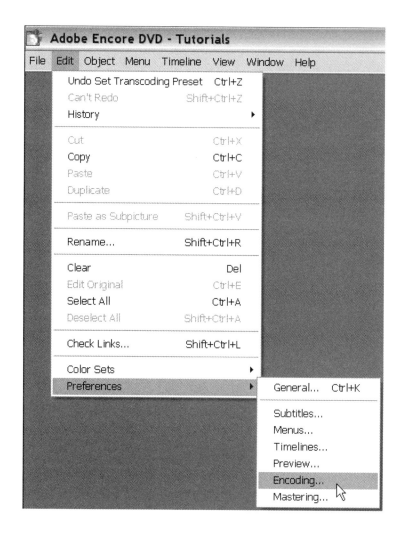

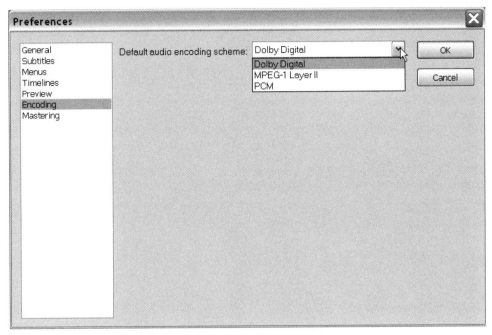

Edit Project Preferences dialog. Note that three different formats are available.

Modify the encoding preferences if you wish to encode to a format other than the default Dolby Digital setting. After the preference has been adjusted, the behavior will be reflected when you open a new project. If you decide you want to change settings in the middle of an existing project, you will need to manually specify transcoding presets by right clicking on the file in the Project window.

Below are some helpful hints on encoding AC-3:

- As with video, use the best quality source material that you can obtain.
- Always have at least 2 seconds of digital black silence at the beginning of the bitstream. This gives the playback system time to lock and start decoding before the real material starts playing. It will provide smoother audio playback. It is not necessary to repeat the process on the tail end of clips.
- Always encode at 348 kbps data rate for multichannel material and at 192 kbps for 2-channel stereo material.
- Do not enable the LFE Channel unless there is dedicated low-frequency effects (LFE) material in the original audio source. Also, if you are planning to create your own 5.1 mix, don't send all of your lower frequencies *solely* to the LFE channel as these frequencies will not be reproduced when downmixed for 2-channel playback. This setting is not chosen in Encore, rather the external AC-3 creation/editing application.

TIP: Most NLEs will not import AC-3 files. Windows Media Player, by default, won't play individual AC-3 files either. If you want to preview AC-3 files, it's best to import these files into Encore. You can also use your favorite DVD playback software for this task.

Importing 5.1 AC-3

This part of the chapter applies to authors who wish to prepare 5.1-channel AC-3 files using external 5.1 AC-3 encoders. Please note that if you don't work with 5.1-channel AC-3, you may skip directly to section on determining bitrates on page 85. Below is a list of common settings that apply to most 5.1 encoders.

Dialog Normalization

Dialog Normalization is used to lower the *average* volume level in an audio stream.

Upon playback, the Dolby Digital decoders in the associated playback device will attenuate playback based on the Dialog Normalization value. This value, specified on an absolute scale ranging from −1 dB to −31 dB, describes the long-term average dialog level of the associated program. Most AC-3 encoders start with a value of −27 db. Higher values (i.e., −26, −25) will attenuate the audio more, while lower values (i.e., −28, −29) will reduce the attenuation upon playback. When a value of −31 is specified, no signal attenuation will be applied.

When playing back audio content that does not contain dialogue, such as music, the Dialog Normalization value indicates how far the average dialog level of the encoded program is below 0 dB. The best way to determine the ideal setting is to encode several smaller files and preview these files using DVD playback software.

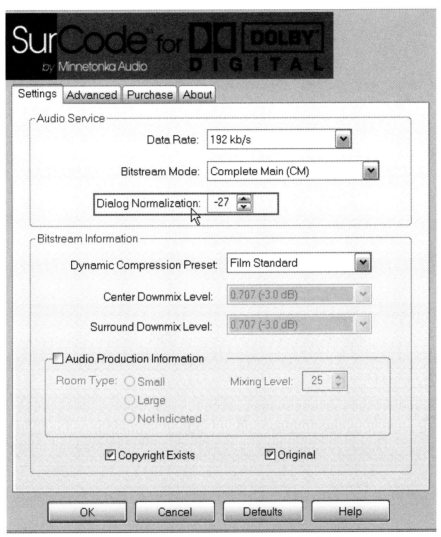

Dialog normalization can be specified directly in the Surcode Encoder provided with Adobe Premiere Pro.

> TIP: If you look at the audio levels in your NLE, 0 dB represents the highest value. Anything above 0 dB will result in permanent loss and distortion. Remember that 0 dB is the peak level and should never be exceeded when preparing audio for DVD.

> TIP: Most material captured and transferred via a DV camera will work best with Dialog Normalization set between −27 and −31 dB.

Dynamic Range Compression Profile

AC-3 encoders use one of six dynamic compression presets to determine how the associated audio stream is compressed. The purpose of this type of compression is not to reduce data rate, but rather to affect the dynamic range of the clip.

Dynamic range compression uses three different bands to isolate different sections of the source according to dynamic levels. These three distinct bands can be used to reduce the loudest levels, boost the quietest, and raise or modify the median levels in an audio stream all at the same time. Six different presets reflect settings that cater to different types of audio content.

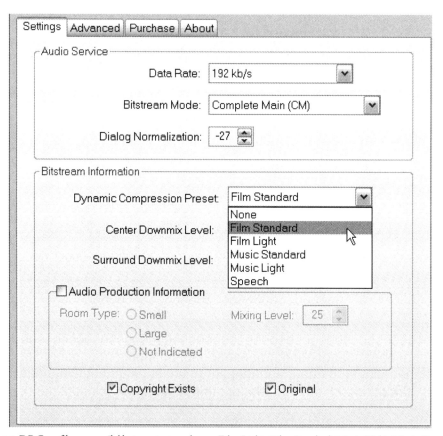

Six preset DRC profiles are available to content producers: Film Light, Film Standard, Music Light, Music Standard, Speech, and None.

TIP: More detailed information on these compression profiles can be obtained at www.dolby.com

Downmixing

If you're planning to deliver your project with 5.1 surround sound, you may have wondered what happens if certain viewers don't have a 5.1-channel surround sound setup. If the viewer will be listening to a 5.1 mix on a television with only two speakers, what happens to the rear and center channels?

This is the purpose of downmixing. When encoding 5.1 AC-3, the encoder will present options that the author can use to downmix the 5.1 stream into two channels. Downmixing won't alter the original 5.1 mix; it simply adds additional information that can be used to cater this stream for viewers with only two speakers.

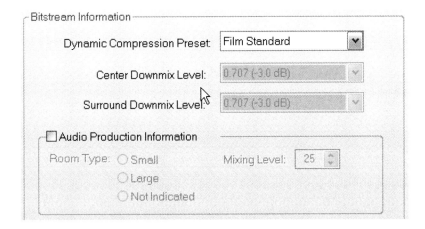

TIP: Downmixing is not an option in Encore as Encore's encoder is limited to two channels. Downmixing applies when using external 5.1 AC-3 encoders.

TIP: Make sure that both Center and Surround downmix levels are specified. The default value of −3.0 dB is recommended and typically produces satisfactory results.

Downmix levels need to be specified for the Center and Surround Channels respectively.

Center Downmix Level

When the encoded audio has three front channels (L, C, R), but the viewer has only two front speakers (left and right), this setting determines the downmix level with respect to the original left and right channels.

Surround Downmix Level

When the encoded audio has one or more Surround channels, but the consumer does not have rear surround speakers, this parameter determines the downmix level for the Surround channels (rear left and rear right) with respect to the Left and Right front channels.

> TIP: When combining audio streams from a 5.1 source, the combination of multiple streams typically increases the volume level when played back. For this reason, most downmix levels are set to −3 dB to compensate.

Determining Bitrates

Now that the limitations of media, capacity, bitrate, and compression have been explored, it's time to get down to the business of determining the perfect bitrate.

To determine bitrate, it's necessary to account for every element that will be used in the finished DVD. Once the elements are laid out in a flowchart, it's easy to determine how much capacity each will require.

Available disc space is the first thing we need to determine. Most will be working with DVD −R/+R media with a maximum capacity of 4.37 gigabytes. However, we will use the "powers of 10" number of 4.7 billion bytes to simplify calculations. For our purposes consider 4,700,000,000 (4.7 billion) bytes as the total capacity of single-sided general media (DVD-R / DVD5).

Next, we'll need to determine the amount of space required for audio, motion menus, PC content, and subtitles. Once these figures are calculated we can deduct from the total disc capacity and devote the remaining bits to encoding the main video streams.

Audio

Audio encoded inside Encore is encoded using 2-channel AC-3 by default. This option uses a bitrate of 192 kbps. Most 5-channel AC-3 files are encoded at 384 kbps.

Subpictures

Subpictures typically do not require much space. A possible exception would be subtitles that run the length of the video file. If you are working with subtitles, you can factor in a bitrate of 10 kbps per stream.

Motion Menus

Because motion menus typically contain more motion than most video, it's best to specify a higher bitrate. Typical bitrates for motion menus are between 6 and 8 Mbps. Of course, if you encoded the motion menus yourself, you'll know exactly what bitrates were specified. Simply use that bitrate or the resulting file size for calculations.

Still Menus

Still menus generally take up very little space and rarely need to be factored into the bit budget. If your project contains a large amount of still menus, deduct 100 kb for each. This will account for the background still image and will also account for the subpticture highlights.

After these assets are accounted for, these numbers are deducted from total capacity. The remaining bits can then be used for encoding video files.

Okay, let's put this into a real-world perspective and break down the math.

This is what we have:

1 single-sided disk
2 still menus
Disc overhead/file structure
A motion menu that is 90 seconds long at 7.5 Mbps
3 language/audio tracks encoded in AC-3 192 kbps
3 subtitle tracks each at 10 kbps
1 movie that is 92 minutes

The movie is what we calculate last, because we want to devote all of the remaining bits to video encoding.

Since data rate is calculated in terms of bits, our disc capacity is 36,700,000,000 bits (4.7 billion bytes × 8).

The still menus are pretty insignificant. Unless you have more than 50, it really doesn't make much of an impact on your bit budget.

Disc overhead, aka "reserve," varies between 5 and 7 percent. We have a very simple menu and file structure, so estimate that only 5 percent of the disc will be used.

5%= .05; .05 × 36,700,000,000 bits = 1,835,000,000 bits

Now we have to take into account our motion menu.
90 seconds × 7.5 Mbps = 675 Mb

Let's not forget that a Megabit is one million bits.
675 Mb = 675,000,000 bits

Now let's figure out the audio tracks. We can safely say a single audio track is 92 minutes long because that is how long our movie is.
92 minutes × 60 = 5520 seconds

Keep this number of seconds handy, because we will be using it in future calculations.
5520 seconds × 192 kbps = 1,059,840 kb

Don't forget we are dealing with bits, and a kilobit is 1,000 bits.
1,059,840 kb × 1,000 = 1,059,840,000 bits

Are we forgetting something? Yes, there are three audio tracks.
3 × 1,059,840,000 = 3,179,520,000

Now let's figure in the three subtitle tracks.
5520 seconds × 10 kbps = 55,200 kb × 1000 = 55,200,000 bits

Again we have three subtitle tracks.
3 × 55,200,000 = 165,600,000 bits

Now we need to add up our bits.

Disc overhead	1,835,000,000
Motion menu	675,000,000
Total audio tracks	3,179,520,000
Total subtitle tracks	165,600,000
	5,855,120,000

We take those bits and subtract them from the total disc capacity.
36,700,000,000 − 5,855,120,000 = 30,844,880 bits

To make things easy, convert the bits into megabits first.
30,844,880 / 1,000,000 = 30,844.88 Mb

We have a 92-minute feature. We will need to convert this into seconds before dividing it into our available megabits.

30,844.88 Mb / 5520 seconds = **5.588 Mbps!!!!**

We'll round that figure to 5.6 Mbps. We've successfully determined our bitrate for encoding video.

Whew! Did you get all that? We've covered some heavy concepts and if you made it through this, the rest will be much easier. As you work with Encore and start burning your own DVDs, these concepts will make more sense and you'll feel more comfortable with adjusting these settings.

Finally time to build a working project!

Chapter 4

Building the Project

If you skipped Chapter 2 or 3, don't worry; the pop quiz isn't until next week. We've covered most of the aspects of the interface and many important technical considerations. Now that we've gotten most of that out of the way, it's time to start working with content inside of Encore.

In this section, we're going to start putting our first basic project together. We'll be working with chapter points, text, and buttons for the first time. We'll create our first menu and we'll link together the assets to build our first working project.

Instead of concentrating on modifying existing menu and button templates, we are going to dive into creating our own, albeit basic, menus and buttons. This is to give you a taste of what can and can't be done inside Encore and should shed some light on when it may be best to use Photoshop instead. Once you go through the process of creating your own custom buttons using simple graphics and building your first menu, creating and modifying your own templates will be a walk in the park.

This chapter will explore many features that can be done in Encore without a second application like Photoshop or Premiere. We will be using assets from the Project DVD included with this book. You can choose to burn these assets to create your own tutorial disc. Of course, that's entirely up to you.

Expect some questions to pop up as you work through this project. We won't cover every aspect of Encore, but we will get you ready for taking the next step. Chapter 5 will clarify many more behaviors and features and will also shed more light on the Photoshop layer behaviors and prefixes used to create and manage menus.

- Project 1
- Navigating in the timelines
- Working with chapters
- Setting chapter markers at GOP headers
- Creating the main menu
- Copy and paste
- Alignment options
- Adding text to the menu
- Working with the character palette
- Working with buttons
- Creating subpicture/selection highlights with layers
- Linking buttons
- Pickwhips
- Specifying start action/First Play
- Preview window

Project 1

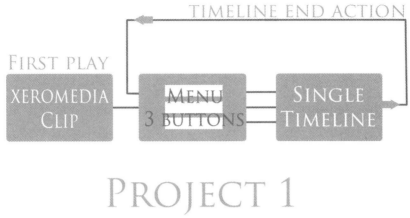

In Project 1, we'll be creating an extremely simple project that showcases some of Encore's main features and behaviors. This project also provides the first look at layer structures and conventions used to create and define menus.

This first DVD project contains two video files and one menu.

The first video file, Xeromedia.avi, will consist of a small logo that plays when the disc is first inserted into the player.

The second video file contains two tutorials that have already been transcoded to MPEG-2 using Adobe Premiere. We'll need to set a chapter point near the center of the tutorial's timeline to provide direct navigation to the second tutorial. Every timeline starts with a chapter point, so we'll end up with two chapter points in our tutorials timeline.

PROJECT ASSETS AND BEHAVIORS

Xeromedia Timeline
We'll use the Xeromedia.m2v clip to create a timeline that will play once the disc is inserted. When the timeline is done playing, it will link to the Main Menu.

Tutorial Timeline
Once the movie is done playing, it will also return to the Main Menu.

TIP: If the Tutorial 1 button is selected, the behavior will mimic the behavior of the Play All button. They both do the same thing. In version 1.0, Encore does not provide an option to alter navigation in the middle of a timeline, so it's impossible to play just chapter one. Once the viewer navigates to chapter one and the timeline commences, The entire timeline will play through to the end. Although the Tutorial 1 button provides the same functionality of the play all button, it is used to achieve consistency and navigation in the menu. In other words, it is not possible to play *just* Chapter 1 and return to the main menu without splitting the clip and putting each clip in its own timeline In order to create a menu that will only play Chapter 1, then return to the menu, multiple timelines would need to be used, each containing individual tutorials. For more information, watch the tutorial clips once you've completed the project.

Main Menu

The Main Menu contains three buttons that provide navigation to chapter points in timelines. There are three buttons with links in the main menu: Play All, Tutorial 1, and Tutorial 2.

Button Behaviors/Linking

Play All: Plays the movie "Tutorial" from the beginning. This button is linked to Chapter 1.

Tutorial 1: Plays the movie "Tutorial" from the beginning. This button is also linked to Chapter 1.

Tutorial 2: Plays the movie "Tutorial" starting at Chapter 2. This button will access the second tutorial contained inside the Tutorial.mp2 clip. This button will be linked to Chapter 2.

Other details:

This DVD is NTSC and distributed in North America only.

No copy protection is required.

The volume label of the DVD should be "Tutorials."

When disk is inserted the Xeromedia clip automatically plays. Once the clip is done playing, it is followed by the Main Menu.

PROJECT 1: STEP-BY-STEP

Creating New Project

1. Choose: File>New Project

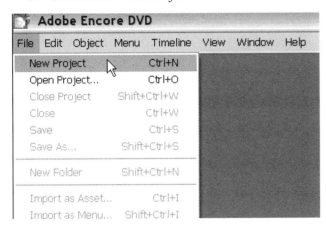

This will open the Project Settings dialog box. Select NTSC as the Television Standard.

Importing Files

The first thing to do after creating a new project is to import assets.

2. Choose: File>Import As Assets

This will bring up the Import dialog box.

3. Select the following files: Tutorial.mp2 and xeromedia.avi.

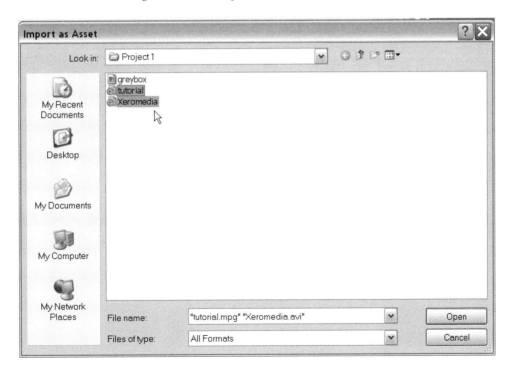

4. Click Open.
5. Next, choose: File>Save As.

This will bring up the Save dialog box.

6. Name the project "project1" and press Enter or click Save.

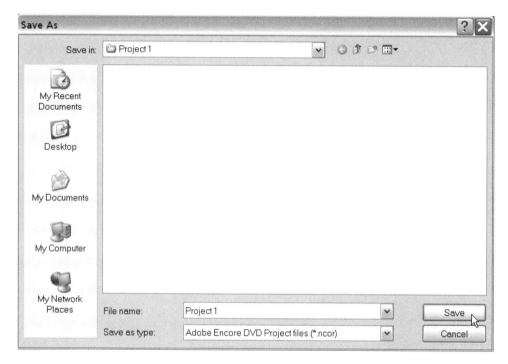

You have now created and saved an Encore project file.

> TIP: This project file keeps track of all the necessary information (assets, menus, chapter points, etc.) Therefore it is important that you save often to avoid losing your work.

Creating the Timelines

Many projects will utilize multiple timelines to accommodate different assets in a project. Each timeline can hold one video clip, or multiple stills.

We need to create two timelines. One for Tutorial.mp2 and one for Xeromedia.avi. Let's start with the Xeromedia clip.

> TIP: If you need to use more than one motion video clip in a timeline, the video clips need to be prepared in advance using a program such as Premiere. Use your NLE to join and export the individual clips as one continuous clip.

7.   From the drop-down menu choose: Timeline>New Timeline.

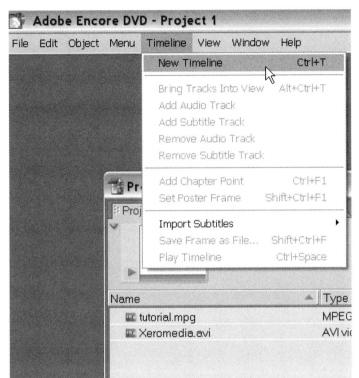

In order to create a new timeline, the project window must be selected.

8. Drag the Xermomedia.avi clip into the blank video track in the Timeline window.

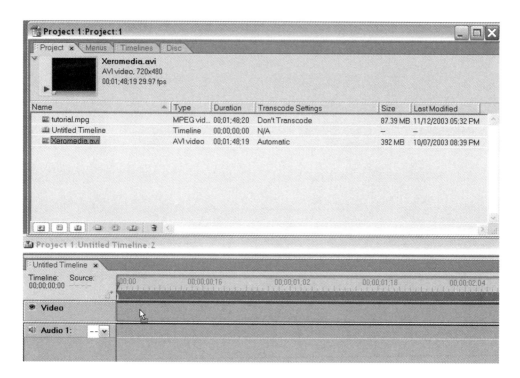

9. Next, we need to name our timeline. Make sure the timeline is selected, then open the Properties palette. In the Name field, change the Timeline Name from "Untitled1" to "XeromediaClip."

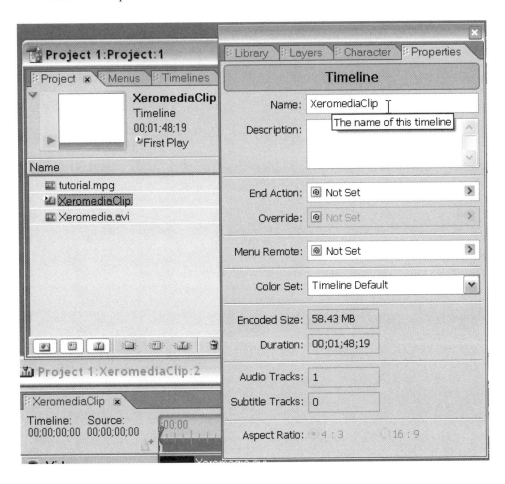

TIP: Keeping detailed, descriptive names for timelines can help with project linking and organization.

TIP: The Window menu can be used to specify which palettes are visible. You can use this menu to open different palettes and windows in Encore.

At this point, if you wish to preview content in a timeline, make sure the timeline window is selected, then simply press the spacebar.

10. Next, we need to create a timeline for our Tutorials movie. This time, instead of using the drop-down menus (Timeline>New Timeline) simply select the Tutorials.mp2 clip within the Project window, then click the new timeline icon at the bottom of the Project window.

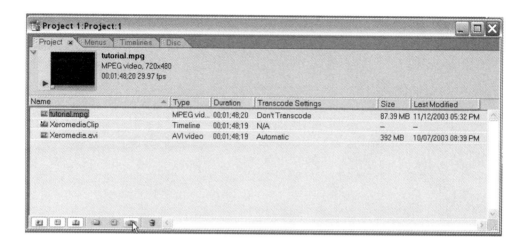

Notice that with the Tutorial.mpg movie selected, the timeline was created with the clip already imported. Using this technique the timeline also automatically inherits the name of the video clip. It is not necessary to rename this timeline.

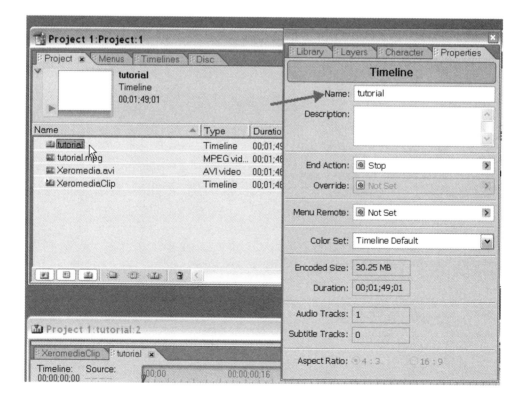

> TIP: The fastest way to create a timeline is simply select the clip you wish to create a timeline for and use the keyboard shortcut CTRL-T.

Navigating in the Timeline

Navigation in the timeline can be accomplished by using a mouse. Simply drag the current time indicator (CTI) to the desired frame.

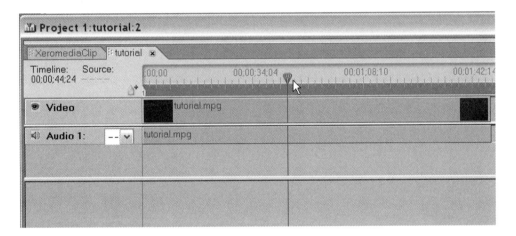

The CTI can also be moved numerically using timecode. Encore uses hot text values that can be clicked and dragged to adjust timecode with a mouse.

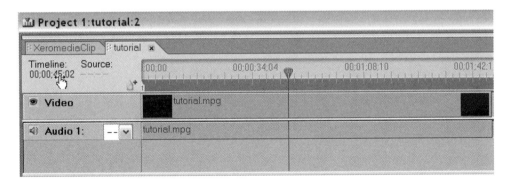

You can also click directly on the timecode and enter a timecode value to jump to that frame.

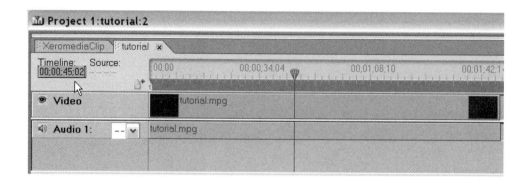

There will also be times when you will want to control the zoom level of the timeline. If you're a mouse fan you can use the Zoom tool in the tool palette. You can also use keyboard shortcuts. When the timeline is selected, CTRL+ will instantly zoom into the timeline, CTRL− will zoom out. You can also bring the entire timeline into view by pressing CTRL + 0 (zero). Use the Home and End keys to navigate to the start and end of the timeline. Right Arrow key to advance 1 frame, Left Arrow key to retreat 1 frame. And don't forget you can use the asterisk key in the numeric keypad (★) to set a chapter point.

TIP: You can view and adjust the properties of individual timelines by selecting the timeline and setting the options directly in the properties palette.

Encore also provides the ability to trim audio and video clips and also allows the author to change the location and duration of still images and subtitles.

Use the Selection tool to hover over the head or tail of the asset. At this point, a red bracket icon becomes visible. The edge of the clip can now be dragged to alter the duration.

Working with Chapters

Chapters can be added to the timelines inside of Encore to specify navigation points for chapter selection. Chapter points usually represent the beginning of a scene or a point of relevant action in the video. Buttons can be linked to individual chapter points in order to provide disc navigation, and menus can have their end actions set to play a chapter point.

> TIP: Encore always creates a chapter point at the beginning of every timeline.

Later on, we'll take a look at exporting markers from Adobe Premiere.

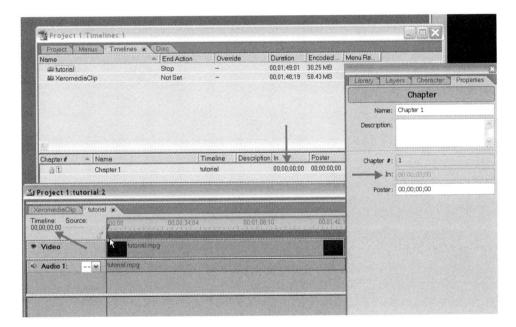

Notice that our tutorial timeline has a chapter point set at 00:00:00:00.

Next, we need to create a second chapter point so we can access our second tutorial.

11.   To create chapter points, drag the CTI (current time indicator) to beginning of the second tutorial and click on the Add Chapter Point icon.

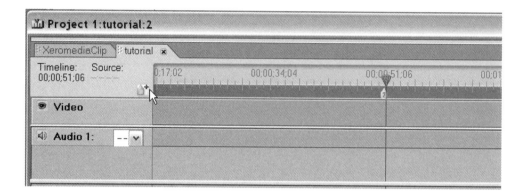

Alternatively, chapter points can be created by right-clicking directly above the Timeline then choosing Add Chapter Point. You can also use the Add Chapter Point in the Timeline Menu or use the ★ key on your numerical keypad.

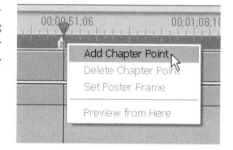

Setting Chapter Markers at GOP Headers

When working with imported MPEG-2 content, chapter markers may only be placed at a GOP header. These GOP headers are represented by the small, white notches made visible by zooming into the timeline.

What Is a GOP?

GOP stands for "group of pictures." DVD players use consecutive GOPs to create a video stream. Think of GOPs as units that MPEG-2 uses to efficiently organize and present the frames, or picture data. GOPs are an essential aspect of MPEG-2 compression used to increase the efficiency of the encoding process by reducing the amount of redundant information that occurs between frames.

TIP: Use the Zoom tool or the keyboard shortcuts CTRL +/− to magnify the view in the timeline. This will bring the GOP headers into view.

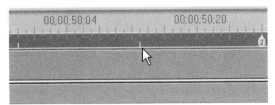

Most MPEG-2 files will be encoded with roughly two GOP headers for every second of content. Therefore, a chapter point can only be placed in two places per second of content.

Chapter points can be added at several different stages. First, markers can be added inside Adobe Premiere during the editing stage. If you're working with an AVI inside Premiere, markers can be placed on any individual frame and these markers will force a GOP header to be created when encoded to MPEG-2.

You can also open AVI files directly inside Encore. Once again, you can place chapter point on any frame you wish. My recommendation would be to make sure you consider chapter placement before you encode your content to MPEG-2. This is the simplest way to eliminate chapter placement restrictions.

Creating the Main Menu

Menus are used to provide access to the contents of a DVD. Inside Encore, graphics can be used to create the background image. Graphics and even motion video can be used to create buttons and video thumbnails. We'll get into motion backgrounds in the Chapter 6. For now, let's look at the basic process of creating a still menu entirely within Encore.

We need a simple menu in order to provide navigation to our Tutorials timeline.

12.   Choose Menu>New Menu

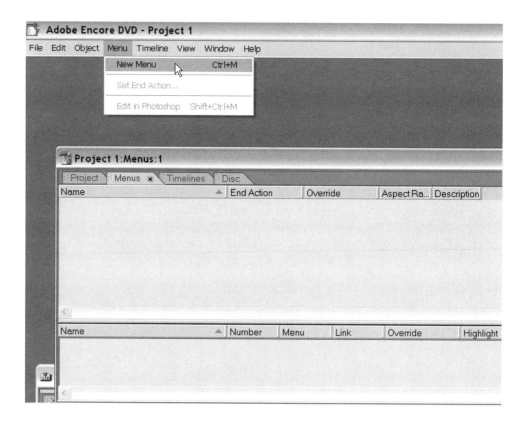

13. Make sure the menu is selected. Go to the Properties palette and change the name to "Tutorials Menu."

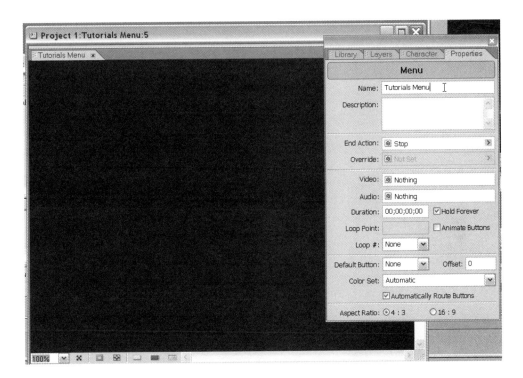

TIP: Notice that Encore creates the new menu using a default menu. The default menu in Encore is not as much a menu as it is a black background. This menu is noted by asterisks to the left of the name in the Library palette. This default menu can be modified by selecting a new file in the Library palette. Right click, then choose Set As Default menu. This process can be repeated to specify a default button.

We'll keep the black background for now. Let's import a graphic that can be used to as a backdrop for the text we'll be using in our buttons.

Working with Buttons

When adding text or graphics to a menu this information is added to the background image of the menu. In order to create buttons or links inside a menu, graphics must be specified as buttons. Encore provides several options to convert graphics into buttons.

We are going to go through creating a button from an imported graphic. However, if you want to use the built-in buttons within Encore, simply select the button you want from the Library palette, and drag it into the Menu Editor. (You can also right click on the button's name and select "Place.") These buttons are ready to be linked and you can skip ahead, but to see more of the possibilities (and limitations) I recommend you build the button for yourself.

14.　Inside the sample file folders, open the Project 1 folder and locate the greybox.jpg file.

At this point, several common Windows behaviors can be incorporated into the workflow.

We can drag and drop using Windows Explorer to import files. This applies to the Project window, the Menu Editor window, the Library palette and the timeline. We can also use standard Windows keyboard shortcuts to select, copy, and paste files.

15.　Using Windows Explorer, drag greybox.jpg directly into the Menu Editor window.

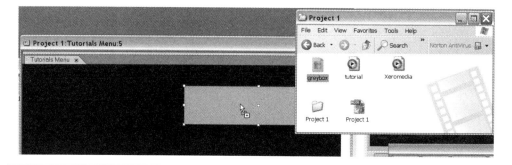

TIP: The Menu Editor can also be resized using the drop-down menu to the bottom left. Use this option to switch between different zoom percentages to accommodate objects in this window. You may also use the Zoom tool.

Copy and Paste

Encore provides cut-and-paste tools directly inside the drop-down Edit menu. However, it's much easier to use standard Windows conventions.

Inside the Menu Editor, simply select the object you wish to copy, Press CTRL-C. This loads the image onto the clipboard. Use CTRL-V to paste the image. CTRL-X can be used to cut and CTRL-D can be used to duplicate.

TIP: Similar to Photoshop, an object can be manipulated by holding down the ALT key before clicking and dragging to a new location. This technique is the simplest method of duplicating an object inside of Encore.

16. With the Selection tool activated, click on the imported greybox.jpg file to select it directly in the Menu Editor window.

Once selected, the bounding box around the greybox.jpg image will be visible. Using the Selection tool, click and drag in the center of the image to position, or click and drag on the corners of the bounding box to resize the image.

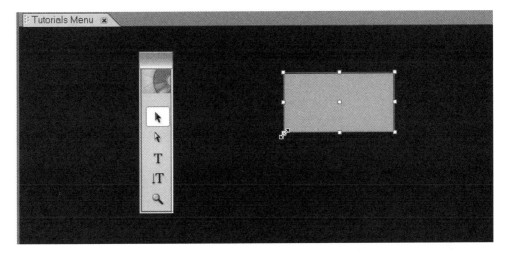

17. Next, while the greybox.jpg image is still selected, press CTRL-C.

This loads a copy of the image onto your Windows clipboard, making duplication possible.

18. Press CTRL-V to paste a copy of this image.

Now two copies of greybox.jpg are visible on the screen.

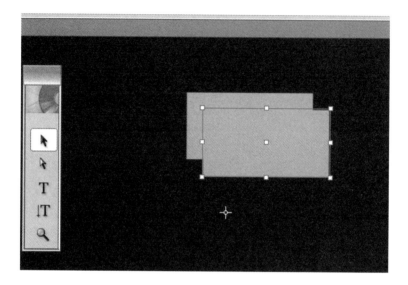

19. Press CTRL-V once again to paste a second copy of the greybox.jpg.

Now three copies are visible in the Menu Editor.

Alignment Options

Encore provides several different alignment tools to help align objects in relation to each other or in relation to title safe areas. You can align according to the left, center, or right edges on the vertical axis, or you can align the top, middle, or bottom of an object according to the horizontal axis. In this case the bounding box, a rectangle, is always used to determine alignment.

Next, we'll use Encore's alignment tools to position these images properly in the Menu Editor window.

Multiple items can be selected by using the SHIFT and CTRL key modifiers. Use these keyboard shortcuts in combination with the mouse to determine which objects are selected.

20.   Hold down the SHIFT key and click on each of the three objects in the Menu Editor.

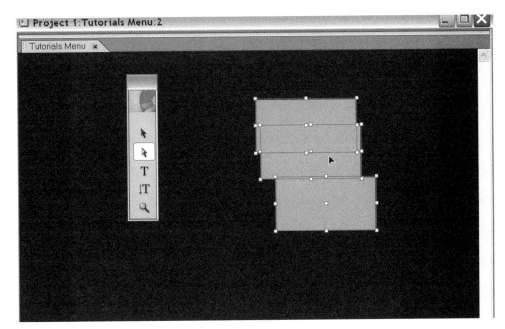

All three objects are now selected.

21.   With all three object selected, from Encore's drop-down menu choose: Object>Align>

This presents options to align these objects.

22.   Next, choose: Align>Relative to Safe Areas

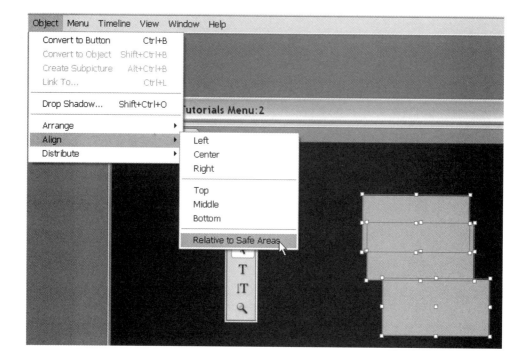

Safe Areas make sure that the buttons are not cut off when displayed on certain TV sets.

23.   Next, choose: Object>Align

Notice that Relative to Safe Areas is still selected.

24.   Choose: Align>Center

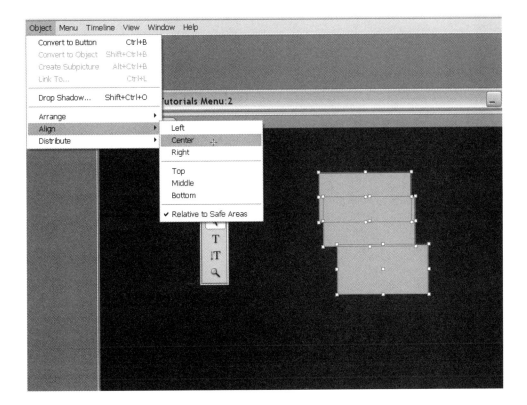

All the clips are now aligned in the center of the screen.

Next, we want to distribute these objects vertically according to title safe areas.

25.   Choose: Edit>Object>Distribute>Relative to Safe Areas.

Notice that when we Distribute, we must also click Relative to Safe Areas.

26.   Once again, choose: Object>Distribute>Vertically.

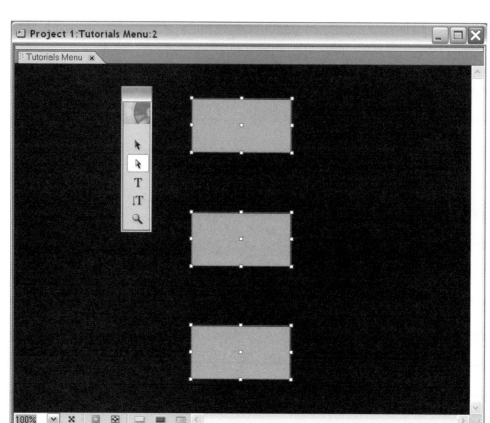

This will space our objects evenly and will keep them all within title safe boundaries.

TIP: If multiple buttons are selected, they can all be moved and/or scaled simultaneously. This will not only improve workflow, but also maintain size and spacing between objects.

Adding Text to the Menu

Adding text to a menu is a very simple process. Simply select the Text tool and click directly in the Menu Editor. Text can be added horizontally or vertically and can be typed directly in the Menu Editor using one of the following two options.

Freely

To type freely, simply click in the Menu Editor window and use the Enter key to specify when the text wraps.

Constrained Text Box

This technique uses a bounding box to determine where the text wraps. To use this method, click with the Type tool and drag to create the desired bounding box. Use the bounding box to specify which section of the menu will be filled with text.

> TIP: Once a bounding box has been created, it can be resized at any time you are editing the text. Resizing will automatically change where and how the text wraps.

> TIP: Text can be aligned, distributed as a graphic, and can also be converted to a button.

Now, we'll create text that can be placed over the grey boxes.

27. Select the Text tool in the toolbar.
28. Click directly in the Menu Editor. A flashing cursor indicates that text is ready to be added to the menu.
29. Type "Play All."

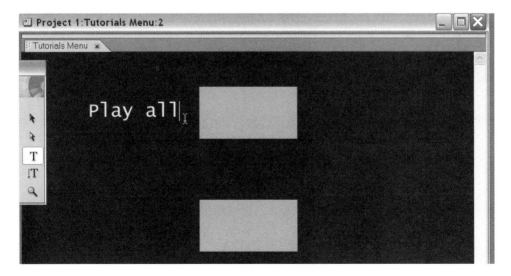

30. With the Text tool still selected, click and drag the "Play All" text to select it.

Working with the Character Palette

The Character palette provides a wide variety of text tools, far surpassing what one would expect for a DVD authoring program. It provides precise control over font, type size, color, leading, kerning, tracking, baseline shift, scaling, text styles, and anti-aliasing.

31. Use the Window menu to open the Character palette. Now, change the font to Microsoft Sans Serif, and 24 point size.

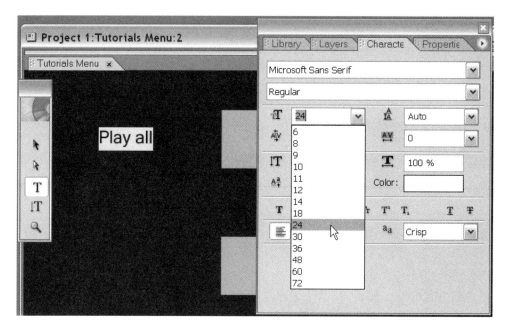

32. Repeat steps 28 through 30 to create the text for "Tutorial 1" and "Tutorial 2."

You'll notice that the text is now in Microsoft Sans Serif 24 pt, so there is no need to repeat steps 31 to 32.

33. Use the Direct Select tool to select and position each block of text over the three grey boxes in the Menu Editor.

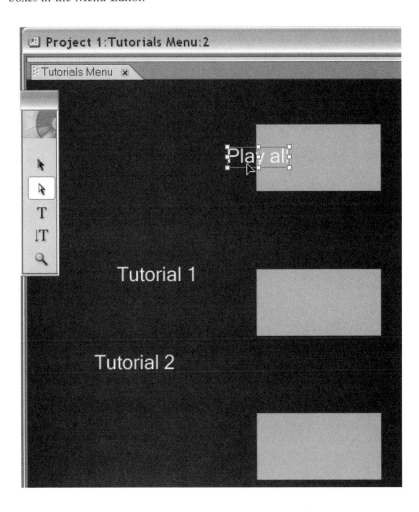

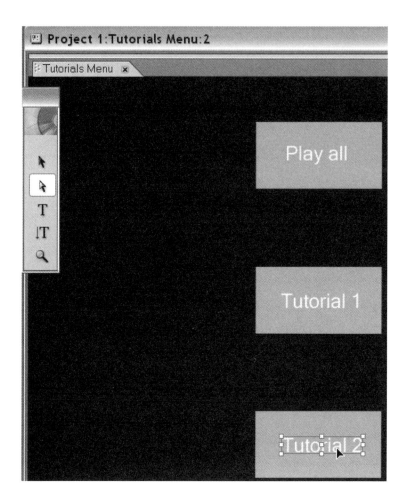

TIP: You can also click on the text with the Selection tool. This displays a bounding box that can be used to resize the text.

34.   Open the Layers palette.

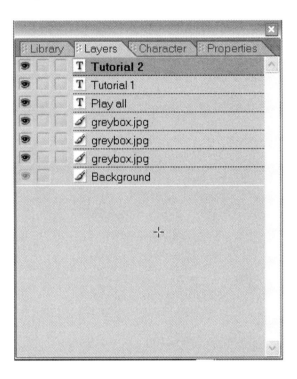

TIP: All palettes can be pulled out and viewed as their own window using this method. You can also consolidate the palettes into one window by dragging a palette into another palette's window. Encore allows you to consolidate windows based on similar functionality. Therefore, you cannot drag, for example, the Layers palette into the Project window. But you can combine it with the Properties and Character palettes. All palettes can be grouped together. All Timeline tabs can be grouped together, all Menus tabs can be grouped together. Find what works for you and incorporate it into your workflow.

NOTE: The Layers palette provides useful information on how Encore identifies the various layers and layer sets. Mastery of the Layers palette is essential to understanding Encore.

Notice that we have created six objects, all created on their own layers. The next part is to convert certain layers to buttons so they can be linked. When an object is converted into a button, a layer set is created. These layer sets represent the structure and naming conventions that Encore and Photoshop use to create menus. We'll cover this in much greater detail in Chapter 5.

In the next section of the project, graphics will be converted to buttons. When a button is created from a graphic in Encore, several layers are created and organized within a layer set. Each layer of a button's layer set represents a different aspect of that button, such as the text, the graphic, the subpicture highlight, and its functionality as a button. Each layer is given a special symbol indicating its function. The layer set, as layers are added, is also given a special symbol. Think of the layer set as the folder and the layers as files in the folder. If this seems confusing at first, don't worry. We will be covering this in greater detail in the Photoshop chapter (Chapter 5). For now, watch the Layers palette and see how Encore adds the layers and changes the layer sets as you create buttons. The chart below shows an expanded layer set with all associated layers.

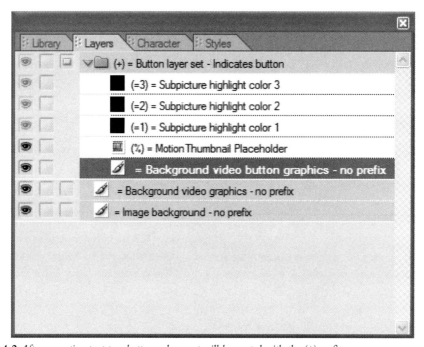

Figure 4.2 *After converting text to a button, a layer set will be created with the (+) prefix.*

TIP: Now and again look in the Layers palette for blank text layers. Inevitably, everyone accidentally creates blank text layers when working with the Text tool (for example, trying to select with the Text tool instead of the Selection tools). Extra text layers can complicate the layering and cause problems later on. Watch for and delete these extra layers.

TIP: Later on in this book, we'll also look at the prefixes used to create video thumbnails.

TIP: You can select buttons or graphics directly in the Menu Editor. Individual objects and buttons can also be selected by clicking on their corresponding layer in the Layers palette. This becomes especially useful when trying to select a specific object or element that is under or nearby another element.

For now, we need to decide which object we want to convert from graphics to buttons. Let's use the titles that we created with the Text tool.

35.   With the Layers palette still in view, select the layer that contains the text "Play All."

36.   Now Choose: Object>Convert To Button

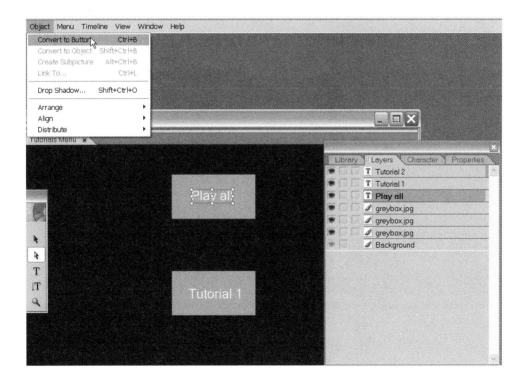

A layer set has now been created reflecting button creation. The "Play All" text is no longer a simple graphic, the (+) symbol in the Layers palette represents a layer set that is used as a button.

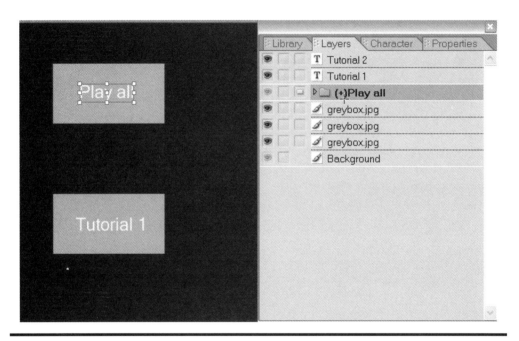

TIP: Using the Create Text Subpicture command, you can have Adobe Encore DVD automatically create a text subpicture layer or update text in an existing subpicture layer. To enable this feature, select the button; in the Properties palette, select Create Text Subpicture. Once enabled, Adobe Encore DVD creates a copy of the text to be used as a subpicture and creates a new (=1) layer. The previous (=1) layer is replaced, updating the subpicture highlight information automatically as text is added or modified.

Creating Subpicture/Selection Highlights with Layers

A subpicture highlight aids in menu navigation by providing the selection and activation states. They can also facilitate linking, providing the ability to navigate menus, timelines, and other buttons. In Chapter 5 we will discuss the subpicture highlight in detail.

Next, we'll create a subpicture for the button that will be used to determine selection states in the final menu.

37. If it is not still selected, select the "Play All" text once again in the Menu Editor, then choose: Object>Create Subpicture.

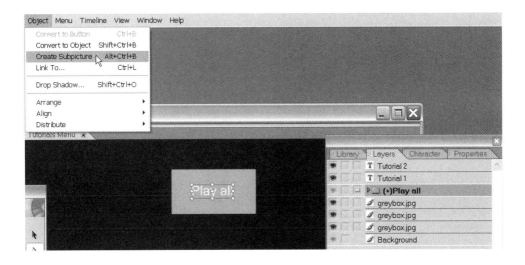

TIP: A layer's set must be expanded to view its individual layers.

The Layers palette now shows another layer added to the layer set. The (=1) symbol represents a layer that is used to determine the subpicture/selection highlight.

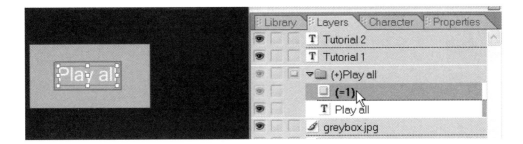

At this point, we need to repeat this process to create our two additional buttons.

38. Select the text "Tutorial 1" in the Menu Editor.

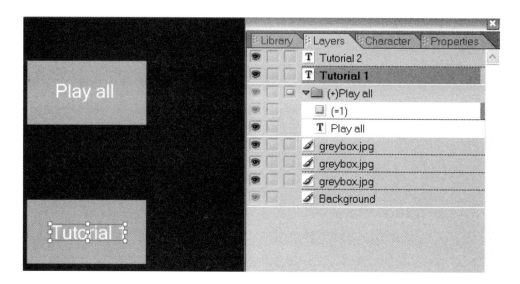

39. Use the keyboard shortcut CTRL-B to convert the graphic to a button.

In the Layers palette, another layer set has been created (+).

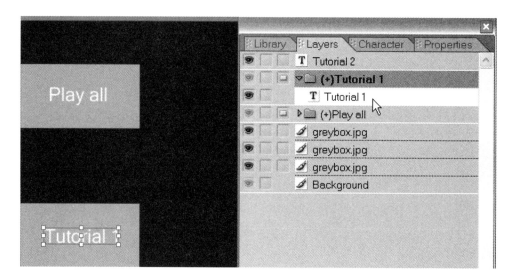

40. Use the keyboard shortcut ALT-CTRL-B to create a subpicture/selection highlight for the second button.

In the Layers palette, inside the newly created layer set, another new layer, (=1), is created that will determine different button states/subpicture highlight selection.

41. Repeat this process to create the third and final button.

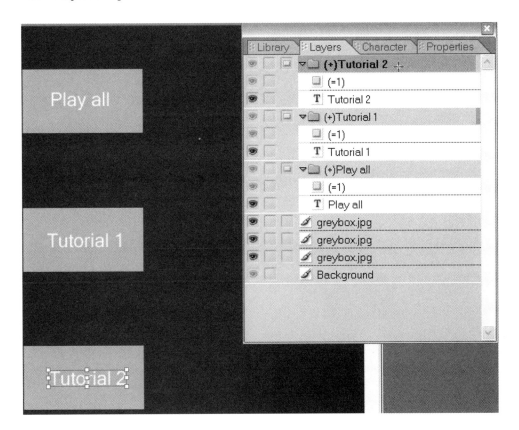

TIP: To increase workflow, multiple buttons and subpicture highlights can be created simultaneously. Simply select all objects you wish to convert to buttons, then press CTRL-B. To create the subpicture/selection highlight, press ALT-CTRL-B.

We've successfully imported graphics, created text, buttons, and subpicture highlights. All without the use of Photoshop. We've also seen how the different layers are named to create different aspects of a menu. For years, Photoshop has utilized layers and layer sets and for the first time, we have seen how Encore has borrowed this same functionality. This not only provides the same functional simplicity, but also full integration between the applications. We'll explore this in greater detail in Chapter 5.

Linking Buttons

Now that we have fully functional buttons, we need to give them something to link to. We are going to go through the different ways of linking buttons, finding the way that works best for you.

42. Using the Selection Tool click on the Play All button. Then right click on the button. Select Link To...

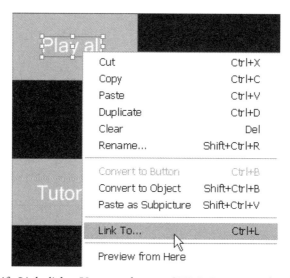

This opens the Specify Link dialog. You can also use CTRL-L to open this dialog.

43. Open ("Twirl down") the Tutorials timeline and select Chapter 1; then hit OK.

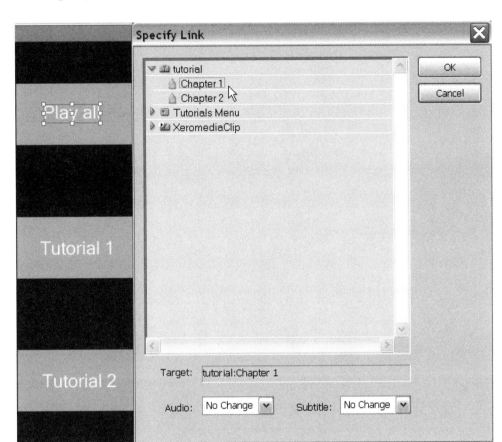

You have successfully linked your first button.

44. Select the Tutorials 1 button and open its Properties palette.
45. In the Link field, click on the Arrow icon.

Now you will see a few options.

46.   Select Tutorials>Chapter 1

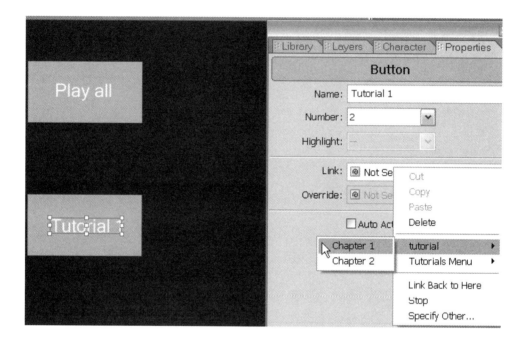

Now the Chapter 1 button is linked the same way as the Play All button. Now remember, the Play All and Chapter 1 buttons shared the same functionality. We could have just created two buttons, Play All and Chapter 2. But for menu consistency we added the Chapter 1 button.

Workflow Shortcut

If you want to link two buttons to the same timeline or menu, there is a quicker way to accomplish this.

In the Menu Editor, hit SHIFT as you select the Play All and Chapter 1 buttons.

In the Properties palette, you will see that buttons, menus, and timelines can be changed simultaneously to Chapter 1.

This multi-selection feature works with menus as well as timelines.

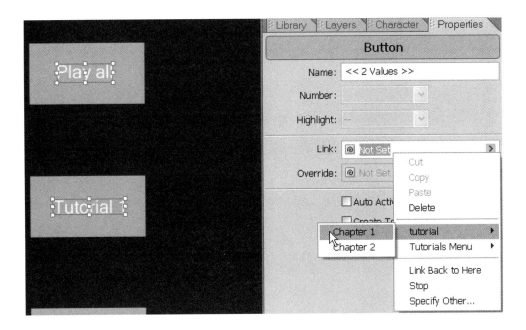

To link the third button, we will try a slightly different method.

47. First, position the Menu Editor in a location next to the main Project Window. Next, select the Timeline tab located inside the Project window. Select the Tutorial timeline inside the Timeline tab.

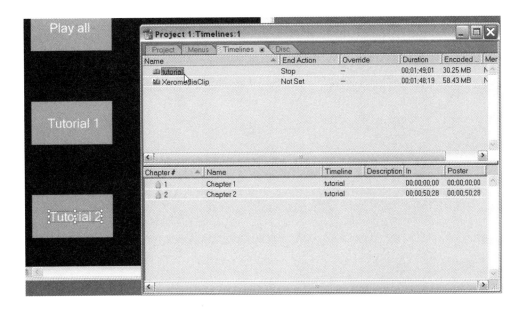

You will see Chapter 1 and Chapter 2 are displayed in the bottom pane.

48. Click and drag the Chapter 2 icon into the Menu Editor window and drop it on top of the Chapter 2 button.

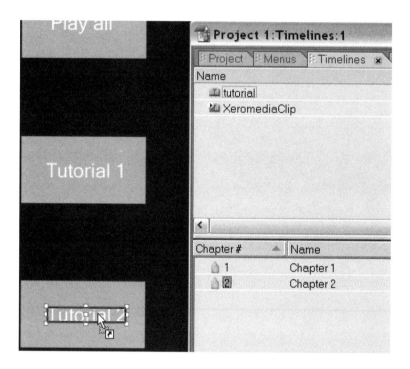

Notice that the bounding box around the Chapter 2 button turns white once you hover the chapter point over it. Release to link the button to Chapter 2.

Pickwhips

If pull-down menus and drag and drop didn't make your life easy enough, somebody just had to invent the Pickwhip. This ingenious little tool makes linking buttons a breeze and can be used to link different buttons and chapter points between the various windows in the interface.

Take a look at the Properties palette for one of your buttons. Next to the Link field, you can see this little icon that kind of looks like a coiled up string (or a snail). This is the Pickwhip. Position the Timeline window so it is visible towards the bottom of your screen with visible chapter points. Click on the Pickwhip and drag it to a chapter point on your timeline.

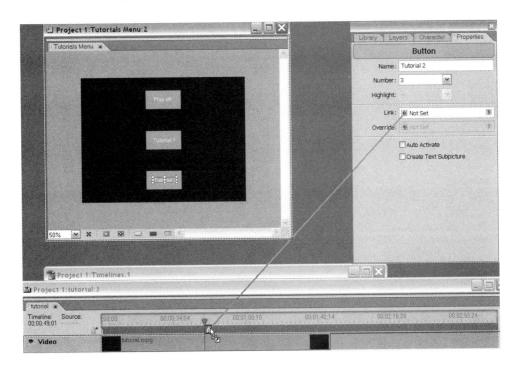

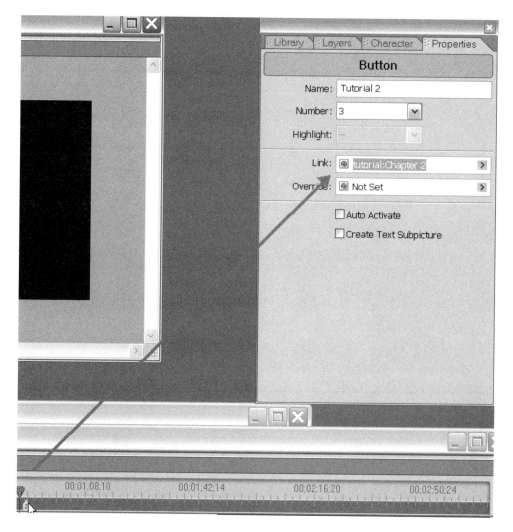

Whoosh! The link is set to that chapter point. You can also set the link to a menu in your Menu tab. Or a timeline in your Timelines tab, essentially linking the button to the first chapter point in that timeline. You can even link a button to another button in the same menu.

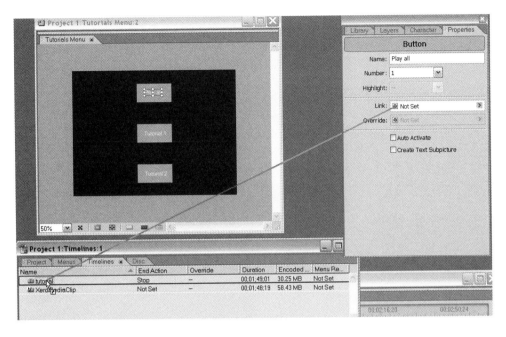

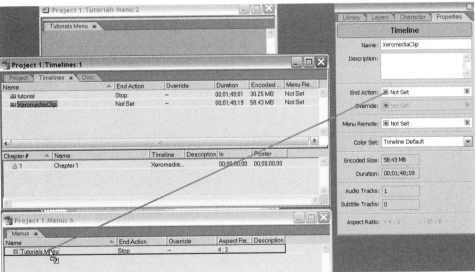

The Pickwhip is for people with great workspace organization, because you must be able to see what you are selecting. If you have to dig through windows to find what you are selecting, chances are it is better to click the pull-down menu in the Link field and use that to select the link.

Pickwhips are also available in a menu's Properties palette and can be used to set the background video, sound, and end action, etc.

If you ever make an invalid choice, the Pickwhip won't select anything at all.

We have now linked all of our buttons to their appropriate chapter points.

It's time to specify the end actions of the timelines. This tells the DVD player where to go after it is done playing a timeline. Without them, the DVD player would stop at the end of a timeline and do nothing. In our case, the Xeromedia clip would play when the disc was inserted but wouldn't go to the menu. Not much of a DVD, right?

49.   Open the Timelines tab and select the Xeromedia Clip timeline.

After this timeline plays to the end, we want the DVD player to navigate to our main menu.

50.   Go to the Properties palette. Right click on the field labeled "End Action." Select Tutorials Menu>Default.

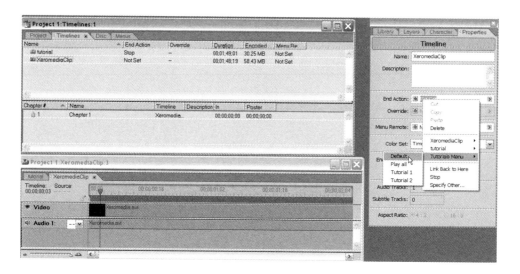

51. Repeat steps 49 to 50 on the Tutorials timeline. Set the End Action to Tutorials Menu>Default.

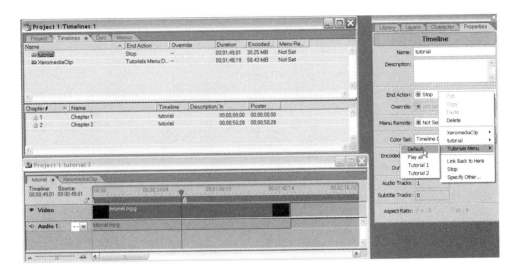

Now both timelines will return to main menu after playing to the end.

Tip: Many beginning authors forget to set end actions. This can create dead spots essentially ruining navigation within the finished DVD.

Specifying Start Action/First Play

Encore provides the ability to specify a start action for your DVD. Also referred to as First Play in Encore, this allows the author to specify which menu or timeline starts playing when the DVD is first inserted into a player. By default, First Play is automatically set to the first timeline created or the first menu imported. However, a First Play action is not required and can be removed quite easily.

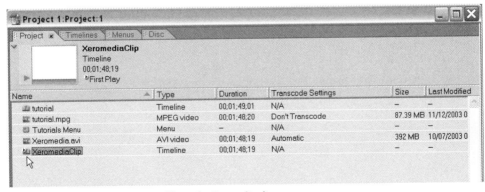

In this project, the First Play icon is visible on the Xeromedia clip.

There are two methods that can be used to specify start action.

Using the File Menu

Select the timeline or menu in the Project window that you wish to modify. Once selected, access the File menu to clear an existing First Play action, or choose Set as First Play to add this behavior to a different clip.

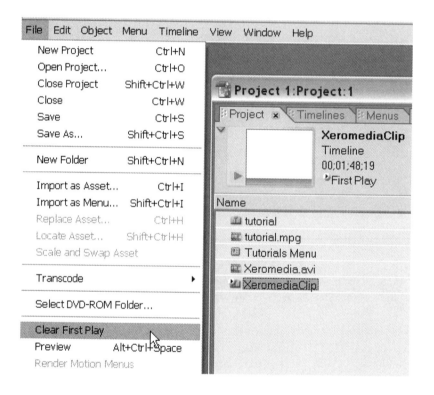

Right Click

Simply right click on any menu or timeline in the Project window. This will provide options to set First Play, or remove this option from a clip that has First Play set.

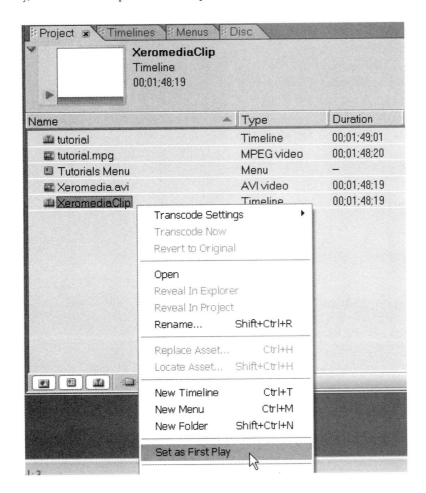

TIP: Remember that, by default, First Play is set to the first timeline created or the first menu imported. If this timeline or menu is deleted, Encore will not automatically reset the First Play to another timeline or menu. In this case, First Play is not specified and the disc will not automatically start when inserted into a player. Certain projects benefit from having no start action/First Play. DVDs without a start action require the viewer to press PLAY.

Now we'll make sure First Play is set properly.

52. Look for the First Play icon in the Project window. A small icon with a PLAY symbol should be next to the Xeromedia timeline. If it isn't, simply right click on the timeline in the Project window and choose: Set as First Play.

This will ensure that the Xeromedia clip will commence playback automatically after the disc is inserted.

Now let's name our disc.

53. Open the Disc Properties palette.
54. In the top field, type the name "tutorial."

Our disc volume is now properly named.

Preview Window

Before burning, it's always a good idea to preview the project. For more information on the Preview window, go to Chapter 8.

55.   Go to: File>Preview

The Xeromedia clip will play, then the Tutorials menu will open.

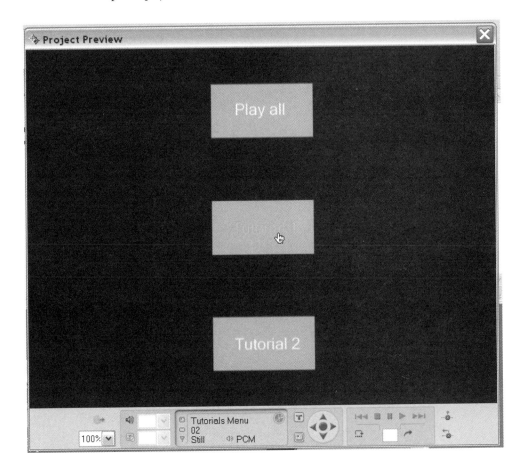

Tip: To open a specific menu in the Preview window, open the desired menu in the Menu Editor. Next, right click on the menu, then choose Preview from here. The menu will now open in the Preview window.

Use the navigation controls to check the links and interactivity of the project. At the end of the tutorials, it will link back to the Tutorials menu.

At this point, Preview should suffice, but if you wish to burn to DVD or to CD, feel free.

Good Job!

We're now finished with our first project. Although it was a very simple DVD, we managed to cover a lot of important aspects of Encore.

So, take one last look at the simple menu. Once you start using Photoshop to create graphics and menus, square, gray buttons with flat text won't ever satisfy you again.

Chapter 5
Photoshop Integration

It's time to investigate one of the most powerful and productive features of Encore—Photoshop integration. This integration between applications streamlines the process of creating menus and buttons. While Photoshop offers the greatest creative potential, both applications use similar methods to create, open, and modify menus and buttons. This is accomplished through the use of layers and layer sets. In this chapter, we'll take a look at this process in greater detail. We'll also cover different techniques that can be used to create menus, buttons, motion thumbnails, and subpicture highlights.

Some of the projects in this chapter illustrate simple points (i.e., creating buttons). Even if this is an area you feel confident in, don't skip these sections. Spend a few minutes and go through all of the projects; you'll be glad you did.

- Pixel aspect ratio .9 vs. 1.0
- Menu fundamentals
- Creating menus in Photoshop
- Naming conventions/menu protocols
- Understanding buttons
- Creating buttons
- Creating buttons with the shape tool
- Creating the subpicture highlight—determining button state
- Color sets
- Creating thumbnail layers in Photoshop
- Poster frame
- Layer styles
- Managing assets/saving work

Pixel Aspect Ratio .9 vs. 1.0

When working with digital video, pixels are the building blocks used to create full frames. Pixel aspect ratio (PAR) refers to the dimension of the pixel length compared to width. It's important to realize that all pixels are not created equal. Computers think in terms of square pixels, while many digital video formats use non-square pixels. In the case of DVD, NTSC, and PAL, the pixels are actually taller than they are wide. This difference in pixel aspect ratio has a direct impact on the image and can cause distortion or stretching to occur. For this reason, understanding pixel aspect ratio is critical when producing content for DVD.

A **pixel** (picture element) is one point in an image. Pixels are composed of three dots: red, blue, and green. Monitors display an image by dividing it into thousands or millions of pixels arranged in rows or columns. An image with hundreds or thousands of pixels forms a single shape.

The **aspect ratio** is the relative horizontal and vertical sizes of an object, typically comprised of hundreds or thousands of individual pixels. If an object has an aspect ratio of **2:1,** then it is wider than it is tall. This term also refers to an image's display resolution. For instance, an image with an **800×600** resolution has an aspect ratio of **4:3.** The standard aspect ratio for traditional television sets and computer monitors is **4:3,** while the aspect ratio for high-definition, wide-screen digital systems is **16:9.**

The **pixel aspect ratio** (PAR) is the width of the individual pixel (x) with respect to its height (y). A square pixel has a ratio of 1:1, but a non-square (rectangular) pixel does not have the same height and width. This concept is similar to the aspect ratio description above, but is applicable specifically to the pixels in the image.

When building images, the size or pixel aspect ratio of the individual pixels is paramount, because this parameter determines how the image is initially created. It's also applicable to how the image is played back. In Figure 5.1, notice the perfect circle has been created using non-square pixels in Photoshop. When viewed with a square pixel aspect ratio, the circle appears stretched horizontally. Notice the circle is not round. When displayed using the .9 PAR, the circle is round. This transition from 1.0 PAR to .9 PAR (i.e., computer to DVD) needs to be considered in advance in order to maintain proper aspect ratios in the finished project.

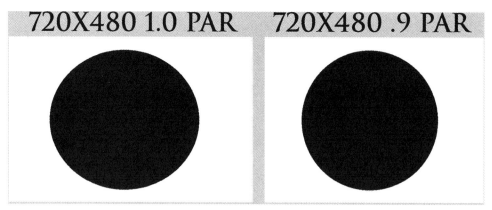

Figure 5.1 *Square pixel images should compensate for the fact that DVD uses a non-square .9 PAR.*

The easiest way to compensate for this difference in aspect ratios is to use project dimensions that account for the difference in PAR. Photoshop includes templates that are designed exclusively for this task. Templates for Widescreen, NTSC, and PAL are all included and drastically simplify the process of creating graphics for DVD. Simply select a preset in accordance with the material you will be using. Once imported into Encore, your graphics will appear as intended.

When creating a new menu or graphic to be used with NTSC DVD playback, it's best to use the 720×534 DV preset inside Photoshop 7. Several templates are provided inside Photoshop offering options for D1, PAL, and HDTV. Before the menu is compressed and exported to DVD, the image is scaled to 720×480 (with constrain proportions unchecked) using a .9 PAR. This can be done in Photoshop, or Encore will automatically rescale a 720×534 1.0 PAR image to 720×480 .9 PAR. This offsets the difference in aspect ratios between the computer-originated pixels and the DVD, and creates an image with the proper dimensions and aspect ratio.

The latest version of Photoshop CS has non-square pixel support and offers new templates designed for non-square applications. It's as simple as choosing project dimensions that match your DVD project (i.e., NTSC DVD 720×480). Many presets offer native non-square pixel aspect ratios, thereby eliminating the need to compensate for square pixels. Photoshop CS also offers the ability to toggle the view between a square and non-square pixel aspect ratio when creating graphics. Encore includes a similar feature to toggle between and view different aspect ratios directly in the Menu Editor.

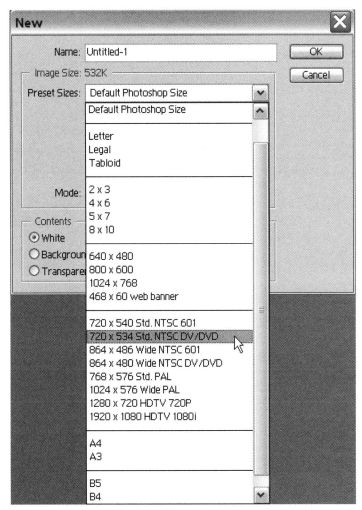

Presets inside Photoshop 7.0.

Photoshop 7 provides presets utilizing square pixel aspect ratios.

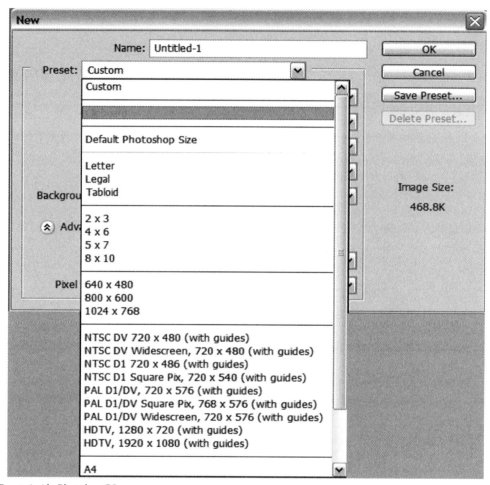

Presets inside Photoshop CS.

Photoshop CS offers non–square PAR presets that reflect DVD-legal dimensions.

Menu Fundamentals

DVD-Video menus consist of very few basic elements. Regardless of how a menu is created in Encore, or any other authoring app for that matter, menus exist on DVD adhering to the strict principles established in the DVD spec. Understanding what the main elements are will help any author understand what is going on behind the scenes in Encore. It will also help avoid some common pitfalls. A good understanding of the mechanics of a menu can also help to provide some creative inspiration.

Every menu consists of two major elements.

Background video. This can be a single still MPEG-2 frame, otherwise known as an I-frame, or a full-motion MPEG-2 clip. This is the key difference between a still menu and a motion menu. It's simply determined by the video used to create the background of the menu.

Subpicture highlights. We'll cover these shortly, but, for now, just remember that these subpicture highlights overlay the background video. The subpicture highlights typically provide visual feedback to the viewer, aiding button selection and navigation.

If this is new information to you, stop for a moment and realize that it's really that simple. Menus are pretty straightforward. They're just like other video that makes up the bulk of a DVD, but they also work with subpicture streams (overlays) that provide navigation and linking functionality. It's a matter of understanding what portions of the menu are in the background video and what portions of a menu exist as an overlay. Once this concept is clear, it's much easier to figure out how Encore works. Understanding these basic elements will also help you understand a lot of the important concepts covered in the next few chapters.

Creating Menus in Photoshop

Every professional DVD author will require a graphics program such as Photoshop to create and manage graphics and assets for DVD production. While other programs exist, Photoshop has been a staple of most authoring houses for quite some time. There's good reason that it's the industry standard graphics program for both Mac and PC platforms. It's a great piece of software.

Encore supports and utilizes several aspects of Photoshop. Photoshop files can be opened and edited directly inside Encore. Menus can also be created in Encore and edited directly in Photoshop. Both applications use the same building blocks, Photoshop files with layers and layer sets; therefore many behaviors are shared.

This type of compatibility allows the author to work freely between both applications. Text and graphics can be created, modified, scaled and swapped using either application...

Below is a picture of a Photoshop file used to create a menu. When the menu is opened inside Encore, notice that the layers and layer sets utilize prefixes that are identical in both applications. This is because a menu IS a Photoshop file. The different prefixes determine and classify the different layers and layer sets that are used to create menus, buttons, and motion thumbnails. They also determine which elements of a menu will be compressed as part of the background video and which elements will exist as a subpicture highlight overlay on the finished DVD.

Encore's Layers palette.

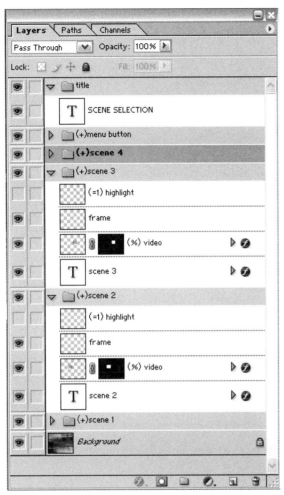

Photoshop's Layers palette.

Notice the layer sets and layers are very similar in both applications. This provides cross-compatibility between applications.

Naming Conventions / Menu Protocols

For years, Photoshop has used layers to separate, create, and modify graphics. With the introduction of Encore, these same layers are now used to create menus. This is accomplished through the use of prefixes that classify individual layers and layer sets. The prefixes are used to specify which layers or layer sets create different elements of a menu or a button (i.e., a thumbnail, a button, a subpicture highlight).

NOTE: Encore menus *are* Photoshop files. These Photoshop files consist of layers that contain the different elements of a menu (i.e., buttons, background, motion thumbnails, text). A Photoshop file can also represent an individual button. In this case, layers are used to specify the different elements of a button (i.e., text, graphic, subpicture highlight).

Layer sets are simply used to group layers into sets. The (+) prefix tells Encore to treat the layer set as a button. The individual layers inside the layer set contain the different elements that create the buttons or a thumbnail. These individual elements of the button are specified by assigned prefixes. Prefixes define whether the individual layer is used to create a subpicture highlight or a thumbnail layer.

Figure 5.2 is a chart detailing the different naming conventions that are used to create menus inside Photoshop.

Open Project 2 to see how all of the different layer set prefixes can be combined to create a menu.

Menu Item	Photoshop Element	Layer Name Prefix
Button Name	Layer set containing button components	(+)
Button Text	Text layers within the layer set	None Required
Button Image	Image layers within the layer set	None Required
Subpicture (optional)	Single-color image layers. Each layer represents one color of the three-color subpicture.	(=1) (=2) (=3)
Video thumbnail (optional)	An image layer within the layer set that serves as a placeholder for video.	(%)
Other design elements or text (such as logo or menu title)	Individual Layer	None required

Figure 5.2 *A useful chart showing how menu items relate to Photoshop elements and layer prefixes.*

PROJECT 2

Layer Prefixes / Menu Protocols

Locate Project_2.ncor in the sample files folder and double click to open in Encore.

Look in the Project window to see if any files are in italics. If this is the case, right click on the files, and then locate them in the sample files folder.

This will ensure that Encore knows where all the files are and we are ready to work with the project.

   1.   **Click on Project2.menu to open the Menu Editor.**

This menu includes several graphics, thumbnails, buttons and subpicture highlights.

   2.   **Click on the first button, labeled "Object."**

In the Layers palette notice there are no prefixes. This is treated as a simple graphic inside Encore.

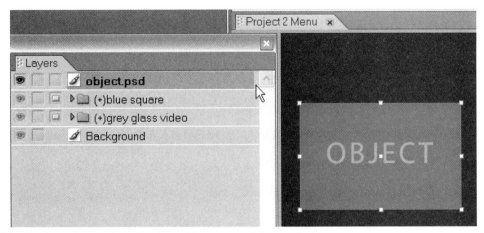

This object button is a simple graphic that will become part of the menu background.

3.   Click on the next button, labeled "Button."

The layer set and the subpicture highlights are defined with layer prefixes.

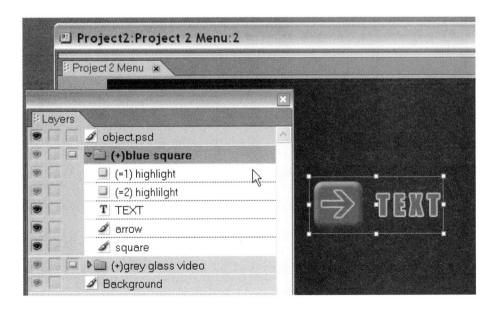

Inside the Layers palette, notice that this button's layer set has the (+) prefix and a (=1) (=2) layer. The (+) prefix indicates that this object is a button, and the (=1) (=2) layers are the subpicture highlights for that button.

4. Click on the button labeled "grey glass Thumbnail."

Taking a look at the Layers palette we can see that in addition to the (+) and (=1) prefixes we can see a (%) prefix in one of the layers. This prefix indicates that this is a placeholder layer used to create a motion thumbnail.

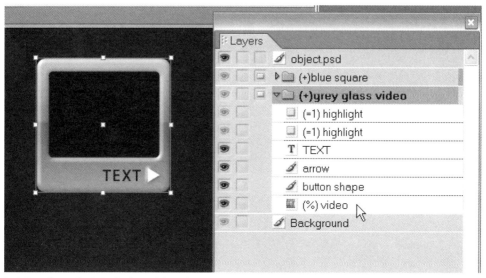

The (%) prefix in the (%)video layer defines the motion thumbnail placeholder.

Once you've explored the project, go ahead and close it. There is no need to save.

Understanding Buttons

When designing buttons for use in a menu, it's critical to understand that buttons can be created using two different methods. Buttons can exist as part of the background video stream, or they can exist entirely as a subpicture highlight.

Inside Encore, after all graphics and text are added to the menu, they are combined and encoded to create a single MPEG-2 clip. Encore converts all graphics to an MPEG-2 format adhering to the DVD spec. If it's a still menu, a single MPEG frame, known as an I-frame, will be created. If it's a motion menu, a motion MPEG-2 clip is created.

The subpicture highlights exist separately and are overlaid on top of the background video stream. They facilitate selection, navigation, and linking for the DVD project. The trick is to understand when to create buttons in the video stream and when to create them in the subpicture highlight. Knowing the difference will aid you in preparing the different elements and will help you take your ideas to the next level.

TIP: Most menus consist of a background video stream (static or motion) AND a subpicture highlight. The subpicture highlight provides the core functionality of the button including navigation and linking. Oftentimes, the background stream can be created to complement the subpicture highlight with a graphic, or vice versa.

Another look at the two major elements of a menu:

Background video. Button graphics can be added to the background video very easily. When a graphic button exists on a DVD-Video disc, it can exist as any other graphic would—as MPEG-2 still or motion video. All graphics imported into your project will eventually be compressed and exist in an MPEG format (unless they exist as a subpicture highlight). Think of the background video as MPEG video that can be complemented with a subpicture highlight to create a menu. Full motion video can be created in external applications like Premiere or After Effects, then imported into Encore to be used in a menu. When compared to a subpicture highlight, the background MPEG-2 video offers far more color depth and better picture quality.

TIP: As the name implies, a subpicture highlight exists on a DVD as subpicture information. When the project is built, all subpicture information is multiplexed with audio and video assets to create the final stream. Although they are separate elements, they are all multiplexed into a single stream that the DVD players use to perform navigation, menus, subpictures, etc.

Subpicture highlights. The subpicture highlight refers to a subpicture stream that is used in a menu. The subpicture highlight is a 2-bit, 4-color overlay used to indicate button selection and determine navigation. These simple and crude subpicture highlights are generated by the DVD player and can be used to create a graphic, an entire button, or a simple accent that complements an object in the background video. A subpicture highlight can use up to four colors, three used to describe different button selection states. These different states help the user determine which buttons are selected, providing feedback for disc navigation. The fourth color is used as a mask to determine transparent sections of the overlay, allowing the viewer to see the underlying video in the menu.

Button in background video.

The complementary subpicture highlight.

TIP. A background MPEG-2 stream and a subpicture highlight are typically used in conjunction; however, it's possible to design a fully functional menu relying solely on the subpicture highlights generated by the DVD player.

As mentioned, most menus typically use a graphic in conjunction with the subpicture highlights. Graphics used to create a button exist on a layer without a prefix and are eventually rendered with other background graphics or video to create the background video for a menu. Other layers in the layer set, named (=1) (=2) (=3), are used to tell the DVD player how to generate subpicture highlights using specific colors that overlay the underlying graphics.

If text or graphics are added to a motion menu with an existing MPEG-2 motion background, the menu will need to be recompressed. This is because the graphic information needs to be added to the original background video. Each menu can only contain one video file, so all graphics must be "flattened." However, if a simple subpicture highlight is added to the same menu, recompression will not occur, because a subpicture highlight is not a part of the MPEG-2 video stream. The subpicture highlight does not alter the MPEG-2 background video, so there is no need for rendering or recompression. This touches on a key point. If all of the graphics, buttons, and motion are created in an external application, adding the subpicture highlight in Encore is a piece of cake. No rendering will be necessary, and the menu will be ready to be burned to disc. This is a perfectly acceptable workflow, one popular with experienced DVD authors.

Now we are going to create a motion menu by simply adding a motion clip to the background of a menu. Then we'll look at a couple different Encore projects that show some creative applications of buttons. The first example shows how subpictures can complement action and buttons that exist in an MPEG-2 motion clip. The second will show how to create buttons using nothing other than subpicture highlights.

PROJECT 3

Understanding Buttons

1. **Go to Open Project and select the Project3.ncor file in the sample files folder.**

Make sure all files are available for the project. (Files shouldn't be in italics.)

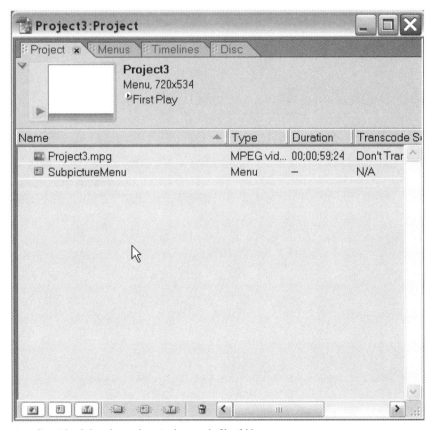

If files are in italics, right click to locate them in the sample files folder.

2. **Locate, then drag and drop Project3.psd from the sample files folder directly into the Library palette.**

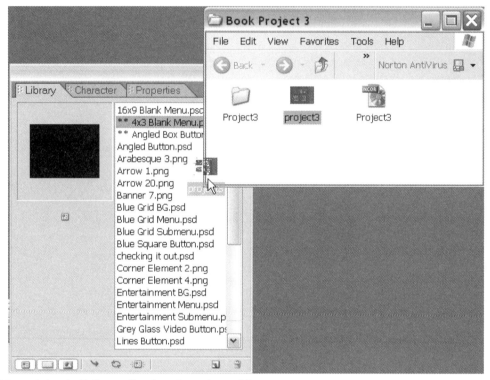

Many windows inside Encore allow the author to drag and drop.

Now the Project3.psd file exists as a menu template in the Library palette.

3. Right click on the new file in the Library palette and choose Create New Menu.

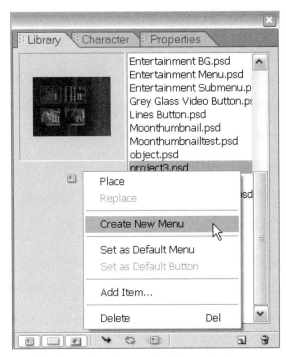

This process creates a new menu from the template chosen in the Library palette.

The new menu is based on our Project3.psd template.

TIP: Encore always generates its own copy of a menu. This allows the author to use existing .psd files as templates. Think of it as non-destructive menu creation. Even when opening menus inside Photoshop, you will be working with "Encore's copy," and this will leave the original .psd files completely untouched. Think of PSD files imported into the Library palette as your master copies, or master templates.

Next, let's select a video clip that will become the background video for our menu.

4. In the Project window, select the newly created Project3 menu and open the Properties palette.

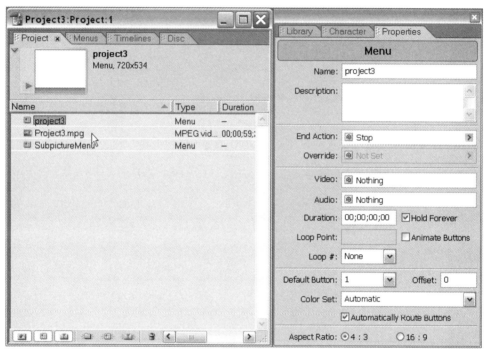

The Properties palette shows the properties of whatever item is selected—in this case a menu.

5. **In the video field, click to drag the Pickwhip to the Project3.m2v file in the Project window.**

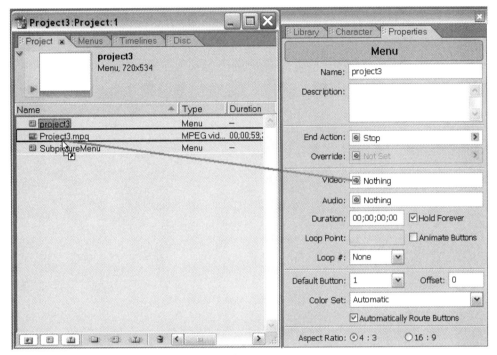

Quick and easy click and drag linking using the Pickwhip.

6. **Next, right click on the menu in the Menu Editor. Then choose Preview From Here.**

The Project Preview window opens and plays the background video we selected, our Project3.m2v clip.

This project was designed with precreated subpicture highlights that supplement the background video.

The buttons exist in the background video clip. The subpicture highlights overlay and complement the underlying video. They also show which button will be selected and provide vital navigation functionality.

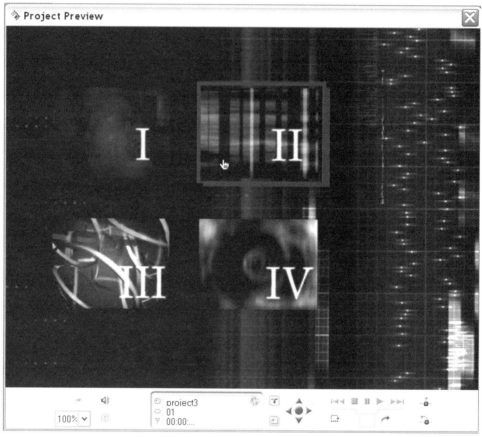

A button in the selected state.

7. **Close the Preview window for now. Let's take a look at the different selected states of our subpicture highlights in the Menu Editor.**

In the Menu Editor, click on the three icons at the bottom, just left of the scroll bar, to toggle between the different button selection states.

> TIP: When using the selection buttons in the Menu Editor, all subpicture highlights are displayed. To view individual buttons as they will appear on the DVD, use the Project Preview window.

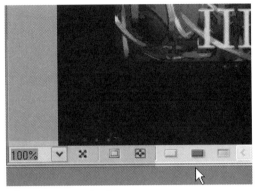

The subpicture preview buttons.

8. Click on the first icon.

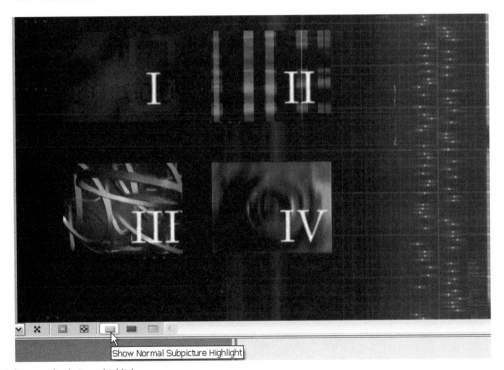

The normal subpicture highlight state.

The first button displays the normal subpicture highlight state for all the buttons. It shows you what the buttons look like when they are not selected. Normal subpicture settings are often set to transparent. In this case, the selected and activated states are used to indicate button selection and activation.

9. **Click on the second icon.**

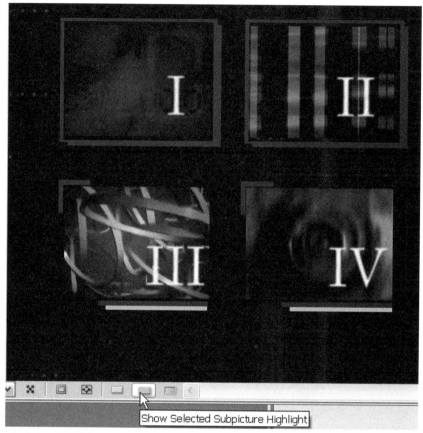

The selected subpicture highlight state.

The second button previews the selected subpicture state for all the buttons.

It shows you what the buttons look like when they are in focus.

Notice two different methods have been used to create accents for the two buttons. Both accents exist as subpicture highlights utilizing slightly different techniques.

10. **Click on the third icon.**

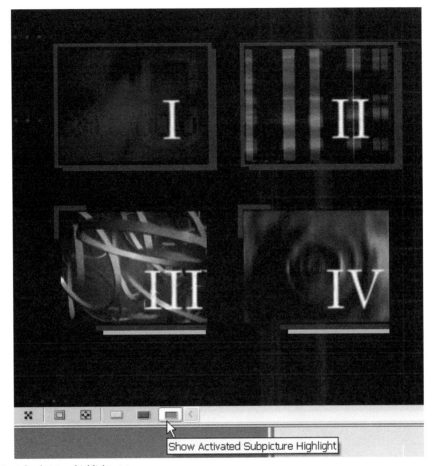

The activated subpicture highlight state.

The third button previews the activated subpicture state for all the buttons. It shows you what the buttons look like when they are activated or pressed.

Next, let's move on and look at another method that can be used to create a button. In our last menu, the buttons existed in the background video in the Project3.mpg clip.

In the next menu, the subpicture graphics have been precreated in Photoshop and assigned the (=1) prefix. Once the prefix is assigned, these graphics will create buttons as part of a subpicture stream.

11. **With Project3 still open, Find subpicturemenu in the Project Window.**

12. Double click to open it in the Menu Editor.

The subpicture highlights are invisible in the normal state.

In this project, we are going to use a customized color set in order to customize the appearance of our subpictures in a normal selected state. Encore leaves subpicture highlights invisible in the normal state. (Remember the last project?) Encore assumes that we don't want subpicture highlights visible all the time or at least when not selected or activated. We will change this behavior, using a custom color set, to display our subpicture buttons.

13.   Choose Edit>Color Set.

This opens the Color Set dialog box.

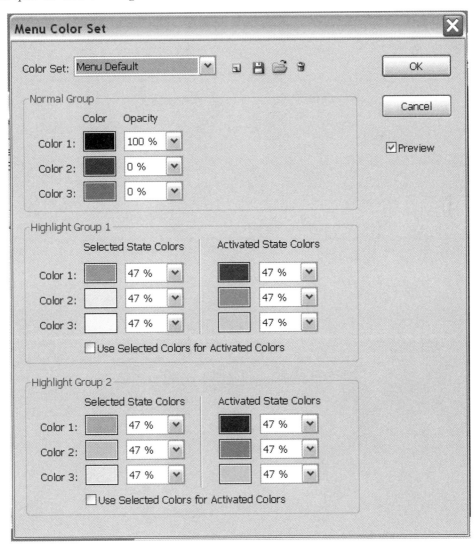

The Edit Color Set dialog box.

14. **Click the folder icon at the top to load a new color set.**

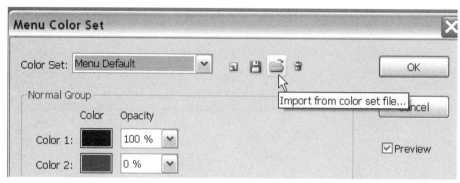

The Import New Color Set icon.

15. **Select subpicturemenucolorset.cs in the Project 3 folder in the sample files folder.**

The color set is now imported into Encore.

Next, we need to make sure that we assign our custom color set to our subpicture menu.

16. **Select the menu and open the Properties palette.**

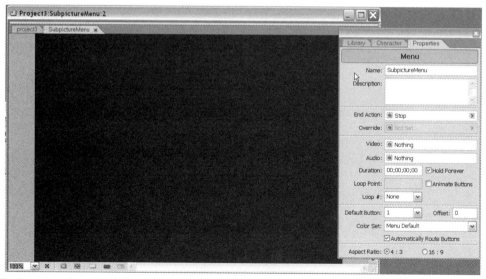

The Properties palette now displays Menu Properties.

17. **At the bottom of the Properties palette, click to open the color set drop-down menu. Select the subpicturemenu color set.**

Assigning the new color set for our menu.

18. **Right click on the menu to view in the Project Preview window.**

Four blue buttons are visible. These are actually subpicture highlights.

As you hover over different portions of the screen, notice different colors are used to indicate selected and activated states.

You'll notice that this menu also consists of four buttons. However, there are no button graphics anywhere in the background of the menu. This button is not part of the background video; in fact, the background video is solid black. The buttons were created in Photoshop using the (=1) layer, so they exist entirely as a subpicture highlight. The subpicture highlights are generated as an overlay by the DVD player.

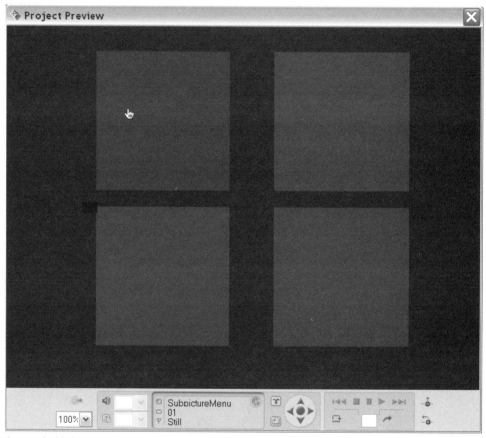

Subpicture highlights used to create simple buttons.

Compare the differences between the automatic color sets and the subpicturemenu color set. Notice that Encore sets, by default, the opacity for normal "unselected" states to zero (automatic setting). This behavior often works best when working with graphics used in the background video. In these situations, normal "unselected" states are not used. The subpicture highlights are typically used to show selected and activated states only.

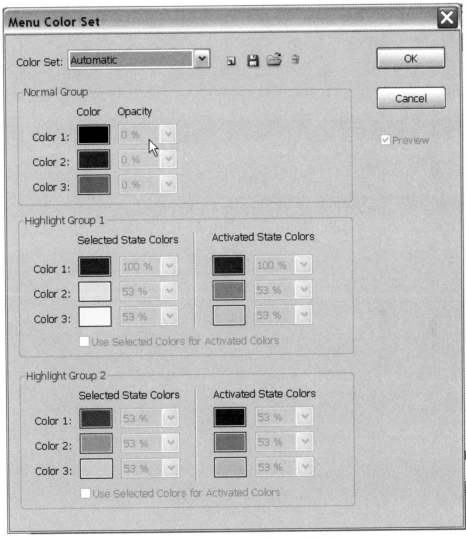

Notice the opacity of the normal unselected state is set to zero in the automatic color set.

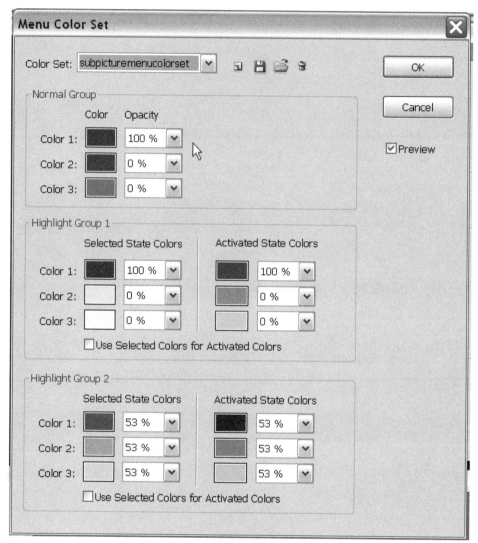

Notice that the normal state is set to 100% in the subpicturemenu color set.

TIP: Notice that the buttons created as subpicture highlights are much more rudimentary than the buttons in the previous project. Color depth and motion limitations make subpicture highlights much more effective as accents or simple icons that complement underlying video. Keep detailed text and graphics in the background video stream when possible.

Go ahead and close the project; there is no need to save.

Hopefully this exercise has sparked a few ideas. Understanding that graphics and subpictures are separate elements should provide valuable insight into how Encore works.

Creative use of subpicture highlights is the key to moving your DVD projects to the next level.

Creating Buttons

While it's possible to create a text button exclusively within Encore, the application does not provide tools to create graphics that can be used to create or complement buttons.

In this next project, we'll use some simple tools inside Photoshop to create some basic buttons, and then we'll import them into Encore.

PROJECT 4

Creating Round and Square Buttons

In this project, we'll be using some of the selection tools inside Photoshop to create some simple graphics that we can use to create a button. These techniques can be used to create buttons that will become part of the background of a menu. They can also be used in a similar fashion to create or modify subpicture highlights.

At the top of the tool palette to the far left, four different tools are available: Single Row, Single Column, Round, and Square.

1. **Open Photoshop.**
2. **Select File>New.**
3. **In the New File dialog box, rename the file "round button."**

As a general rule of thumb, always specify a name for files. It will help with project organization and planning.

Toward the bottom of this window, we have some options for content.

4. **Choose a white background.**
5. **Specify 400×400 pixels for the width and height.**

No need to use NTSC or PAL templates. We're not creating a menu; rather a small button.

6. **Click OK to open the new Photoshop file.**

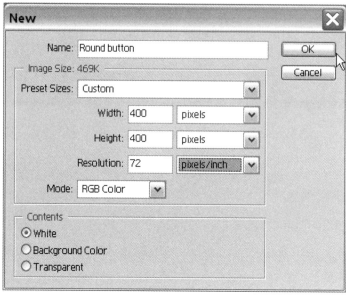

Many choices are presented when opening a new Photoshop project.

7. **From the Layer menu, select New>Layer Set.**

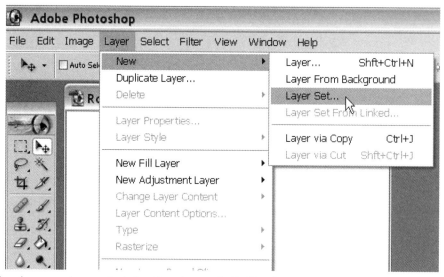

The drop-down menu is one method of creating a layer set inside Photoshop.

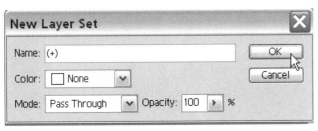

8. Type a name for the layer set, beginning with the prefix (+). Click OK.

The prefix (+) tells Encore that this layer set is a button.

Typing the prefix and name while creating the layer set eliminates the hassle of renaming it later.

NOTE: A name can also be added after the prefix to help differentiate and organize the different layers. For example, (+)first button.

Next, we'll need to create a layer for our button graphic.

9. From the Layer menu, select New>Layer.

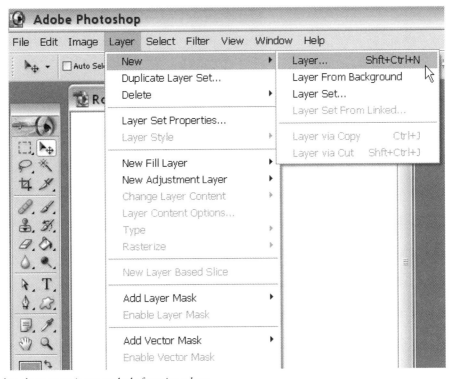

The drop-down menu is one method of creating a layer.

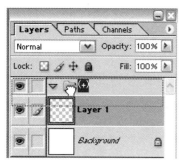 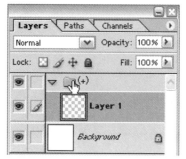

The new layer should automatically appear in the layer set. If not, drag the layer inside the layer set.

Next, we'll create a circular selection area.

If your layers do not automatically fall under your new layer set, drag the layer into the layer set.

10. From the Toolbar, select the Elliptical Marquee Tool.

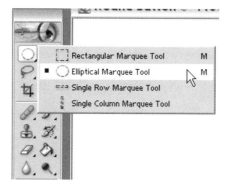

Marquee Tool options.

If you want a square button, select the Rectangular Marquee Tool.

11. **Click and hold on the canvas, pull the circle to the shape you want, and then release the mouse button.**

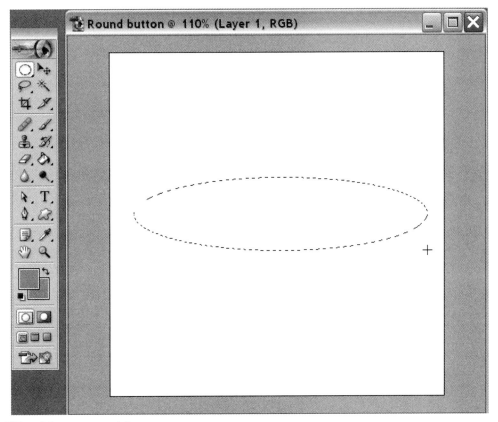

Click and drag to create a circle.

While holding the mouse button, press SHIFT to constrain the proportions; the Space Bar will allow you to reposition the shape around the canvas. Experiment with these features until you get the shape you want.

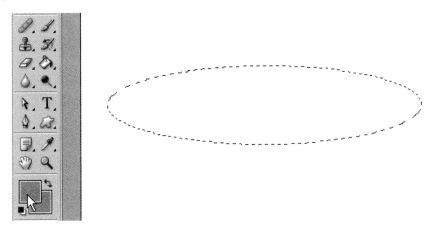

12. Click on the foreground color palette in the Toolbar. Select a color, and hit OK.

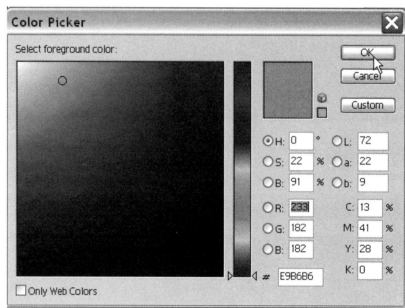

Choose a fill color using the color picker options.

This will determine the fill color for your shape.

13. Go to Edit>Fill>OK.

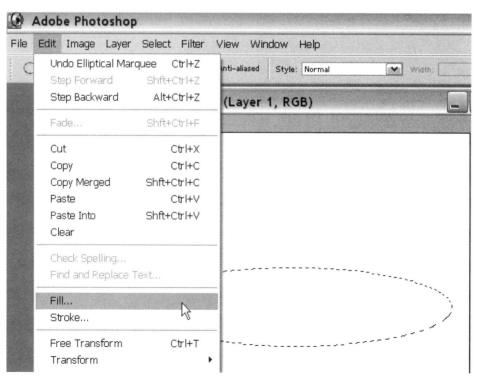

TIP: You can also use the Paint Bucket tool to fill the selected area.

This will apply the foreground color to the inside of the shape.

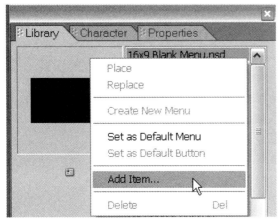

Right click to add an item to the Library palette, or simply drag and drop into the window.

14. **Go to File>Save As and save the file to your desktop.**
15. **In Encore, go to the Library palette. Right click and select Add Item. Select the roundbutton.psd file and click Open.**

If the file is dragged from Windows Explorer into the Project window, it will be imported as an asset. In this case it would be imported as a still image, not a button.

By adding the .psd file to the library, it is recognized as a button. Encore logically assumes that a .psd file with one layer set is a button. If more than one layer set is used, Encore will assume the .psd is a menu.

You can also drag buttons directly into the Menu Editor.

Before we can add a button to a menu in a project, obviously we need a menu and a project.

16. **File>New Project.**
17. **Select NTSC.**

18. **Right click on the blank 4×3 menu template in the Library palette. Choose Create New Menu.**

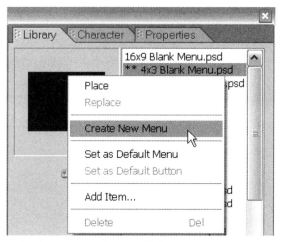

This will create a blank menu that is ready to have buttons added.

We're now ready to add our button to the blank menu.

19. **Click and drag roundbutton.psd from the Library palette into the Menu Editor window.**

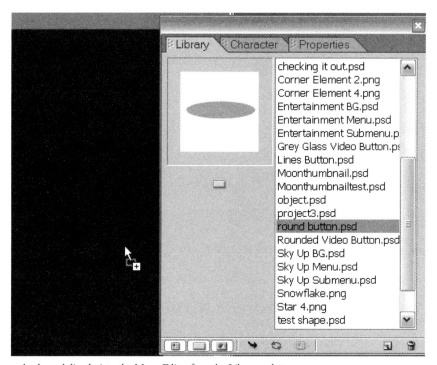

Buttons can be dragged directly into the Menu Editor from the Library palette.

A bounding box should now appear around the button. If you don't see a bounding box, click to select the button. Use this to resize the image or reposition the image as you wish. Holding SHIFT while resizing the bounding box maintains the proportions of the original graphic.

Resize your buttons using the bounding box.

Did you notice that the white background from Photoshop does not appear in Encore when the button is added? Why is that? Encore knows the .psd file is a button. With buttons, the background layer is disregarded. This is not the case with menus; more on that shortly.

20.   Open the Layers palette.

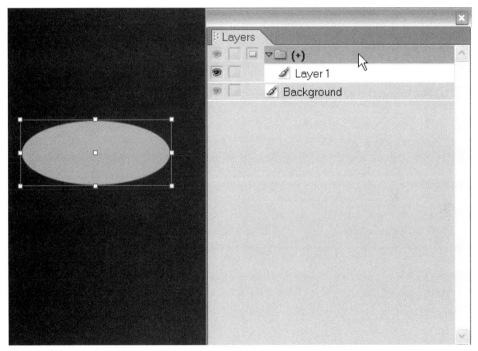

A (+) prefix defines the button layer set.

Notice that the (+) prefix we specified in Photoshop is preserved in Encore's Layers palette.

It's not always necessary to open the Layers palette, but it aids you in understanding how layers are used and preserved between the applications.

At this point if you want to experiment and create your own subpicture highlight, feel free. This can be a simple accent or graphic that will be used to indicate selection states for buttons. Using Photoshop, simply add another layer to the layer set and use the (=1) prefix.

A simple subpicture highlight can also be created in Encore.

21. **Select the button and press CTRL ALT-B to create a simple subpicture that reflects the dimensions of the button graphic.**

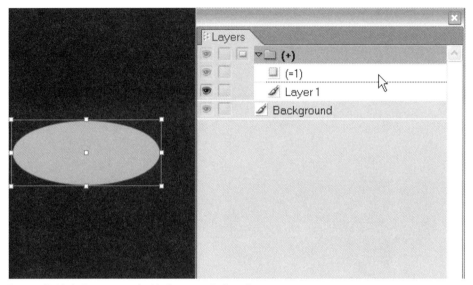

A subpicture highlight layer is created with the proper (=1) prefix.

When finished, close the project. There's no need to save it unless you wish to keep the project.

Final Note: The Marquee tools are also perfect for creating subpicture highlights. Anti-aliasing can be disabled, eliminating the feathering effect that automatically occurs with many tools inside Encore. We will get more into subpicture highlights in a moment.

Creating Buttons with the Shape Tool

The Shape tool offers an almost endless supply of shapes that can be used to create buttons. The Shape tool uses vectors to create shapes that are later rasterized, or converted to pixels. This process is performed automatically when graphics created with the Shape tool are imported into Encore.

When working with vector images, paths are used to create objects. The Pen tool can be used to adjust any shapes created with the Pen tool.

PROJECT 5

Creating a Button with the Shape Tool in Photoshop

We'll create a new Photoshop file the same way we did in Project 4.

1. **Open Photoshop.**
2. **Select File>New.**
3. **In the New File dialog box, rename the file "Arrowbutton."**
4. **From the Preset Sizes select 400×400 pixels for the width and height.**
5. **Select the contents as White.**
6. **Click OK.**

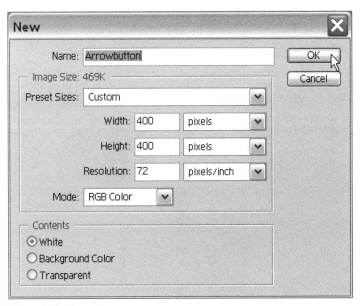

All options specified correctly for the project.

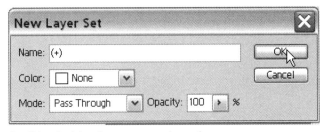

Specifying the (+) prefix creates a new button layer set.

7. **From the Layer Menu, select New>Layer Set.**
8. **In the Layer Set dialog, rename the layer (+). Hit OK.**

Once again, this prefix is necessary to designate this layer set as a button.

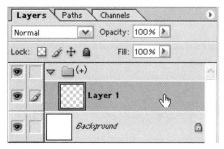

Make sure the new layer exists inside *the layer set.*

9. From the Layer Menu, select New>Layer.

Once again, make sure this layer is in the layer set. We're almost ready to create another button using the Shape tool.

10. Double click the foreground color in Photoshop's Toolbar.

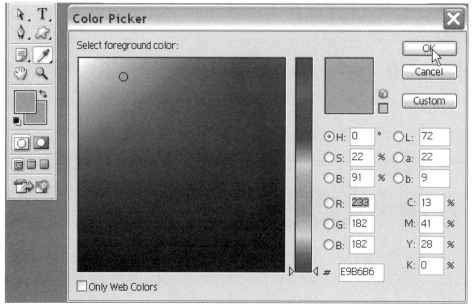

Choose a color for the Shape tool.

11. Select a color.

With the Shape tool, the foreground color is automatically filled after you make the shape. That's why it's best to select your preferred color/pattern in advance.

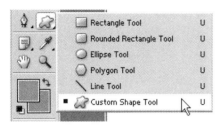

The custom Shape tool hides two spots above the Zoom tool.

12. **From the Toolbar, select the Shape tool.**

13. **Select the arrow 9 shape from the available shapes.**

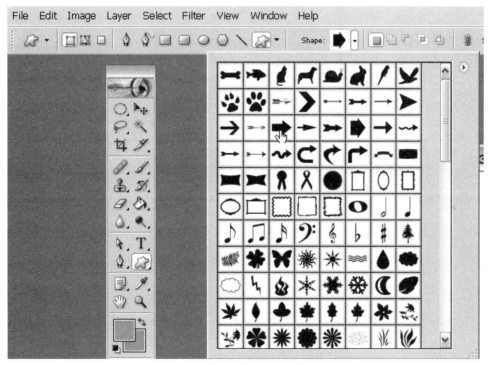

Select the black arrow (arrow 9) shape.

14. **Click and hold on the canvas and pull the arrow to the size you want, then release the mouse button.**

TIP: Similar to the Marquee tool, the Shape tool allows you to adapt the tool using keys while holding the mouse button. SHIFT constrains the proportions and the Space Bar allows you to reposition.

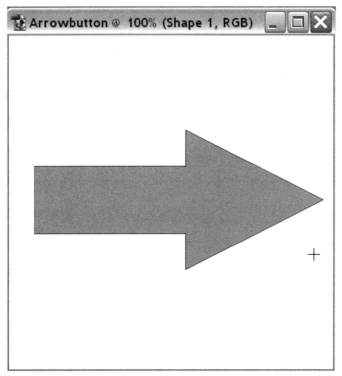

Holding SHIFT keeps the arrow's original shape.

TIP: Vector graphics are transferred to Encore intact and can be positioned and resized.

---

15. Save the Arrow button to your desktop and close Photoshop.

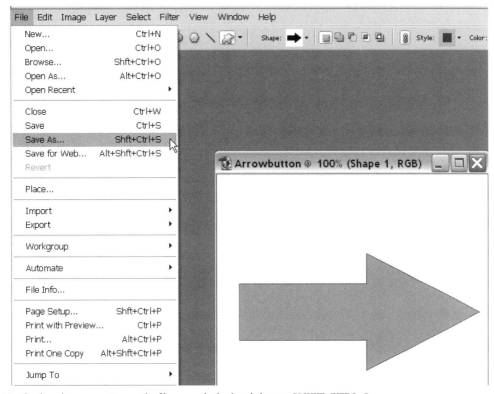

Use the drop-down menu to save the file or use the keyboard shortcut SHIFT CTRL-S.

Just like the Round button you can import the Arrow button directly into Encore by using the Library palette. Remember, Encore will treat the Arrow as a button and disregard the white background if you import it using the Library palette.

We have created very simplistic buttons in Photoshop, but the rules are the same for complex graphics. Let your imagination run free and experiment with creating your own buttons. The take home message is the (+) prefix creates a button layer set. And lastly, when imported properly, Encore will interpret Photoshop files with more than one button layer set as a menu.

Now that we've created some basic buttons, it's time to spend a little time going over subpicture highlights. We'll create highlights and address some key considerations in the next chapter.

Creating the Subpicture Highlight—Determining Button State

Photoshop is the tool of choice when complete creative control over subpicture highlights is desired. Three different subpicture layers can be used to create subpicture highlights for a button. The subpicture layers are created by assigning prefixes to the three individual layers: (=1), (=2), and (=3).

Many beginning users assume that the (=1), (=2), and (=3) prefixes used to create subpicture highlights are related to button selection states. This is not the case. These prefixes simply allow the author to create 3 separate images, using 3 individual colors, existing as 3 separate subpicture layers. The individual subpicture layers will be displayed in a menu using one color apiece.

This allows authors to create highlights that uses more than one color. It's a simple matter of using more than one subpicture layer. While only 1 layer is necessary, up to 3 layers can be used to specify up to 3 separate colors in the highlight. All three layers can be combined to create a multi-colored subpicture highlight.

Bottom line: These prefixes do not determine button selection—they just give the author the ability to create subpicture highlight overlays that display more than one color at a time.

When designing the individual layers for use in the subpicture highlights, care must be taken to keep the edges clean and crisp. The entire subpicture (including all 3 subpicture layers) is limited to 2 bits and can utilize a maximum of 4 colors. This includes the 3 separate colors that can be assigned for subpicture highlights: (=1), (=2), (=3). The remaining color is critical as it's reserved to determine the transparent pixels in the overlay. Encore takes care of this automatically, so don't worry too much about the fourth color.

Pixels in the each subpicture layer will either represent transparency or the subpicture itself. Essentially, this means that there can be only ONE color in each individual layer. Gradients and anti-aliased images do not work well because the intermediate colors used to feather the image are not preserved when imported into Encore. All pixels in the subpicture layer are mapped either to transparency or the single solid color used to create the image in each layer. You can also think of the individual layers as having pixels either on or off—no intermediate values. See Figure 5.3. We'll also demonstrate this in Project 6.

Think of the individual subpicture layers as image maps. Encore refers to these graphics to determine which pixels will be used to create the subpicture overlay. Each subpicture layer utilizes one color. It really doesn't matter what color is used to create these subpicture layers. Encore simply uses the subpicture layers as a reference to determine which pixels will be filled with color later. Encore uses the subpicture layer to determine which pixels will be "on" and which pixels will be transparent ("off").

> TIP: As a rule of thumb, use only ONE color, without any feathering or anti-aliasing, on each individual subpicture layer.

MUTLI-COLORED GRAPHIC

AFTER CONVERSION TO 1-BIT SUBPICTURE LAYER

Figure 5.3 *When a feathered image is converted to a subpicture layer, all pixels are mapped either to transparency or the sole color used to create the subpicture. All intermediate colors are discarded.*

Individual subpicture layers can be used in many different ways. In addition to representing a single color, each layer can also contain a different graphic, opening a myriad of creative possibilities.

After subpicture layers are created, Encore uses colors defined in a color set to determine the opacity and color of the subpicture layer graphics. We'll cover color sets shortly.

In Project 6, we'll explore some important considerations when it comes to working with subpicture highlights. Understanding certain quirks and limitations of subpicture highlights will help you make critical design decisions that will improve the appearance of your menus.

TIP: When creating subpicture highlights inside Photoshop, it's best to use tools that don't introduce anti-aliasing. This will create sharp edges that will look better after being flattened and encoded to DVD. It also makes working with the blocky solid colors more predictable.

Photoshop and Encore do not maintain a completely live link between applications. If continued changes need to be made to a menu while toggling between applications, the Edit Original command must be used repeatedly.

To edit a menu in Photoshop, select the desired menu. Choose Menu> Edit in Photoshop.

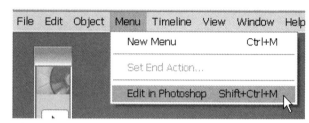

At this point, Photoshop will open. Make desired changes, then save. After returning to Encore, the changes will be visible. However, once you return to Encore, the link is broken.

The Edit in Photoshop command in Encore.

Continued changes to the Photoshop file won't update unless it is re-opened using the Edit Original command in Encore.

PROJECT 6

It's been established that each subpicture layer should be designed with one solid color. This example will help cement why this is important.

1. **Open Project6.ncor in the sample files folder.**

Make sure all files are available for the project (no files should be in italics).

2. **Find the subpicturegradient menu in the Project window and double click to open in the Menu Editor.**

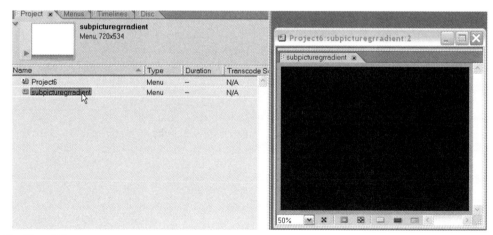

The Menu Editor.

192

Use the selection buttons to view the subpicture highlights in their different selection states. Notice they are solid blocks of color.

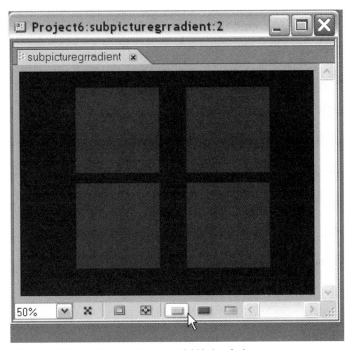

The squares are created using subpicture layers and exist as solid blocks of color.

3. **Make sure the menu is selected and choose Menu>Edit in Photoshop.**

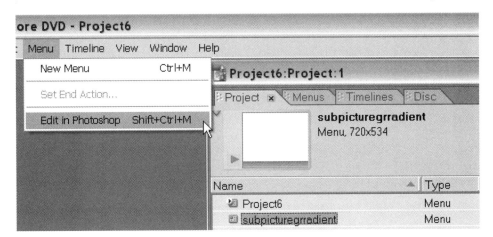

4. **Inside Photoshop's Layers palette, click to expand one of the layer sets.**

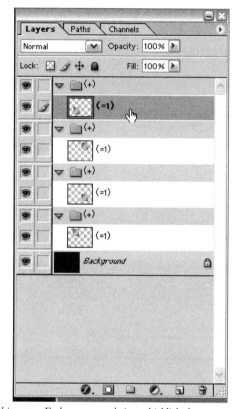

Four button layer sets exist in this menu. Each uses one subpicture highlight layer to create the square overlay.

Analyze the different subpicture layers (=1). *Notice that more than one color has been used to create the different buttons.*

This was created to show the flattening or quantizing effect that will occur when importing individual subpicture layers into Encore.

When imported into Encore, it will show a quantized image consisting of only 1 color. Remember how we discussed whether the pixels are "on" or "off"? As far as Encore is concerned, each pixel will be fully transparent or opaque. Transparent sections of the layer will be "off"; any colors used to color pixels will be turned "on." All of the yellows and orange colors are mapped to one color when imported into Encore.

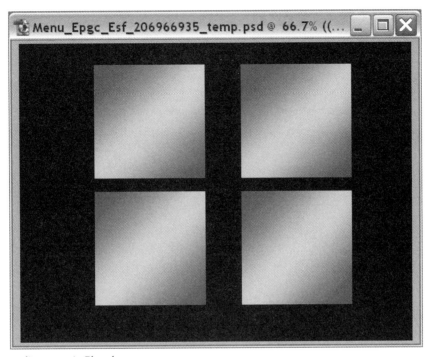

Subpicturegradient menu in Photoshop.

Subpicturegradient menu in Encore.

So, why were the buttons orange and yellow in Photoshop and blue in Encore? Good question! This menu was assigned a custom color set that specified that all pixels would be mapped to blue. This was done intentionally to demonstrate that the colors used to design subpictures in Encore could be easily overridden through the use of custom color sets. If we had used the automatic color set, the colored pixels would have all been mapped to yellow.

Now that we know we only have "1 color" available for each subpicture layer, let's take a look at a project that utilizes all three subpicture layers to jazz up a menu.

5. Back inside Encore, double click to open the Project 6 menu.

Use the buttons in the Menu Editor to preview the selected and activated states for the subpicture highlights.

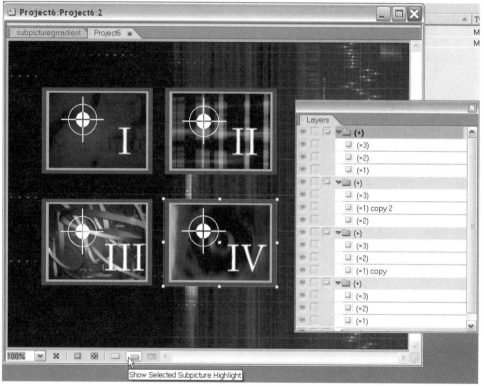

Although somewhat hard to see in black and white, 3 different subpicture layers are used to create 3 different colors for the subpicture highlight overlay.

Notice that 3 colors have been used for each button. Take a moment to analyze the layer set and layer prefixes. Make sure to view the individual subpicture layers.

6. Close Project 6.

There is no need to save this project.

ADVANCED TIP: Feathering can be accomplished to some degree by using three similar colors. However, this requires that all three subpicture layers be used. For an example of this, see project subpicturefeather.ncor in the sample files folder. Once this project is opened, look for the menu subpicture feather and analyze the different layers used to create the menu. This is similar to the anti-aliasing/stroke technique that Encore uses to create subtitles. For more information, refer to the subtitle section in Chapter 7.

Color Sets

Once the subpicture highlights have been created, the next step is to specify which colors will represent the subpicture information on each layer. Fortunately, Encore automates this process when importing subpicture layers from Photoshop. Encore parses color information from the original Photoshop file. It analyzes what colors were used to create the subpicture highlights and transfers this information into the automatic color set. For example, if a subpicture layer is created using red, Encore will pass this information along to the automatic color set. When imported in Encore, it will indeed be red. However, the exact color used to design the subpicture layer isn't critical. These subpicture colors can be changed at any time by creating and assigning a new color set to a menu.

A color set includes a maximum of 15 colors, each with its own opacity setting. Each button can utilize a maximum of 9 colors to describe a maximum of 3 different subpicture layers each with 3 different selection states.

Six additional colors can also be used to create a second color group. The author can then choose which color group is used for individual buttons in a menu. This simply provides a bit more variety and can create differentiation between different buttons.

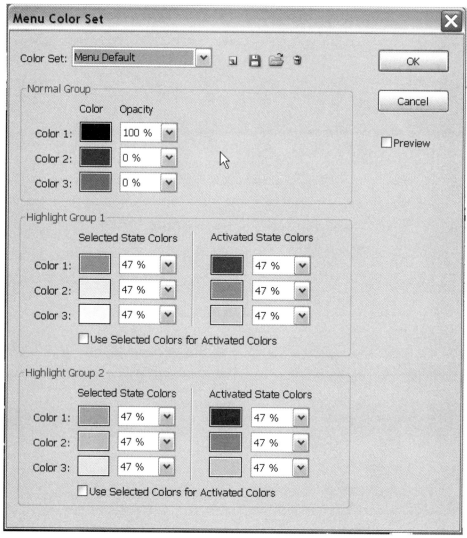

Color set palette.

TIP: While each menu can only use one color set, several color sets can be used for different menus in the same project. Simply create and name individual color sets, select a menu, then specify the desired color set in the Properties palette. Multiple color groups can now be selected for the various buttons in the menu.

TIP: It's not necessary to return to Photoshop to change colors in the subpicture layers. The color sets in Encore provide manual settings that can override the colors used in Photoshop.

It's important to understand the default behavior of automatic color sets within Encore. Many beginning users mistake the color set dialog for a global setting. The most important thing to realize is that in order to change the color set, a new one must be created, then assigned to the desired menu. Let's take a look.

PROJECT 7

1. **Open Photoshop and import the file colorset.psd from the sample files folder.**

This opens a file that we'll use to create a menu in Encore.

2. **Click the twirl downarrow to expand the button layer set and look at the different subpicture layers.**

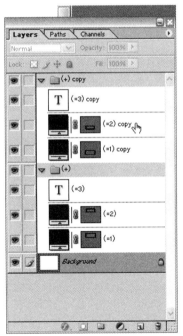

The Shape tool was used to create graphics for the individual subpicture layers.

Notice each subpicture layer is created using black.

3. **Close this file and return to Encore.**
4. **Locate Colorset.ncor in the sample files folder. Open the project in Encore.**

This project doesn't have any files imported yet.

5. **Choose File>Import as Menu.**

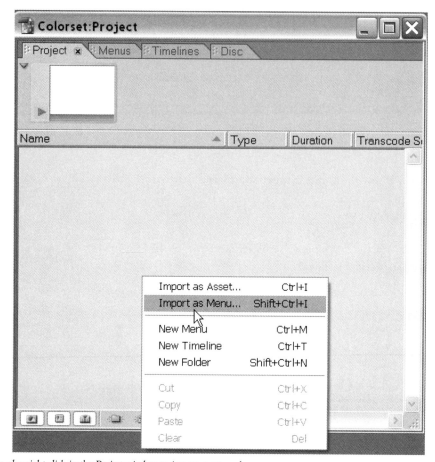

You can also right click in the Project window to import assets and menus.

6. **Select the same Photoshop file, colorset.psd, from the sample files folder.**
7. **In the Menu Editor once again use the different selection buttons to view the different selection states.**

Notice the behaviors of the automatic color set. Encore parsed the color information from the .psd file and adjusted the color set automatically. The selection state for all layers is displayed black, as designed in Photoshop.

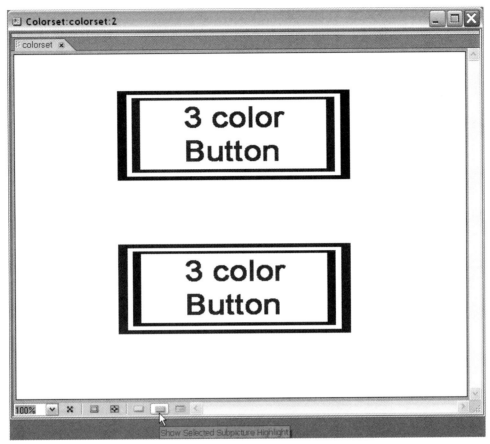

All subpicture layers are currently displayed in black.

If we opened the file in Photoshop and changed the colors of the subpicture layers so they were not all black, Encore would adjust the automatic color set upon import. However, this is not necessary. To specify the colors used in the subpicture layers, it's best to create a custom color set inside Encore.

8. **Choose Edit>Color Set.**

9. **Click the folder icon to import a new color set.**

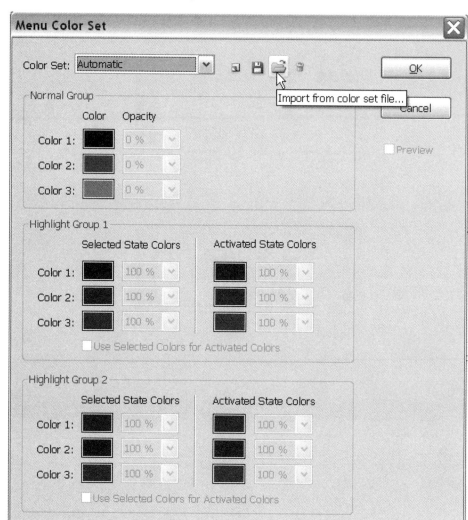

Click the folder to import a custom color set.

10. **Once the Import dialog pops up, locate the file project7.cs.**
11. **Click OK.**

Next, make sure that this color set is assigned to our colorset menu.

12. **Make sure the colorset menu is selected and open the Properties palette.**

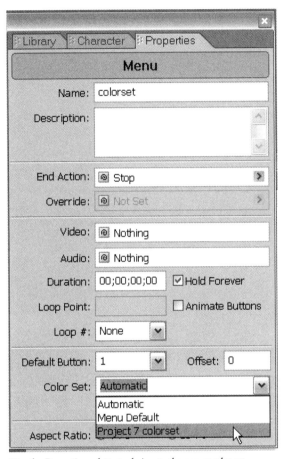

Use the Properties palette to designate the proper color set.

13. Make sure the project7 colorset is specified for the colorset menu.

Return to the Menu Editor and preview the changes to the different selection states. Even though all subpicture layers were created using the color black, this was easy to change inside Encore. Also notice that the selected subpicture is partially transparent. Experiment with different colors and opacity levels to get a feel for how the color sets work.

Next, let's assign one of the buttons in the menu to a different color group.

14. Make sure one of the buttons is selected and open the Properties palette.

15. In the Properties palette, find the field labeled "Highlight."

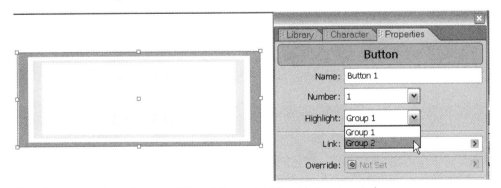

Two color groups can be used to create different behaviors for different buttons in a single menu.

This is where we can choose between the two different color groups for each button.

16. **Select color group 2 and click OK.**
17. **Return to the Menu Editor and preview the subpicture highlights once again.**

Notice that the two buttons now display different colors for the selected and activated states.

Just for practice, create and save your own color group.

18. **Choose Edit>Color Sets>Menu.**

TIP: The second color group does not affect the normal state. Only selected and activated states can be adjusted for color group 2.

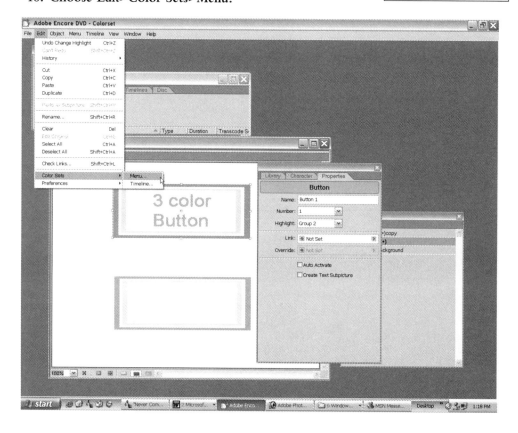

19. Click on the first icon toward the top to create a new color set.

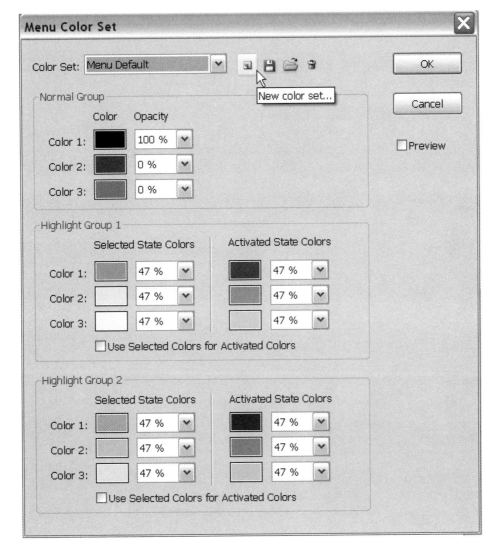

Click the New Color Set icon to create a new color set.

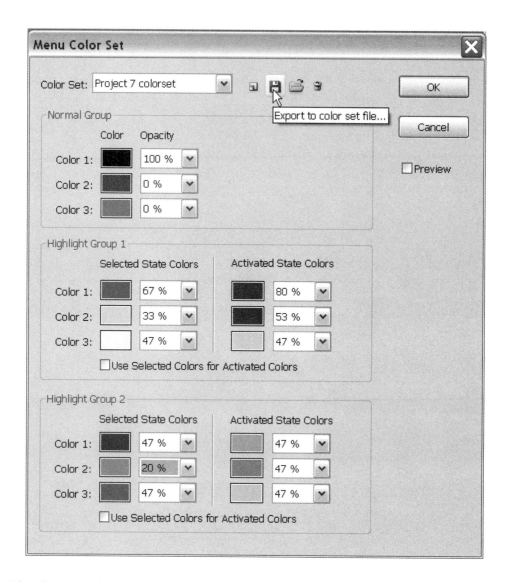

After the new color set is specified, you can change the normal state color (and opacity), the selected and activated colors (and opacity) for both color groups.

After all adjustments to color set have been made, choose OK. The color set will be saved and you will be able to specify this color set for menus in the Menu Properties window.

You may close this project and save it if you wish.

Creating Thumbnail Layers in Photoshop

Buttons can contain a thumbnail image of the video that it is linked to. This thumbnail image can be a simple still graphic representing one frame, or a full motion video that plays a specified amount of time.

Thumbnails are built by creating a placeholder layer inside of a regular button layer set. The button layer set is designated with the (+) prefix, while the thumbnail placeholder is created on an individual layer within the layer set designated with the (%) prefix. Inside Photoshop, the image in the thumbnail layer serves as a placeholder. This placeholder determines where the thumbnail graphic will occur in the menu. The placeholder can be a very simple graphic. It simply determines where the thumbnail exists in the image. If the placeholder image used in the thumbnail layer is not rectangular, Encore will do its best to fit the rectangular video within the boundaries of the placeholder.

Once the placeholder graphic is created in the (%) layer, a mask can be applied to the layer. The masks in the thumbnail layer can be applied to the placeholder graphic to create custom sizes and shapes. This mask determines what portions of the placeholder graphic are preserved, effectively determining a custom shape for the motion thumbnail.

Once the thumbnail is created, the button can be opened in Encore and added to a menu. The next step is to locate the video that will be linked to the button. To link the video to the thumbnail, simply select a chapter point in the timeline with the video to be linked, then drag the chapter point to the blank placeholder in the Menu Editor.

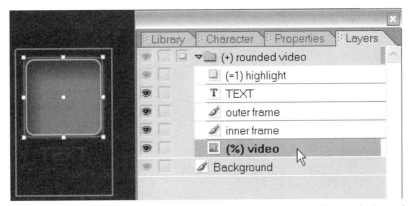

Remember that a thumbnail exists as a button. Therefore it exists as a separate layer inside a regular button layer set.

This process of creating motion thumbnails inside Encore essentially creates a new MPEG-2 file that is used to supply the background video for the motion menu. When the disc is created, all video, thumbnails, and graphics are rendered inside Encore to create the new MPEG-2 clip.

TIP: If background video is used in addition to motion thumbnails in a menu, this will cause the background video to be recompressed. All elements in the menu need to be rendered to MPEG-2 and the subsequent recompression of the background video may create a visible reduction in quality if MPEG-2 source files are used. In this situation it's best to use a high-quality AVI file for the background video.

Background video for menus can also be created using programs such as Premiere or After Effects. These external applications offer more precise control over placement of elements, including video files that provide the same function as a motion thumbnail in Encore. There are almost unlimited motion controls for every element, and superior preview options. They also open a myriad of creative possibilities through the use of creative filters and effects.

PROJECT 8

Thumbnails

In this project, we are going to create a motion thumbnail button using Photoshop. We'll start by creating a placeholder and using a vector mask to give our motion thumbnail a unique cloud shape. Then we will import our button into Encore and link our four chapter points to four buttons. Finally, we'll take a look at our menu inside the Preview window.

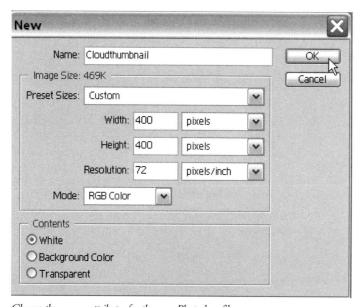

1. Open Photoshop. Go to File>New.
2. In the New File dialog, name the file "Cloudthumbnail."
3. Set the dimensions to 400×400 pixels.
4. Make sure the mode is RGB Color.
5. Select a White background.
6. Click OK.

Now we need to create a new layer set with the (+) prefix, to create a button layer set.

Choose the proper attributes for the new Photoshop file.

7. **Go to Layer>New> Layer Set.**
8. **Name the Layer Set "(+) Cloud."**

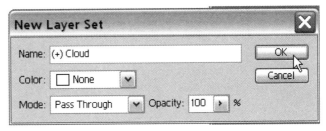

Steps 1 through 8 should feel familiar. Next, we need to create the placeholder layer and define its shape with vector masks.

Use the (+) prefix to create a new button layer set.

9. **Go to Layer>New>Layer.**
10. **In the New Layer dialog, rename the layer "(%)Placeholder."**

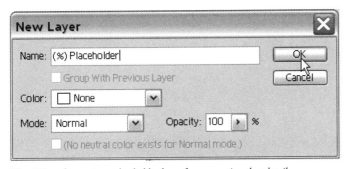

The (%) prefix creates a placeholder layer for our motion thumbnail.

The name "Placeholder" is unessential, but the (%) prefix is vital. This layer is where Encore will place the video pixels inside the button.

The Placeholder layer should appear directly under the layer set we created. If not, drag it up into the (+) Cloud layer set.

11. **Select the Rectangular Marquee tool.**

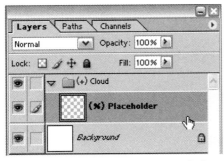

Make sure the thumbnail placeholder is inside the layer set.

Choose the rectangular Marquee tool.

12. **With the (%) layer selected, click and drag the Rectangular Marquee tool over the canvas. Once you get the shape you want, release the mouse button.**

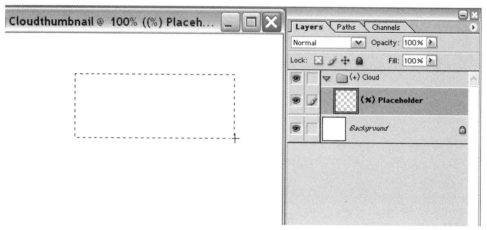

Drag to create a box for the placeholder graphic.

13. **Select the Paint Bucket tool and click inside the rectangle.**

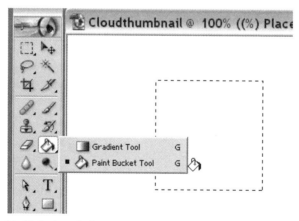

Use the Paint Bucket tool to fill the box selection.

Right now, you could save this and you'd have a basic motion thumbnail ready to import. But we are not going to create a square thumbnail, we want a different shape altogether. Why do we need to create this square placeholder first? Excellent question. Encore wants to place a square video into a square box. By creating this square we give Encore its square box. However, through the use of vector masks we keep the square box but only let a portion show through.

Next, let's create a vector mask on the placeholder layer.

14.   Go to Layer>Add Vector Mask>Reveal All.

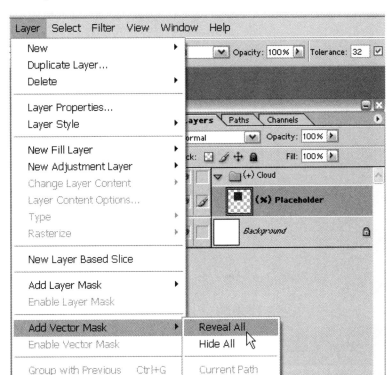

Use the drop-down menu to create a vector mask.

Another box appears on the placeholder layer. This is the vector mask.

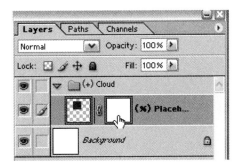

The vector mask should appear in the thumbnail layer.

15. **Select the Custom Shape tool from the toolbar. Find the Cloud Shape. (The solid shape—not the outline; we'll use that outline later to create the subpicture highlight.)**

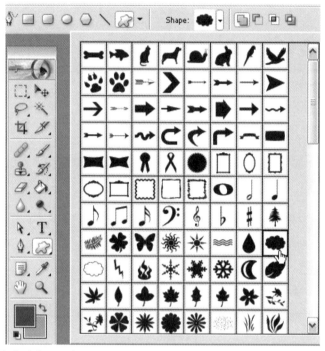

Choose the solid black cloud shape tool.

16. **Click directly on the vector mask to select it within the placeholder layer. Click and drag the Shape tool within the square.**

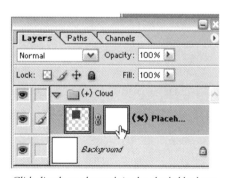

Click directly on the mask in the placeholder layer.

Try to keep the shape within the square. If a part of the new shape extends past the placeholder, it will reveal the edge of the video clip. Use the SHIFT key to constrain the proportions of the shape and the Space Bar to reposition the shape while dragging. This will help you out immensely when we create the subpicture.

17.   Release the mouse button once you have the desired shape.

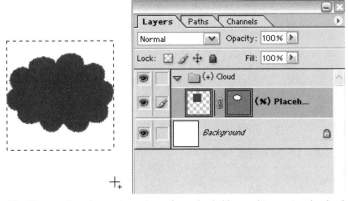

The Shape tool masks certain sections of our placeholder graphic, creating the cloud shape.

Instantly the square box becomes a fluffy cloud. Nice work! Not only have you created a motion thumbnail, but you have used vector masks to make a unique shape for the video to show through. But why stop here? If you have a nice thumbnail, you should have a subtle subpicture highlight to complement it. Right?

18.   Layer>New>Layer.

19.   Rename the layer (=1)subpicture.

The (=1) prefix creates a new subpicture highlight layer.

Of course, this defines this layer as the subpicture highlight.

Next, make sure the Shape tool is selected.

20. From the Custom Shape toolbar, find the Cloud Outline.

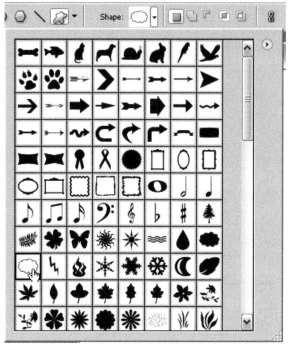

Locate the hollow cloud with a black outline.

If you really want to change the color of the outline, you can. But remember, the subpicture highlight is controlled by a colorset inside Encore. You can always adjust the color later.

21. Click and drag the shape so that your placeholder fits inside the outline. Release the mouse button when you have the desired shape.

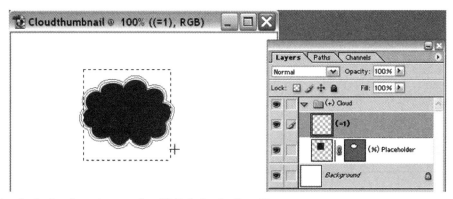

Position the cloud outline so it accents the solid black thumbnail graphic.

This may take some work, especially if you didn't constrain the proportions of the placeholder shape. Work with it a bit until you come close. If you find you can't get the shape completely outside the placeholder, don't worry, you can always adjust the opacity of the subpicture highlight in Encore, and make a very subtle accent. Or you can use the shortcut CTRL-T to access the transform feature.

Okay, now that we've created a fully functional motion thumbnail, it's time to save and put it inside Encore.

22. **Save the Cloudthumbnail.psd file to your desktop.**
23. **Start Encore DVD, open thumbnail.ncor from the sample projects folder.**

As always, check to make sure none of the assets are in italics.

24. **Open up the Thumbnail menu in the Menu Editor window.**

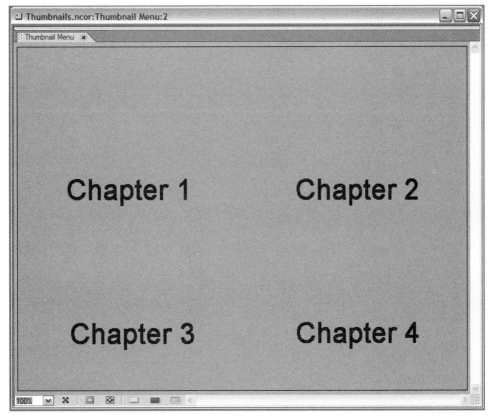

The Thumbnail menu in the Menu Editor.

As you can see in the Project window, a menu has already been created for you. Now we need to add thumbnail buttons.

25. Open the Library palette, right click, and choose Add Item...

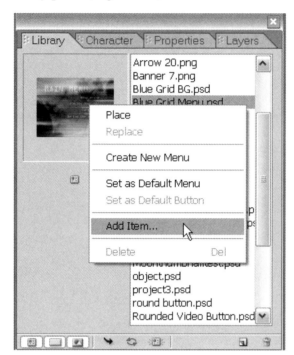

Right click in the Library palette to import the Cloudthumnail menu.

26. Choose the Cloudthumbnail.psd from your desktop and click OK.

Importing buttons in this manner ensures that the .psd file is recognized as a button.

27. From the Library palette, drag the Cloudthumbnail into the Menu Editor.

28. **Using the bounding box and the SHIFT key, resize the button until it seems appropriate for the menu.**

Position and size the button using the bounding box.

You might notice that the color disappears when you resize the box. As noted earlier, the color of the placeholder image is inconsequential and isn't preserved.

We have four chapters, we should have four buttons. You can continue to drag the other three buttons out of the Library palette. Or use the ALT key in conjunction with the selection tool when selecting your button, and Encore will duplicate the button with the exact size and proportions.

Take this opportunity to view the selection states for your buttons. You'll notice that they're not the same colors as they were in Photoshop. Just like in Project 7, we are not using the automatic color set. It's a good idea to get in the habit of creating and importing your own color sets.

A timeline has been created with four chapters. We will use these chapter points to link the placeholders to the proper chapters.

29. Open the thumbnail timeline.

Once opened, we need to drag the chapter points to the placeholders in the menu.

30. Drag Chapter Point 1 onto the upper right button.

31. Drag Chapter Point 2 onto the upper right button.

Drag and drop the chapter points from the timeline into the proper thumbnails in the Menu Editor.

32. Drag Chapter Point 3 onto the lower left button.

33. Drag Chapter Point 4 onto the lower right button.

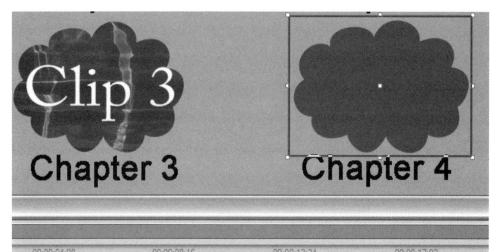

Repeat the drag and drop process for the last two thumbnails.

Notice the placeholders have now been replaced with video. If chapter points or poster frames are adjusted in the time-line, the video frame in the menu will reflect the changes.

34. Bring the Properties palette into view and click inside the Menu Editor. With the menu selected, click on Animate Buttons.

If you do not activate the buttons in the Menu Properties palette, Encore will treat the thumbnails as still images.

To create a motion thumbnail, the Animate Button box must be checked.

35. Inside the Menu Editor window, right click and select Preview from Here.

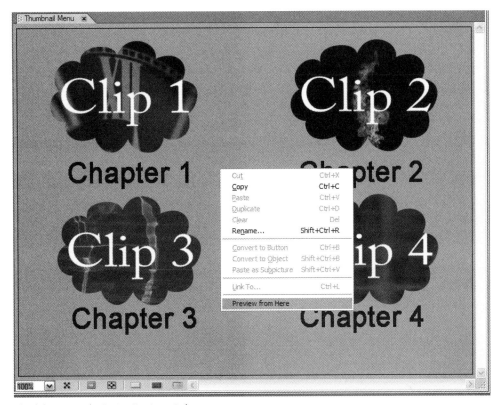

Right click to open the Project Preview window.

Since we have changed the visible dimensions of the MPEG-2 clips, the thumbnails do not automatically move. They must be rendered into a new background video stream.

36. Click the Render button in the Preview window.

Click the Render icon to the far left.

Now you can see the thumbnails set into motion.

37. When you are finished previewing, close the Preview window and go to File>Save As.

We will be using this in the next section, so we will save your progress as a different project file.

38. **Inside the Save As dialog, change the name to Project 9 and save the project to your sample file folder.**

TIP: If thumbnails in your project don't display properly in the Project Preview window, make sure the menu is rendered. To render the menu, you can select the Render button in the Preview window. After the project is rendered, the thumbnails will be set into motion.

Poster Frame

The poster frame feature gives the author the ability to choose a specific frame that best represents the related video. In the case of a motion thumbnail, the poster frame usually determines the starting frame for the video it is linked to. By default, the thumbnail starts at the first frame of video that corresponds to the chapter point in the linked timeline. However, clicking on the related chapter directly in the timeline presents the poster frame option in the Properties palette. Once the chapter point is selected in a timeline, the properties window can be used to adjust the in point as well as the poster frame. You can also set a poster frame directly inside the Timeline window using the Timeline Marker.

We will use our last project we saved as Project9.ncor for a quick demonstration of poster frames.

PROJECT 9

Poster Frames

Let's create our own poster frames. We start this process in the Timeline window.

1. **In Encore, open the Project9.ncor you created in the last section.**
2. **Open the Timeline window.**

Notice that the chapter points are already set. The video thumbnails, by default, start at the chapter point. A good chapter point is between transitions, but that isn't always the best representation of the content in the chapter. Using home movies as an example, a shot of sleepy kids walking out of their rooms on Christmas Day doesn't say much, but a scene of them ripping open presents speaks volumes. Since we want our menu thumbnail to show the best representation of that chapter, we need to create a poster frame at a notable place in the chapter.

In this example, let's say we don't want the thumbnails to display the text at the beginning of the chapters. Let's assume this just doesn't work for the aesthetic design of the menu. Poster frames can be changed to display a section of the footage that displays a good visual representation of the linked footage. It's easy to scrub to a section of the clip that doesn't contain the text, essentially removing the text from the thumbnails in our menu.

3. **Select the first Chapter Point directly in the timeline.**

4. **Next, move the CTI cursor to a frame that best represents the chapter.**

Scrub in the timeline to find a frame that best represents the chapter content.

5. **With the CTI cursor set at the appropriate frame, move the mouse to the chapter point and right click. Then select Set Poster Frame.**

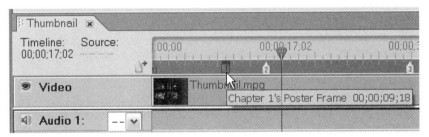

The Poster Frame icon.

TIP: You can also use the Properties palette of a chapter point to specify the poster frame's timecode.

Notice that a poster frame has been created at the CTI cursor position. If you wish, repeat steps 2 to 3 for the remaining chapters.

6. Return to the Menu Editor window.

Notice that the frame in the thumbnail is now the poster frame you selected in the timeline window. If you are using motion thumbnails, the action within the thumbnail begins on that frame. If you are using simple thumbnails, the poster frame is the still image.

The Properties palette can be used to specify a poster frame.

If you create/change the poster frames of a menu, you must render it again in the Preview window, since the video has changed.

Layer Styles

Seasoned Photoshop users will definitely appreciate Encore's ability to respect layer styles. These layer effects are linked to individual layers inside Photoshop and are preserved when imported into Encore.

Layer styles provide a variety of effects such as shadows, glows, bevels, overlays, and strokes that let you quickly change the appearance of a layer's contents. They can even be applied to motion thumbnails, providing the ability to texturize or tint full motion video! If opacity is adjusted for layers in Photoshop, this is applied in Encore as well.

The effects that you apply to a layer become part of the layer's custom *style*. The layer style is marked with an "f" icon (𝑓) that appears to the right of the layer's name in the Layers palette. You can expand the style in the Layers palette to view and edit all the effects that comprise the style.

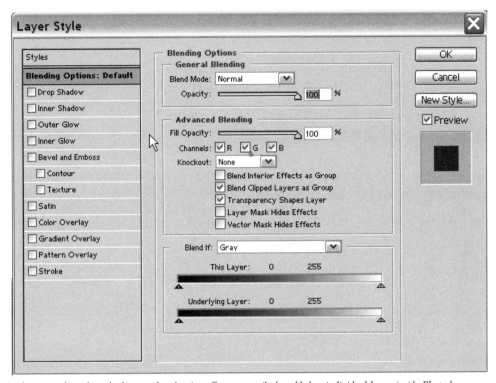

Gradients, overlays, drop shadows, and embossing effects can easily be added to individual layers inside Photoshop.

TIP: Double clicking a layer in Photoshop automatically opens the Layer Style dialog box.

Managing Assets / Saving Work

So far we've used the Library palette for importing buttons and pulling out menus. What we've overlooked is something that you'll discover over time. The Library palette is an incredible tool for organizing and managing your work. As you work with it, it becomes more than a list—it's your tool chest.

The different menus and buttons offered in the Library palette provide professionally designed graphics that can be incorporated into projects with minor modifications. Using templates is a great way to save time, especially for the professional DVD author. If several of your DVD projects have the same format, then templates are invaluable. Oftentimes creating a complex menu requires a significant investment of time and resources. Fortunately, menus and buttons can be saved and reused in future projects. This allows authors to develop a collection of commonly used menus that can be used over and over again.

Many new users will fall into the habit of taking templates and reworking them the same way, several more times than they have to. Perhaps they wonder why they can't just update their templates in Encore. One of Encore's strengths is whenever it opens a menu or button from the Library palette, it creates a working copy of that file with a different file name. That way you can't corrupt or change the template accidentally. But what if you know that your modified template serves your needs better than the built-in template?

> TIP: It's always a good idea to keep important templates organized and stored safely in a directory on your hard drive.

Using Photoshop you can realize that potential. If you use the Edit Original command in Encore, Encore sends the working copy to Photoshop. All you have to do is change the file name of the working copy to correspond to the file name of the original template in the Library palette. Next, import it into the Library palette and Encore will save over the original template. It's that simple.

> TIP: A tidy Library palette is key. If after several months of using Encore, it gets cluttered—organize, prioritize, and eliminate. Next to a well laid out workspace, the importance of ready access to commonly used files in the Library palette is a close second.

Working with the templates inside Encore is not only easy, but it can provide insight into menu creation. New users should explore those menus and buttons in Photoshop and shouldn't be afraid to change them to suit their needs.

It's pretty clear that it would be hard to get by creatively in Encore without Photoshop. Photoshop is a versatile piece of software that unlocks the potential of Encore. Now it's up to you to experiment with these key concepts and find what works for you.

If you want to take DVD authoring to the next level—with full motion menus and spectacular transitions and effects—After Effects and Premiere are waiting.

Chapter 6
Working with After Effects and Premiere Pro

So you're tired of the same old boring static DVDs? Motion thumbnails just not offering all the options that you're looking for? If you haven't already, you may want to look into the world of Adobe After Effects.

In this chapter, we'll assemble a real-world project using clips created with After Effects, Premiere, and Encore. Among other things, it will give you some insight into creative linking and the fundamentals of motion menu design. The project will illustrate how motion video clips created in After Effects can be used to form the foundation of a creative motion menu. After all, the background video clip used in a motion menu offers more creative potential than any other aspect of a DVD.

Later on, looping and override features will be incorporated to maximize effectiveness, interaction, and appearance of the project. We'll finish by covering a few important details when preparing assets and creating basic animations in Premiere Pro.

- Motion menus
- Working with AVIs
- Rendering and previewing motion menus
- Motion menu project
- Looping functions
- Delaying subpicture highlights
- Override
- Inserting audio into the background menu
- Preparing clips in Premiere
- Exporting MPEG files from Premiere
- Working with chapters

Motion Menus

The most effective way to create advanced motion menus is to prepare the background video in an external application. Although Encore can create motion thumbnails, it can't create the motion IN the thumbnail. It simply doesn't offer precise control over placement, compositing, filters, or effects. For maximum control over motion menu creation, a program such as After Effects is an ideal solution.

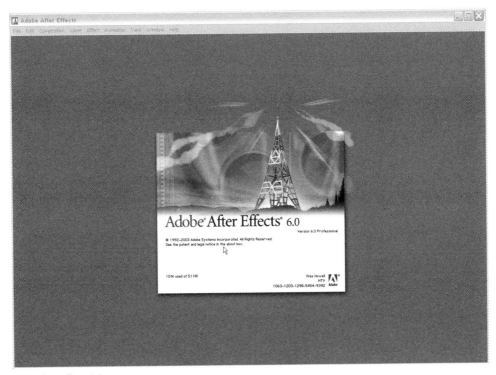

Adobe After Effects 6.0.

With After Effects multiple video clips can be created, then linked together to create animation, interactivity, motion, and action. Buttons can be zoomed in and out, effects can be added, and clips can be faded in or out of view.

After Effects offers endless options when it comes to animation and creative design. However, it's well beyond the scope of this book to provide a comprehensive understanding of After Effects. After Effects is a relatively complex program and requires a good amount of time to master the application. The intent of this chapter is to demonstrate how AE incorporates with Encore, cover common issues, and provide a road map for those interested in advanced motion menu creation.

Working with AVIs

Encore can automatically track changes made to clips imported from After Effects. Once a clip has been imported, Encore keeps track as changes that are made externally. Changes will be updated automatically and reflected inside Encore. How does Encore do this? The official way is to embed a project link in AE when you save the AVI file. After importing the AVI into Encore, choose Edit Original to open the original After Effects project.

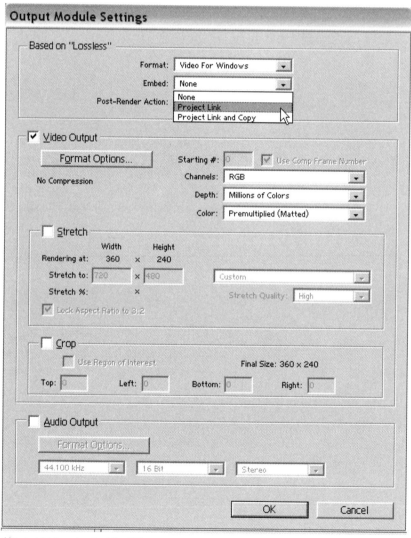

The Embed Project Link option in After Effects.

Rendering and Previewing Motion Menus

TIP: When possible, use a slightly higher bitrate (7–8 Mbps) when encoding video for motion menus. Considering the content has excessive motion, higher bitrates will produce better results. These clips are usually fairly short, so the higher bitrate won't use much disc space.

As a general rule of thumb, Motion video intended for use in a motion menu should not require additional modification or added graphics once imported into Encore. This is much more critical if the motion video is already encoded to MPEG-2. When possible, all graphics should be added to the clip *before* it's rendered and imported into Encore. This will help eliminate excessive recompression and will help maintain image quality.

It's important to understand when menus will be recompressed. This will help eliminate unnecessary transcoding and will increase the quality of your DVD projects. Let's take a look.

Recompression of a menu WILL occur when:

- Video used in the menu is not DVD compliant.
- Motion thumbnails are added to the menu.
- Still thumbnails are added to the menu.
- Text or graphics are added to the menu.

TIP: If you find yourself rendering a ton of motion menus in Encore, you should try to use high-quality AVIs rather than MPEG-2 clips for the source video.

Anytime multiple elements and graphic layers are added to a menu inside Encore, recompression is required. In this situation, the motion menu will need to be rendered before Encore can generate a preview.

Recompression WILL NOT occur:

If an MPEG-2 DVD compliant clip is specified for the background video and no other text or graphics are added to the menu, the motion menu will not need to be rendered inside Encore. DVD-legal video can be previewed instantly inside the Project Preview window. No rendering! The menu may just need some simple subpicture highlights; this can be accomplished using Photoshop and Encore together. This is a great workflow for those who regularly create their own motion clips.

TIP: If the menu does not need to be rendered, the render motion menu option will not be available inside Encore.

TIP: As discussed earlier, subpicture highlights are simple overlays and will not cause a menu to be recompressed.

AVI clips also can be previewed without rendering if all of the graphics are contained inside the video clip. It will be need to be rendered to MPEG-2 before being burned to disc; however, the

TIP: If text or graphics are added, anything other than subpicture highlights, the menu will need to be rendered in order to view the full motion video in the Project Preview window.

point here is that Encore can provide an instant preview for menus that utilize recommended AVI files.

It's very easy to preview menus directly inside Encore. Simply right click on the menu: choose Preview From Here. The Preview window will pop up and simulate playback. If the Project Preview window isn't working as expected, you probably need to render the motion menu. We'll cover the Project Preview window in greater detail in Chapter 8.

Recompression

When working with motion menus or motion thumbnails, there will be times that Encore will need to render, or recompress, the images and video in order to create a "flattened" MPEG-2 file for the menu. If the images or clips in question have already been compressed to MPEG-2, recompression can reduce quality. As mentioned earlier, MPEG-2 is not ideal when it comes to recompression. A high-quality AVI file is a much better choice for this situation. A good rule of thumb is to encode to MPEG-2 only once, whenever possible.

Certain workflows can improve the quality of your production. If you plan on building menus that combine several video streams, sometimes it's better to build these menus inside a specialized program like AE. For example, rather than adding motion thumbnails or graphics to a motion menu in Encore, it can be advantageous to prepare and animate the entire video with After Effects. After Effects provides complete creative control over placement, animation, effects, and color correction. It also offers a wide range of codecs and uncompressed options for export.

TIP: AE can access the original high-resolution clips and output a high-quality file that only needs to be encoded to MPEG-2 once. This can produce much higher quality results than importing MPEG-2 assets separately and forcing recompression. Regardless of the software you choose to work with, try to use high-quality AVIs rather than MPEG-2 clips when building multi-layered menus that will require recompression.

Motion Menu Project

At this point, we're ready to put some of Encore's more advanced features to work. This project also provides a good example of the creative use of subpicture highlights in conjunction with motion graphics prepared in After Effects. At this point, a lot of the fundamentals covered earlier will fall into place. We'll be linking menus and timelines together to create an animated interactive experience.

This should prove to be a quick, fun, and enlightening project. And the good news is: No, you don't have to create the motion clips. All clips are ready for use, already compressed to MPEG-2 and patiently waiting for you in the sample files folder.

Motion Menu Project 10

1. Open a new NTSC project in Encore.
2. In the sample files folder, locate the MPEG Clips folder in Project 10.
3. Open the folder and drag the 5 clips into the Project window.

Next, let's import our menus.

4. Locate two Photoshop files in the sample files folder: INTROmenu.psd and 3ChapterMenu.psd.
5. Choose File>Import as Menu to import both menus into the Project window.

> TIP: If you prefer, you can also hold the ALT key while dragging and dropping the Photoshop files into the Project window. The ALT key will import the files as menus rather than assets.

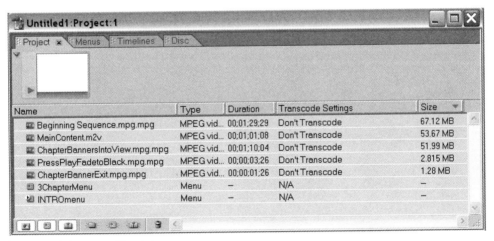

The Project window up to this point.

Not much is visible in the menus at this point as there is no background video. Both menus have precreated subpicture highlights, so feel free to use the preview buttons in the Menu Editor and the Layers palette to view these.

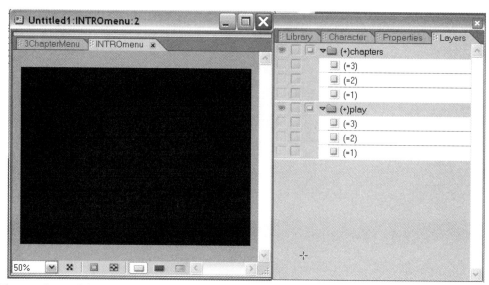

The normal state of the INTROmenu.

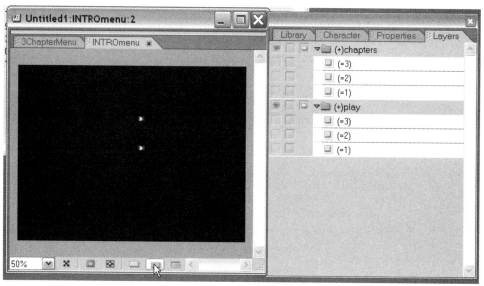

The selected state of the INTROmenu.

Next, we need to add the background video to both of these menus.

6. Select the INTROmenu and open the Properties palette. Keep the Properties palette open to the side of the Project window so the Pickwhip can be used to link the background video.

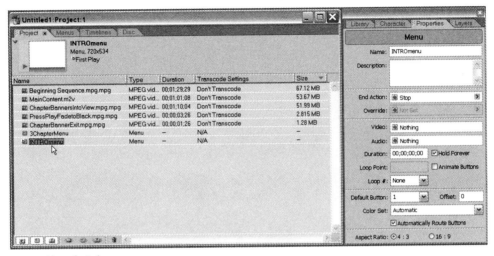

Proper position of windows.

7. Drag the Pickwhip to link the video field in the Menu Properties to the BeginningSequence.mpg clip in the Project window.

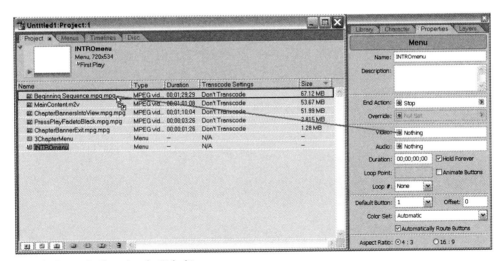

Linking background video using the Pickwhip.

The menu should now display the beginning sequence clip.

The beginning sequence clip shows in the menu. Toggle the Show Selected Subpicture to see the subpicture buttons.

Next, we'll repeat this process to specify the background video for the 3ChapterMenu.

8.   Select the 3ChapterMenu and make sure the menu properties are visible in the Properties palette.

9. Drag the Pickwhip from the video field in the Properties palette to the ChapterBannersIntoView.mpg clip in the Project window.

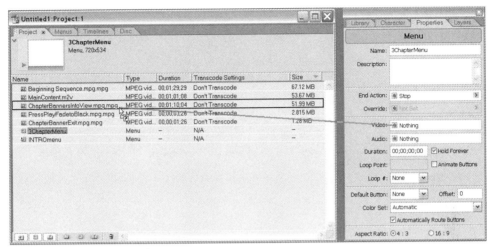

Linking the video clip to the second menu.

Use the preview buttons in the Menu Editor to view the different subpicture states of both menus. Notice that the subpicture highlights seem out of place in the 3ChapterMenu. This is because our subpicture highlights correspond to action that occurs later on in the background video. If this is confusing, right click on this menu and choose Preview From Here. Notice that subpicture highlights were designed to correspond to the banners in the background video. The menu looks a bit strange and the subpicture highlights have some issues. We'll address these concerns shortly.

Next, we'll create a timeline that will act as a transition to the first chapter point on the main timeline.

10. Select the PressPlayFadeToBlack.mpg clip in the Project window and click the New Timeline icon at the bottom of the Project window.

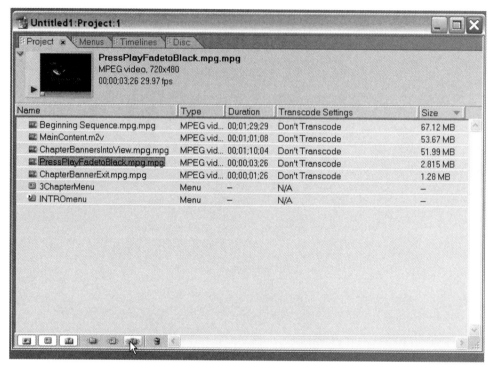

Creating a new timeline with the New Timeline icon.

While we're at it, let's also create two more timelines.

11. Select the MainContent.m2v clip. Once again, press the new timeline icon at the bottom of the Project window to place it inside its own timeline.

12. Next, select the ChapterBannerExit clip and press the New Timeline icon to place it inside its own timeline.

New timelines should now be created for the PressPlayFadeToBlack.mpg, MainContent.m2v, and ChapterBannerExit clips.

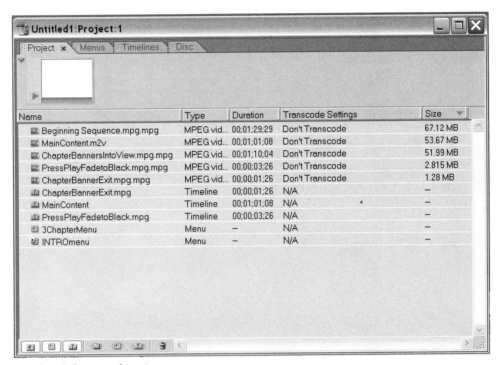

Our project window up to this point.

Back to setting links for the buttons in the INTROmenu.

13.   Open the INTROmenu and select the top button.

All navigation and linking in the INTROmenu is accomplished through the use of subpicture highlights. In this project, the subpicture highlights *are* our buttons. To view and link these sub-picture buttons, we can simply click the selected state preview button in the Menu Editor. Once the selected state is activated, we can click the subpicture highlights directly to position and set properties for the different buttons.

14.   Select the top button, then link this button to the PressPlayFadeToBlack.mpg timeline.

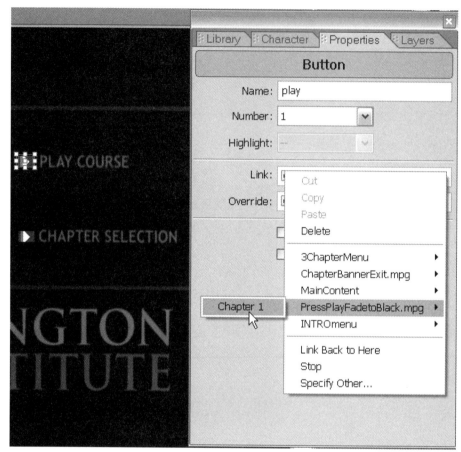

Notice that there is only one chapter to choose from.

This clip was created to act as a simple transition from the INTROmenu to the main timeline. It simply creates a fade to black, then links to the first chapter in the main timeline. Its main purpose is to provide a smooth transition to the main content of the DVD when chapter selection is not desired.

After the PressPlayFadeToBlack timeline finishes playback, we need it to link to the first chapter of the MainContent timeline. Otherwise, we would end up with a broken link.

15. Select the newly created PressPlayFadeToBlack timeline in the Timeline tab and open the Properties palette. Set the end action to the first chapter of the MainContent timeline.

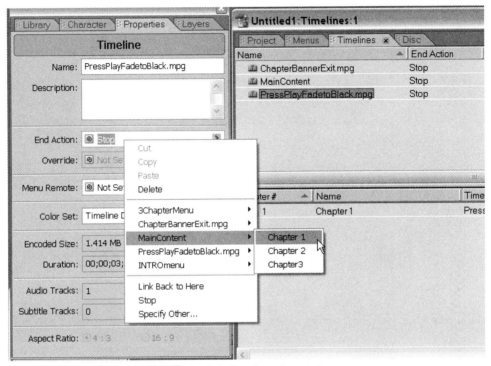

Selecting an end action for the transition clip that links it to the main content.

Let's also create a link for the bottom chapter selection button.

16. Go back to the Menu Editor for the INTROmenu. Select the bottom button, then use the drop-down menu in the Properties palette to select the 3ChapterMenu.

Notice that another menu opens to the side, allowing us to choose which button will be selected when the menu opens. We can choose between the three different banners. These are not chapter points, but rather options to determine which button will be selected after the button is pressed and the 3ChapterMenu becomes visible.

17.   Choose Banner 1.

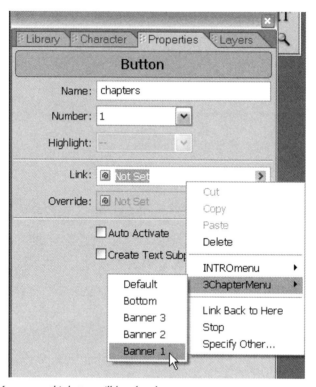

When the 3ChapterMenu opens, this button will be selected.

This determines the selected button for the menu *from this link*.

TIP: Button 1 in all menus is the default selected button. If you want another button to be selected as the default, select it in that menu's Properties palette. This way you don't have to remember which button you want when you link to the menu, just select the default when linking your buttons. This is also an added bonus when your menu is set as the First Play on the DVD.

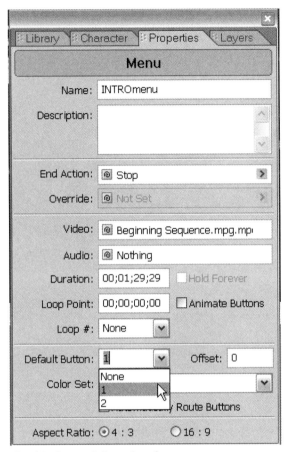

The default button can be selected in the menu's Properties palette.

We've now linked first menu to the second menu. The background video in both menus matches up seamlessly and creates an animated interactive experience.

18. Right click on the INTROmenu and choose Preview From Here.

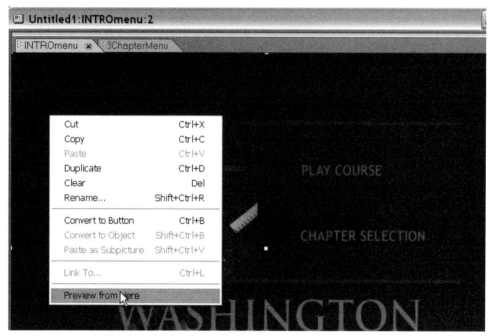

To test the interactivity of your project or menu, right click and choose Preview From Here.

TIP: To get an idea of how this menu will look in a DVD player, you can build the project to a folder. This will create a DVD directory that can be previewed with a DVD software program. Alternatively, you can also burn to disc and test / preview in a set top player.

When previewing, pay particular attention to the INTROmenu.

Notice the subpicture highlight is visible next to the Chapter Selection text. This is because the menu defaults to display the selected state of the first button. The chapter selection button is actually labeled as "Button 1" in Encore.

19. Close the Preview window.
20. In the Menu Editor select the Chapter Selection button and open the Properties palette.

21.   Change the button number from Number 1 to Number 2.

The chapter selection button is improperly labeled as Button 1. Change it with the pull-down menu.

22.   Next, select the top button; notice this has changed and is now listed as Button 1.

23. Preview the project again; notice the default button is now the top button.

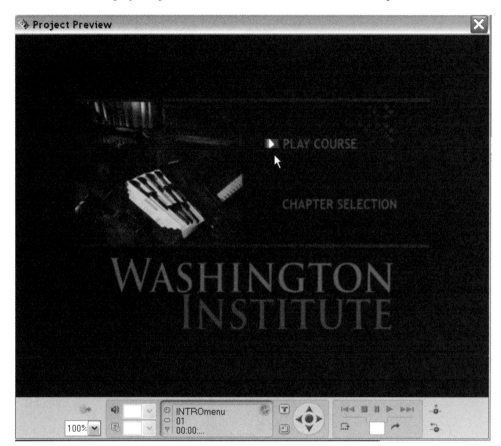

The initial selection is now on the first button instead of the second.

TIP: Changing a button number to 1 is probably the worst way to make it the default button. Use the default button option in the menu's Properties palette instead. It's better to make sure the buttons are numbered properly as this can affect direct button selection when using a remote control.

There are other problems with the project as well.

1. Subpicture highlights are in view *EVEN BEFORE* the INTROmenu comes into view.
2. Subpicture highlights are visible too soon in the 3ChapterMenu as well.
3. The buttons in the second menu are not linked yet.
4. Button routing is not working properly.

This project definitely needs some work. Don't worry, we'll be finishing this project later on in this chapter. Let's cover some important considerations first.

Looping Functions

To access looping options for a menu, select the desired menu and open the Properties palette. Once the Properties palette is open, four different settings can be used to customize looping options for the menu.

> TIP: Previewing in Encore may cause some glitches between timeline or when looping menus. Quite often, this glitch is more noticeable inside Encore when compared to most set top players. If it's a critical project, it's usually best to burn the project to disc for the final preview or building a disc volume and previewing with DVD playback software.

> TIP: Using Premiere, fades to and from black can be created at the beginning and end of clips to compensate for the glitch that occurs in most players when transferring from one timeline to another. If the content fades in and out, this creates a smooth transition and helps to eliminate glitches between timelines.

Let's take a look at some of the different looping functions inside Encore.

Hold Forever

Hold Forever checkbox.

By default, menus are set to hold indefinitely, waiting for input from the viewer. This is typically ideal when working with still menus.

Duration

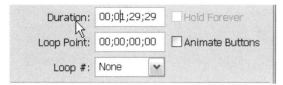

Duration field.

For still menus, duration determines how long the static image is displayed before the menu loops or executes the end action.

For motion menus, the duration typically matches the length of the background video in the menu. This setting can be reduced to shorten the duration of the menu, shortening the duration of the background video. Duration can also be increased to extend the duration of the menu. If the duration is set longer than the background video clip, this will cause the last frame of video to display until an end action is executed or the menu loops.

Loop

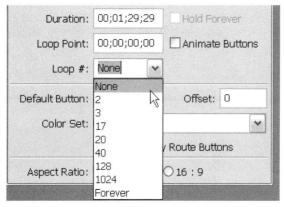

Looping options can be accessed using the drop-down menu.

By default, setting loop # values will cause the contents of the menu to start over, playing from the beginning of the menu. This behavior can be changed by using the loop point setting. This setting determines how many times the menu will loop. Authors can use values from the drop-down menu. To create a continually looping menu, you can choose Forever. You can also choose from the other values, or specify a value directly in the Properties palette.

Loop Point

Loop point.

After the menu plays through once, the loop point determines where subsequent loops occur. This setting reduces the duration of the menu and can be used, for example, to offset the starting point of the loop. The loop point also determines when the subpicture highlights become visible.

Delaying Subpicture Highlights

Imagine a menu fading from black. Five seconds later, buttons converge from the edges to fill the screen. Slight problem... by default, the button highlights are displayed from the beginning frame of the menu. In this case, the highlights would be visible before the buttons even come into view! Fortunately, Encore has a subpicture delay feature incorporated "under the hood."

Subpicture delay is provided through the use of the looping feature in the Properties palette. The loop point serves two different purposes. As mentioned previously, the loop point determines where the menu returns after playing through once; it also determines when the subpicture highlights come into view.

Let's get back to the project we were just working on. It does a good job of demonstrating the practical application of this feature.

Project 10

Time to tie up some loose ends on our AE project.

The first thing we want to do is create some looping behaviors for both of our menus. Both menus have background video. The duration of the clips we previously added are listed in the Menu Properties palette.

The current behavior for our menus is to play the background video one time. After the menus reach the end, the link is broken. Avoid this at all costs. This can spell disaster for a DVD.

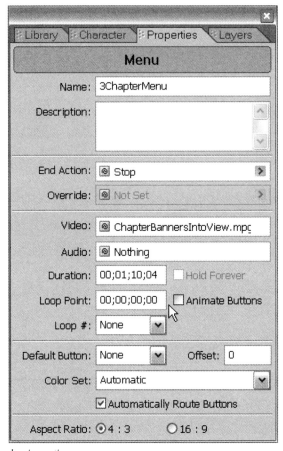

Menu properties displaying looping options.

Let's add some looping to our menus, so when they reach the end they will return to the point we specify. This will give the viewer plenty of time to make a menu selection.

1. Select the INTROmenu and open the Properties palette.
2. In the Loop# field, choose Forever.

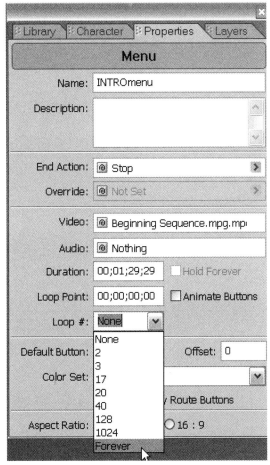

Specify Forever in the Loop# field.

Let's set the same looping behavior for the 3ChapterMenu.

3. Select the 3ChapterMenu and open the Properties Palette.
4. Once again, in the Loop# field choose Forever.
5. Right click on the INTROmenu and choose Preview From Here.

The background video is a relatively long clip. Notice that when it reaches the end, it returns to the beginning of the background video clip. The 3ChapterMenu will exhibit these same behaviors.

We are experiencing two major problems with these menus.

First of all, the subpicture highlights are visible from the first frame. They need to be delayed a few seconds until after the action in the video stream has subsided.

The other major problem is that when the menus loop, they return to the first frame and this causes the menus to rebuild themselves. At this point, the menus are not seamless and this is not ideal behavior. It would be much better if the loop point returned to the portion of the clip *just after* the elements settle into place. This is even worse with the 3ChapterMenu. We don't want the banners sliding in and out every time the menu loops.

Fortunately, we can resolve all of these issues by specifying a loop point.

6. Select the INTROmenu and in the loop point field type in 3 seconds—00;00;03;01.

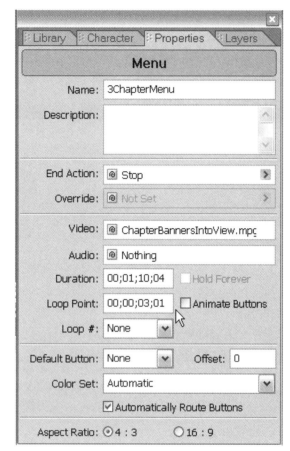

Input a new timecode value directly in the loop point field.

This sets the loop point just a touch over 3 seconds into the video stream.

Next, repeat this exact process for the 3ChapterMenu.

7. Select the 3ChapterMenu and in the loop point field, type in 3 seconds—00;00;03;01.

This establishes the loop point just after the action subsides in both menus. It also automatically changed the behaviors of the subpicture highlights.

8. Right click on the INTROmenu and choose Preview From Here.

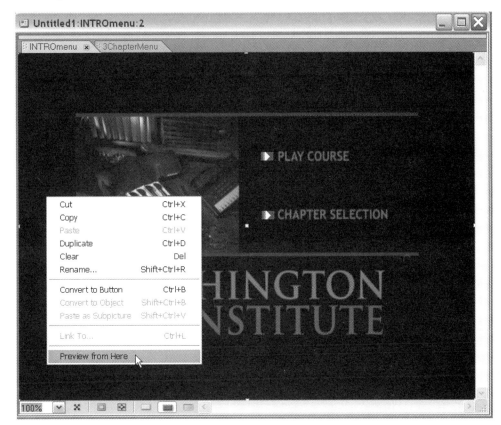

Open the Project Preview window.

Notice that changing the loop point has created a subpicture delay. The first time the menu plays, the subpicture highlights do not come into view until the loop point is reached.

Subsequent loops are also timed to occur after the action has subsided. PERFECT! Just what we needed.

Use this feature to time subpicture highlights in complex motion menus.

The last thing we need to do for this project is set the linking for the buttons in the 3ChapterMenu. We're going to be using the Override feature to accomplish this.

Override

Override substitutes, or overrides, the existing end action of a linked menu or timeline. Imagine yourself linking a button to timeline. Assume the timeline that you are linking to already has an end action specified. Override allows you to override the existing end action of this timeline. This is set using the button properties. Keep in mind that many buttons could access a single timeline, so the override function makes complex navigation much simpler by allowing the linked object to access several different timelines or menus. In the case of our menu project, the override is used to create a transition from the animated chapter menu to several chapter points on the timeline.

Let's take a look.

TIP: Override can also be used to select different buttons when linking to menus from different areas of the project. This can make navigation more intuitive by allowing the author to specify which button is in a selected state when returning to a menu. Override can also be used to improve functionality of multilingual projects (more in Chapter 7).

PROJECT 10

Now it's time to finish the project. Let's link up the three buttons in our 3ChapterMenu.

1. Click on the 3ChapterMenu to open it in the Menu Editor.
2. Next, use the Preview buttons at the bottom of the Menu Editor to bring the subpictures into view. This simply makes them easier to select.

Now let's set linking for our three buttons.

To create the proper interaction for the DVD, we want the chapter banners to slide off the screen after a selection has been made. In this situation, we will use the Override function. This will allow us to use a single timeline to provide a transition for all three of the different buttons to the desired chapter point in the MainContent timeline.

Let's take a look.

Since we want all of our buttons to link to the ChapterBannerExit timeline, we can save ourselves some time by selecting all of them simultaneously.

3. Using the Selection tool, drag a long selection box through the buttons to select them all.

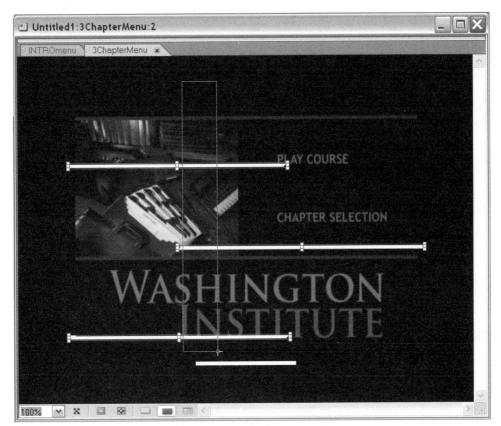

Multiple selections make adjusting several buttons at once simple and convenient.

Notice in the top field three values are listed in the Properties palette. This allows us to link all three buttons at once.

4. In the Properties palette, drag the Pickwhip from the link field to the ChapterBannerExit timeline in the Project window.

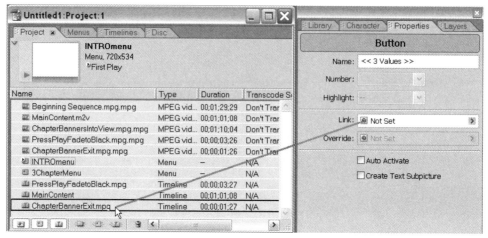

Now all three buttons are linked to the same exit clip.

When the buttons are activated, they will now link to the ChapterBannerExit timeline. This will cause our banners to slide out of view as desired.

Using the Override feature, we can use the same ChapterBannerExit timeline for all three buttons. We'll use Override to create different end action behaviors for each button. The Override feature allows us to specify different end actions to the ChapterBannerExit timeline. We're able to access 3 different chapter points, all depending on which button links to and overrides the end action of the ChapterBannerExit timeline. Each button will link to the ChapterBannerExit timeline, but Override will allow us to customize what happens when the ChapterBannerExit timeline reaches the end. It allows us to customize, or override, the end action individually for all three buttons.

Since each button corresponds to a different chapter point in the MainContent timeline, we have to set the overrides separately.

5. Open up the Timelines tab in the Project window and select the MainContent timeline so the chapters are shown in the bottom panel.

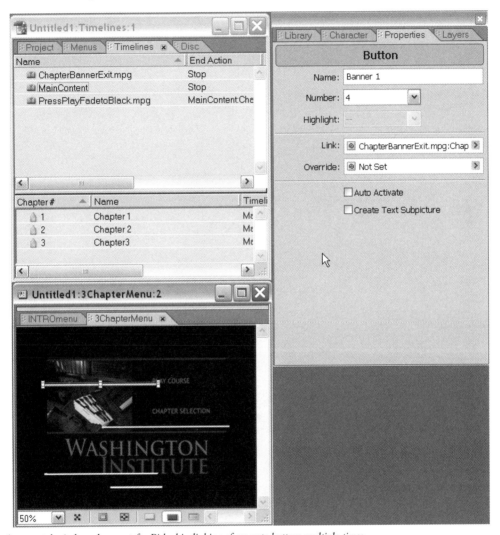

A suggested window placement for Pickwhip-linking of separate buttons multiple times.

6. With the first button selected and properties displayed, drag the Pickwhip from the override field to the first chapter point in the Timeline tab.

The Timeline tab lists chapter points for menus in the bottom portion of the window. In this situation, the Pickwhip can be dragged directly to chapter points in the timeline window as well.

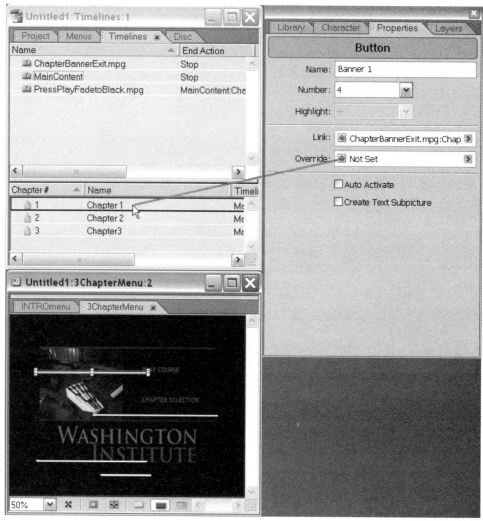

Creating links with the Timeline tab.

Let's set the override for the next button.

7. Select the second banner/button.

8. Next, drag the Pickwhip from the override field to the second chapter point in the MainContent timeline.

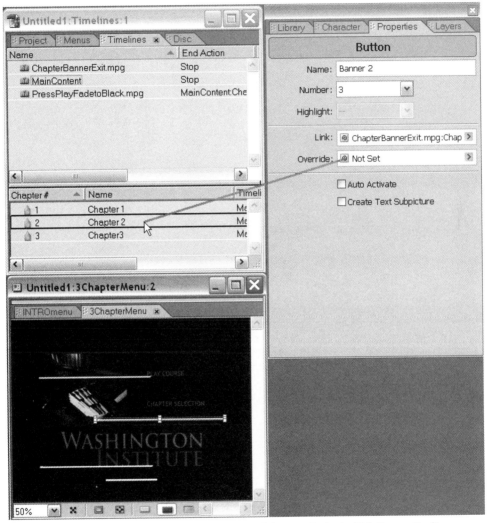

Create an override link for button 2 that is linked to the second chapter point in the MainContent timeline.

This changes the end action to link to the second chapter point in the MainContent timeline.

Repeat this process for the third and final button, setting the override to link up with the third chapter point on the MainContent timeline.

Override simplified!

Finishing Steps

These last steps have been covered quite well in this and previous chapters, so we will leave it to you to complete them. When you are done, compare your project to a finalized project, Project 10.ncor, in the sample files folder.

Make sure the buttons are assigned proper numbers by selecting the buttons and viewing the button properties (like we did for the first menu).

Make sure to set an end action for the MainContent timeline. Set the end action to link back to the INTROmenu.

Click on the Disc tab to name the disc. This palette also allows you to create a link for the title button.

The one thing we haven't covered is up next in Chapter 7, but the concept is pretty simple. Click on the MainContent timeline, view properties, and set the menu remote button to the INTROmenu. This way, when the menu button is pressed it provides direct access to the INTROmenu.

Congratulations. You have used full-motion menus to create a DVD menu. This was an advanced project, so give yourself a pat on the back. We've used some of the more technical features in Encore and added a new spin to creating motion DVDs.

Inserting Audio into the Background Menu

Inserting audio in the motion menu couldn't get much easier. It's very similar to the process of specifying video for a menu. Simply select the menu that you wish to add the audio to and open the Properties palette. Next, access the audio field and select the desired audio file.

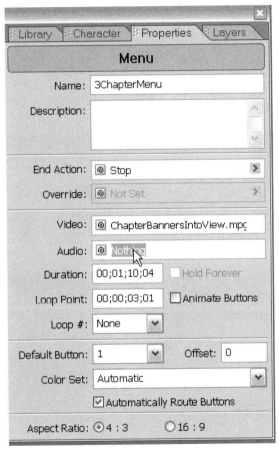

Linking background audio.

You don't want to go overboard when it comes to looping audio. Sometimes menus with looping audio can be downright annoying. It may be a good idea to create your motion menu with a section at the end that doesn't contain audio. In this situation, the clip plays through with audio once, then loop point can be used to offset the starting point of subsequent loops, bypassing the beginning (and potentially annoying) audio section.

Preparing Clips in Premiere

In this section, we'll look at the pros and cons of incorporating Premiere into your workflow. Premiere can be used to generate simple motion graphics, prepare assets, and encode content. It excels when it comes to frame-accurate control over editing, titling, audio sweetening, and surround sound mixing.

As discussed in previous chapters, a non-linear editor is used to prepare assets or for simple animations and basic effects. This is where clips are prepared and optimized for DVD. NLEs, like Premiere, can be used for color correction, noise removal, effects, or to ensure content is broadcast legal. An NLE can also be used to encode assets directly to MPEG-2, eliminating the need to transcode within Encore.

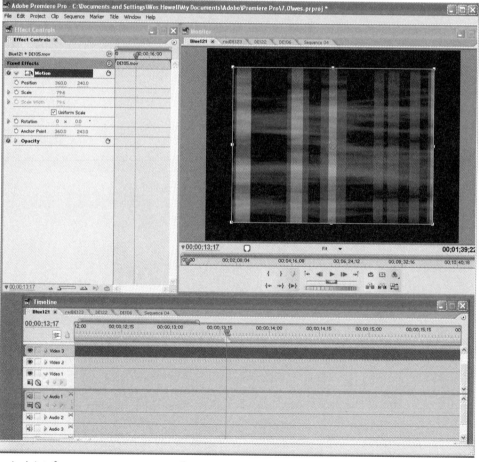

Premiere's interface.

Exporting MPEG Files from Premiere

Premiere and Encore use the same MPEG–2 encoder, so similar results can be expected. However, as detailed earlier, when preparing multilayered graphics or titles in Premiere, exporting directly to MPEG–2 can produce better results by eliminating unnecessary transcoding to an interim codec.

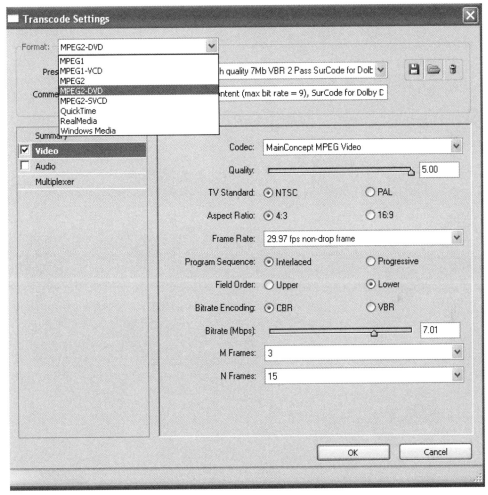

Premiere's encoder.

MPEG–2 files exported from Premiere can take advantage of the Edit Original feature. Like After Effects, this feature is enabled by embedding a project link when you save the AVI file.

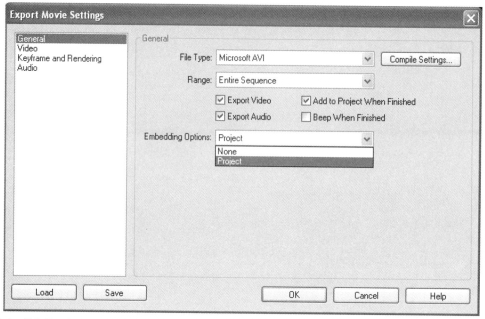

Project link Premiere.

After the AVI is created and imported into Encore, select the clip; then, from the Edit Menu, choose Edit Original. Premiere will open, displaying the project used to create the original clip. At this point, the clip can be modified and changes will be reflected inside Encore. If chapter points are changed, Encore will provide the option to update changes.

Source vs. Delivery codec

A DV AVI from a digital video camera is an example of a source codec. The DV codec was designed to maintain image quality even after several generations of compression. It was also designed to be used as source material that would be edited at a later time.

MPEG-2 and MP3 are examples of delivery codecs. These codecs were designed to deliver content when efficiency and bandwidth are paramount. Delivery codecs are typically quite lossy and not designed to be used as source material. Most non-linear editors do a poor job of editing and repurposing MPEG-2 video.

For this reason, it's best to avoid relying on DVDs or MPEG-2 video for archiving. If the product will eventually require more editing, keep the original source files, batch lists, and project files so that the project can be reconstructed at a later date.

Working with Chapters

Chapter points are typically used to direct navigation to specific scenes or timelines in a project. Buttons, menus, even other timelines can be linked to specific chapter points.

Every timeline used in Encore is created with a chapter point at the first frame. Other chapter points can also be added by positioning the timeline marker, then clicking the Add Marker icon in the timeline, or by using the keyboard shortcut, (the asterisk*) on the numeric keypad.

As chapter points are added, Encore automatically numbers them sequentially, and will even renumber chapters if additional points are added between two existing points.

Chapter Marker Placement

When working with files already encoded to MPEG-2, Encore allows chapters to be placed at GOP headers. GOP headers are indicated by the small tic marks in the timeline.

If absolute precision is required for chapter placement, it's best to specify chapters BEFORE the material is encoded to MPEG-2. This can be accomplished inside Premiere or by importing an AVI file into Encore. If using Premiere, markers can be used to specify chapter points. When exported as an MPEG-2 file, this will create frame-accurate chapter points that force GOP headers to be placed with perfect precision. These chapter points will also be recognized by Encore when imported. The only catch.... Before exporting from Premiere, a name must be specified in the name field of the marker.

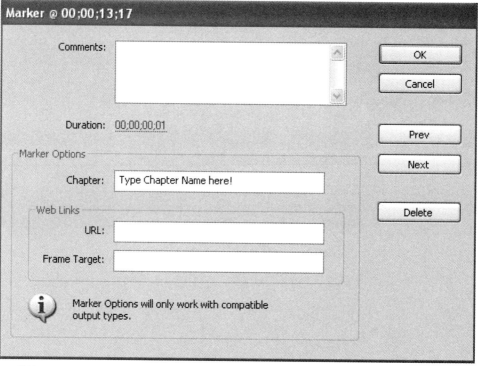

Name field.

TIP: Make sure all chapter points are at least 12 to 15 frames apart.

PROJECT 11

Project 11 shows how a motion menu was created using basic motion controls inside Premiere Pro. The Effects Control window makes motion controls easy to access and now provides direct sizing, scaling, and positioning of clips in the monitor window. There's no reason why you can't use a program like Premiere to create small clips ideal for use in motion menus.

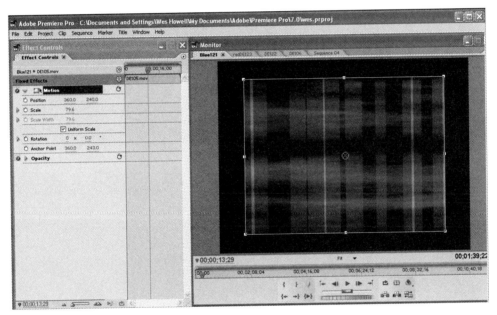

Effect Control window.

Notice that the Project 13 folder contains a Premiere Pro project file. Double click to open this file and look at how different tracks were used to create an effect similar to motion thumbnails. Simple resizing and positioning using an NLE is an effective method of adding basic animation and customizing your own menus and motion clips.

Feel free to open this project and view how it was created.

TIP: This example project creates a video clip similar to the background video clips used in Chapter 5. Project 13 also includes several full resolution clips generously provided by Artbeats (www.Artbeats.com). Many of the clips are perfect for use as motion video backgrounds, especially if you're still learning your way around After Effects. If you need stock footage, check out their website; the variety and quality of their footage cannot be beat.

Well that's it for now. You've created a motion menu with clips from After Effects, and you've had a look at using some of the tools inside Adobe Premiere.

In the next chapter, we are going to take a look at special considerations inside Encore such as working with multilingual audio tracks, subtitles, aspect ratios, and more.

Chapter 7

Finishing Touches

In the last couple chapters we'll be tying up some loose ends and looking into some of the more specialized features of Encore. The first few sections in Chapter 7 will cover the process of linking and will also detail some common menu types used in DVD production. We'll also take a look at optimizing remote control navigation using the Title, Menu remote, and the offset features. Lastly, we'll look into the process of using still photos to create a DVD slide show.

For those who work with multiple languages, or produce products that appeal to a diverse audience, we will explore setting up multiple audio tracks for multilingual discs and/or commentaries. We'll also add take a look at complementing these projects with subtitles.

Finally, we'll cover 16:9 menu and timeline considerations and working with 23.976p footage.

- Managing links
- Menu and title buttons
- Using the offset feature
- Menu types
- Slide shows
- Multilingual DVD
- Working with subtitles
- 16:9 considerations
- Creating 16:9 menus
- 23.976p support (NTSC)

Managing Links

Encore provides several different varieties of links that stitch the different elements of a project together and provide navigation options to the viewer.

Links come into play in several situations:

- When a timeline finishes playing, the end action link determines what happens next. This end action link can refer to another timeline or a particular button in a menu.
- Buttons use links to determine what happens when the button is activated. This link can be set to activate automatically when the button is selected (without requiring activation).
- Menus can use links to determine what happens if a button is not selected. An end action can be specified that will come into effect when a motion menu finishes playing, or after a still menu plays for a specified amount of time. This value can be specified in the duration field of the Properties palette.

Links can be set for menus, timelines, and buttons. There are also specialized links that can be specified for the title and menu function of a DVD player, typically activated on the remote control.

Menu and Title Buttons

Menu and Title buttons are link settings specified inside Encore that correspond to and provide functionality for the corresponding Menu and Title buttons on a set top player's remote control. The Title and Menu buttons are typically used to quickly navigate to the Main Menu or individual submenus inside a project.

Think of the **Title** button as a global setting for the project that typically allows the viewer to return to the Main Menu or the starting point of the disc with the press of one button on a remote control keypad.

To set the Title button: Select the Disc tab (next to the Project window). Next, open the Properties palette. The title button field is visible toward the bottom and can easily be changed to correspond to the main menu in the project.

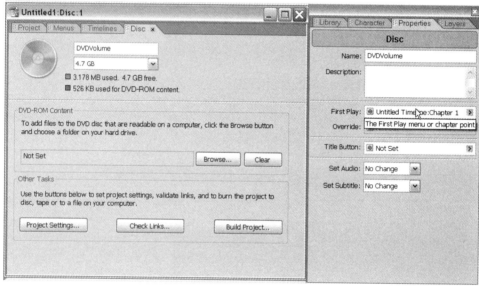

Setting the Title button in the Disc Properties palette.

The **Menu** button is similar in certain way to the Title button. The Menu button allows the viewer to create a link that is typically used to link to specific timelines. When viewing a time-line, menu buttons can be assigned to provide instant links, typically to a submenu. Different menu button links can be specified for various timelines and subjects in a project.

The Menu button exists as a property of the timeline window. To set the Menu button, select the desired timeline and open the Properties palette.

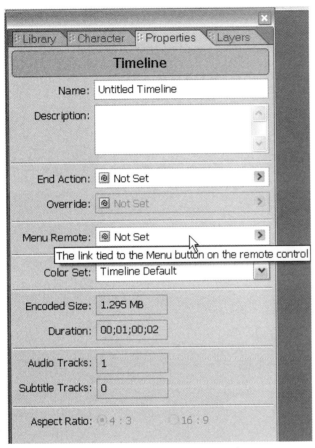

Setting the Menu button in the Timeline Properties palette.

Using the Offset Feature

The offset feature was designed to enhance the functionality of direct button selection in menus when using a set top player's handheld remote control. Many menus will contain several individual pages (additional menus), each containing several buttons. Numbers can be assigned to particular buttons in each menu and can be as activated by typing in the corresponding number on the remote control. (In this case the first button could be linked to a number 1, second, number 2, etc.) This provides a "direct selection" capability.

As far as the DVD player is concerned, all buttons in every menu start at 1, but there will be times when multiple menus are used to list several chapters and not every page will contain buttons starting at 1. Imagine if you have progressed to work on the second part of a two-page menu. Each part contains three buttons. The three buttons on the first page of the menu correspond properly to the numbers 1, 2, and 3. However, the second page starts with button 4. The button offset is the perfect solution for these situations.

PROJECT 12

Button Offset

1. Open Project12.ncor in the sample files folder.
2. Click to open Menu1 in the Menu Editor window.

Notice we have three buttons.

3. Select one of the buttons and view its properties in the Properties palette.

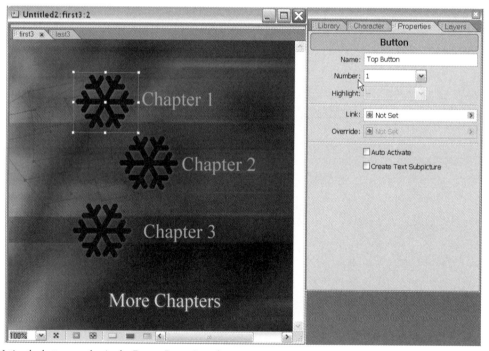

Notice the button number in the Button Properties palette.

Encore automatically assigns a number to each of these buttons—1, 2, and 3, respectively. The button number is displayed and can be adjusted in the Button Properties palette. These buttons correspond directly to the number pad on a set top DVD player's remote control. Pressing Number 1 will activate button 1, Number 2 will activate button 2, etc.

Notice toward the bottom there is a link to a second menu. This button is linked to Menu2 and opens more chapter selection options.

4.   Click on Menu2 to open it in the Menu Editor.

What happens when the user selects next page and is presented with buttons 4, 5, and 6? Users may want to access these buttons in the same manner using the number pad on the remote control.

Encore, by default, treats the buttons in this menu the same as buttons in the first menu. It sees three buttons and assumes that we want these to start at 1 and follow up with 2 and 3. Obviously this isn't what we want. We want these buttons to coincide with the number 4, 5, and 6 keys on the remote keypad.

This is what we use the offset feature for. It simply determines how menu buttons are interpreted and how they interact with direct button selection.

5.   Select Menu2 and open the Properties palette.

Notice the offset field toward the bottom of the Menu Properties palette.

6. Specify an offset value of 3.

The direct selection buttons on a remote will now work properly.

Menu Types

Most authors are going to be designing menus to accomplish specific tasks. Below, some of the most common menus are listed.

Main Menu

This is the most common menu in Encore. It's also the simplest to understand and implement. The main menu usually provides an index, or a list of different submenus on the disc. The main menu is typically linked to several smaller menus that provide options for setup, scene selection, or a direct link to the main video content.

Setup Menu

A setup menu provides options to choose between different playback options. The setup menu allows the viewer to configure playback according to their individual situation and preference. Audio, subtitles, and aspect ratio are common options available inside a Setup menu. Setup Menus are used inside Encore to control which audio track, subtitle, and even which video clip will be played.

Scene Selection Menu

With a scene selection menu, the viewer is presented with options to select from specific chapters or scenes. Seamless timelines with large sections of video content can be accessed from these menus. Multiple chapter points provide access to different sections of these timelines. After linking to a specific section in a timeline, playback continues until the timeline finishes. This behavior is normal and expected.

Outtakes Menu

Most outtakes menus provide links to small video clips. Inside Encore, some authors will want to link to a small section of video contained within a larger timeline. Unlike scene selection methods, if the viewer accesses a section of the timeline (i.e., a chapter in the middle of the timeline), the viewer does not want the timeline to continue playing all the way to the end. As mentioned in a previous chapter, this can cause a slight problem as most viewers will expect to return to the main outtakes menu after seeing an individually selected outtake. This is not possible if all the clips are located on a single timeline because Encore does not provide the ability to alter navigation *within* a timeline. End actions are only activated at the end of a timeline.

The workaround is to create smaller timelines that represent individual outtakes. In this case, after a specific outtake has been selected, it's easy to link the end action back to the outtakes menu. The drawback of this technique is that if the individual outtakes are on separate timelines, there is no way to play all of the outtakes seamlessly. The only alternatives are to create fades to black on each timeline, eliminating the viewable glitches between timelines, or to create an additional timeline that holds one clip containing all the outtakes.

TIP: In order to accommodate different menus and eliminate the glitch between timelines during playback, many authors will inevitably create multiple timelines to accommodate different menus and linking scenarios. Although this can be an acceptable workaround, one simple rule always applies:

In Encore 1.0, two timelines with the same media will burn the same media twice onto the DVD.

Slide Shows

Slide shows are used to display still frames or a sequence of still frames for a specified amount of time. Slide shows display static video accompanied by background music, although audio is not required.

Encore provides the ability to add several stills to a single timeline. Multiple stills can be selected in the project window and dragged down into the Timeline. Once added to the timeline, Encore lines the clips up sequentially and automatically inserts chapter points at the beginning of each still (up to 99 per timeline). The chapter points provide simple and easy navigation for the viewer.

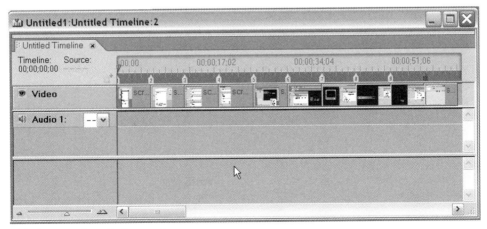

A slide show's timeline with chapter points.

If you know the desired length of all stills before import, the default still duration can be specified in Preferences. Duration can also be adjusted for individual clips directly on the timeline. Simply hover over the head or tail of the clip, then click and drag with your mouse to manually adjust duration.

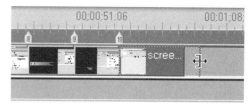

Slide show duration adjustment.

For the most part, images used to create slide shows are prepared and adjusted just like any other asset in a timeline. The main difference is that with slide shows, the timeline can accommodate more than one file, whereas video timelines can only accommodate one clip. Just like any other timeline, up to 8 audio streams can be added, allowing the author to utilize multiple languages.

> TIP: Slide shows can save a significant amount of disc space by displaying a single still image over time. This replaces the need to create a full motion clip containing multiple frames over time. Encore encodes individual frames to disc and includes data that tells the player how long to display them. This technique requires much less disc space than manually creating video clips from still frames in external applications.

> TIP: Keep in mind that 1 gigabyte is the maximum amount of space that menus can occupy on any DVD-Video disc.

Multilingual DVD

Several different audio and subpicture streams can be used to provide additional content in a DVD project. This can include director's comments, subpicture graphics, text captions, or multiple languages.

The DVD spec allows up to 8 audio streams and 32 subpicture streams to be multiplexed into the main DVD-Video stream. Encore supports this functionality, allowing authors to use multiple languages and subtitles in a single timeline. This allows the viewer to complement a single video stream with their choice of optional subtitles and language tracks.

Only one audio and one subtitle track can be viewed at a time, so it is critical to understand how to create setup menus that allow the viewer to choose from the available subtitles and audio streams.

Audio tracks and subtitles are turned on and off through the use of buttons. These buttons facilitate the navigation and linking options required to select the desired subtitles or audio streams in the timeline they are linked to. This allows the viewer to use buttons in a menu to choose streams that represent the desired language.

The default behavior is to play audio track one in conjunction with the video stream in the respective timeline. This behavior can be altered in a menu by selecting the button that links to the timeline and using the "Specify Other" option in the link field. To access the "Specify Other" options, open the Properties palette and click the arrow to the right of the link field.

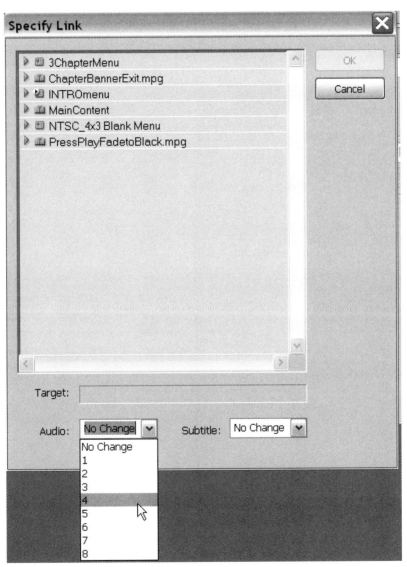

The "Specify Other" options in the Link To dialog.

Once the "Specify Other" option has been chosen, a dialog pops up allowing the author to specify subtitle and audio tracks. This behavior is controlled through the use of the linking options. Once the link is set, Override option becomes available below the link field. This feature makes many more navigation and linking behaviors available to the author.

After a subtitle or audio track has been activated using the "Specify Other" properties, the player will keep track of this setting. If the project contains subsequent timelines, the player will keep this setting, assuming all timelines utilize the same number and placement of audio tracks/subtitles. *For example, if a new timeline comes into play that does not have the same tracks as the first timeline, the player will reset the default back to the first audio track.*

When working with subtitles, if subsequent timelines do not contain the specified track, the subtitles will disappear.

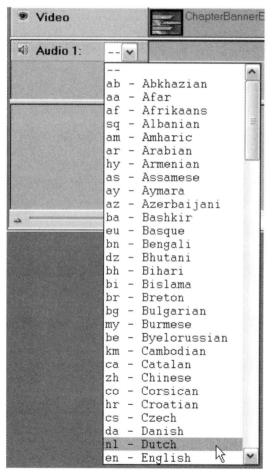

Language settings in the timeline.

The point here is to make sure that all audio tracks and subtitle tracks are consistent between timelines. For example, keep all English audio streams on the same numbered audio tracks. This will ensure consistent playback throughout the DVD. Also when possible, make sure all timelines utilize the same track structure and order.

When adding multiple audio tracks and subtitle tracks to the timeline, drop-down boxes are used to specify the language directly in the subtitle or audio track. This tells the DVD player which tracks represent specific languages and enhances the functionality of the DVD player's setup menu. This information is often displayed by a stand-alone DVD player in the front panel LED display so the viewer can see what tracks and languages are selected.

TIP: Menus only support one audio stream. In order to create menus for multilingual projects, multiple menus are created with buttons that can be linked to menus with the desired language. Buttons can be linked and the Override feature can be incorporated to activate different audio and subtitle tracks.

PROJECT 13

To view an example of a multilingual project, open Project 13.ncor in the sample files folder. We'll reference and elaborate upon this project using one of the video tutorials included with the accompanying DVD.

In the meantime, feel free to start investigating and reverse engineering this project. Select the buttons in the setup menu and access the "Specify Other" settings. Notice that once an initial link is specified, the override options are accessible. Notice the different settings and preview the menus to analyze the different behaviors. Also, notice how Override controls the end action destination of the timeline, directing it to a specific menu.

Working with Subtitles

Subtitles are text captions that are overlaid on top of video content. They can provide a text translation for a foreign language used in the main dialogue and can also provide valuable functionality for the hearing impaired. In Encore, subtitles are created as individual clips that occupy sections of a subtitle track in the timeline. Up to 32 different subpicture streams can be used in a timeline; however, a DVD player can only play one subpicture stream at a time.

Similar to subpicture highlights, subtitles are 2-bit, 4-color overlays that are generated by the DVD player. Like subpicture highlights used for menus, subtitles can be created with three colors plus transparency.

The color of subtitles can be controlled through the use of color sets. This process is similar to setting color sets for subpicture highlights. As covered in Chapter 5, color sets can be specified for menus to determine subpicture highlights. In the case of subtitles, a timeline color set is used to determine color, stroke, and partial anti-aliasing for the subtitles.

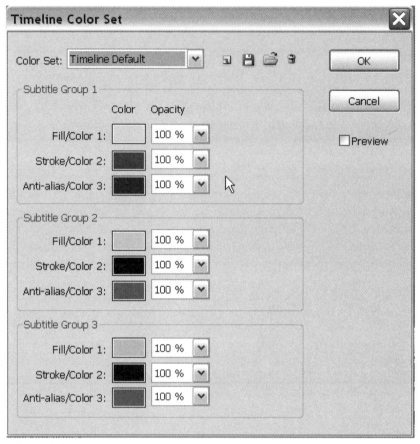

Timeline Color Set dialog.

Subtitles color sets provide three color groups (compared to two for menus) that can be assigned to timelines. Only one color set can be assigned for each timeline; however, each timeline and its individual subtitle clips have full access to any of the three color groups in the color set. In addition, multiple color sets can be used in the same project.

Like subpicture highlights, subtitles are not incorporated into the background MPEG-2 video, and exist only as overlays. This allows the viewer to choose between separate individual subtitles that can be laid over the top the same piece of video.

Encore provides many different options for working with subtitles. Subtitles can be created within the application or they can be prepared in an external application. Several file formats are supported, including text script, FAB format, and Captions Inc files.

When importing text script subtitles, there are a few format considerations. Text script must be either ASCII, UTF-8 (Universal Text Format), or UTF-16 file formats. The text script must be in an ordered, timecoded format. See Figure 7.1.

To import subtitles created in an external application, right click on the timeline; then choose Import Subtitles. You can also use the Timeline Menu; Timeline> Import Subtitles. You can then choose between the three import options. After selecting the file to import, Encore will present you with options to select font, colors, position, and orientation for the imported subtitles.

Color group selection in the Subtitle Properties palette.

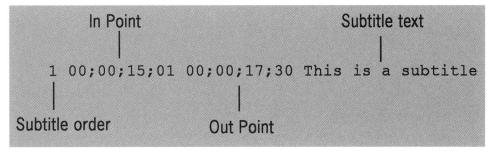

Figure 7.1 *Text script must be in this format.*

TIP: Remember that in order to add subtitles, a subtitle track must be created first.

PROJECT 14

Subtitles

Subtitles can be created inside Encore by creating a subtitle track, then typing directly inside the Monitor window with the Text tool. No file is provided for this project, but you may use any of the previous projects that has a timeline.

1. To create a subtitle track, simply right click on the timeline and choose Add Subtitle Track.

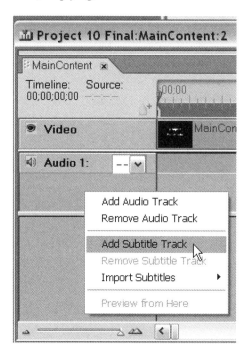

Adding a subtitle track.

2. Once the subtitle appears in the timeline, position the timeline marker where you want the subtitle to start.
3. Next, choose Window>Character Palette.

The Character palette will open allowing you to specify font, type size, orientation, and many other type attributes.

Choose the type size and font that you wish to use for your subtitle.

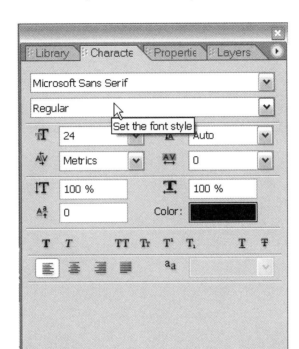

The Character palette allows you to adjust the font.

4. Next, select the text tool (vertical or horizontal), then click directly in the Monitor window to add a subtitle.

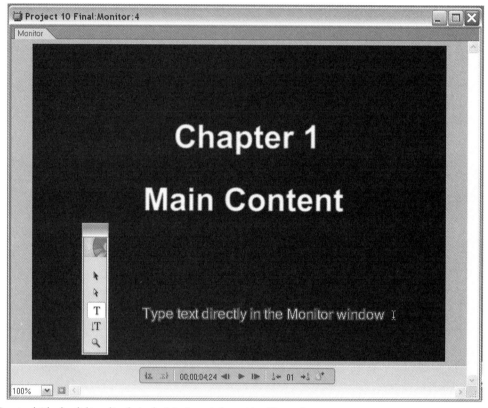

Insert subtitles by clicking directly in the Monitor window with a Text tool.

When adding a subtitle, a bounding box appears in the Monitor window. Subtitles can be scaled and positioned just like other graphics inside Encore.

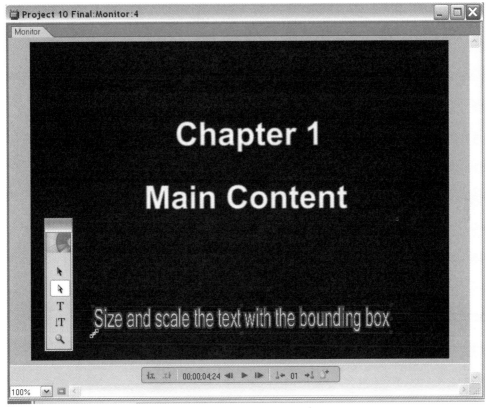

The bounding box allows you to scale and position subtitle text.

When a timeline is selected, the properties can be adjusted using the Properties palette. The Character palette can also be used to change type attributes. In fact, multiple subtitles can be selected and adjusted at the same time.

Color sets for subtitles are adjusted using color sets. This is very similar to the process of creating color sets for menus.

TIP: There is a known problem in Encore 1.0 in which subtitle text that extends outside the Monitor window can cause errors when the Monitor window is open. A couple of things can cause this. First, inserting text in the middle of a subtitle clip can cause the bounding box to expand beyond the Monitor window frame. Changing text attributes on a range of subtitle clips can cause some clips to expand beyond the Monitor frame as well.

To edit subtitle colors, choose: Edit>Color Sets>Timeline. Choosing Timeline brings the default timeline color set into view.

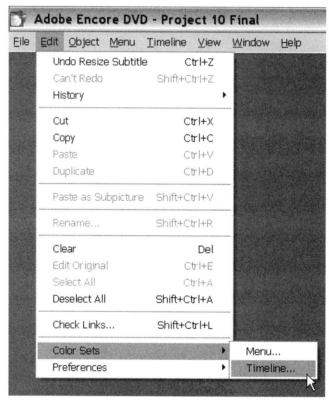

Pulling up the Timeline Color Set dialog.

At this point, adjustments can be made to the default color set, or an entirely new template can be created.

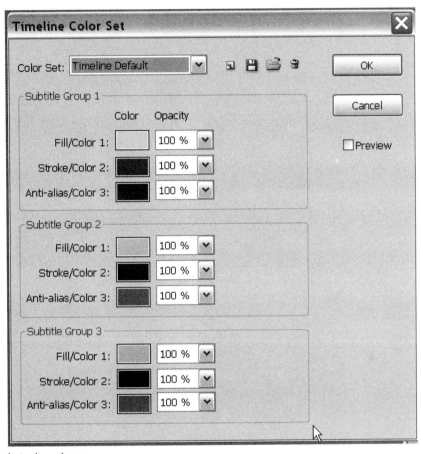

The default timeline color set.

TIP: After a custom color set is created for a timeline, make sure it is specified in the timeline's Properties palette.

Only one color set can be specified for each individual timeline. However, each subtitle can use one of three individual color groups.

To specify color groups for individual subtitles, select the desired subtitle and view its properties in the Properties palette.

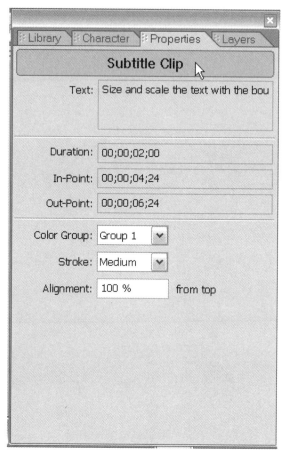

Subtitle Properties palette.

Once the Properties palette is open, the color group can be specified. This allows the author to display various subtitles in the same menu using three distinct color groups.

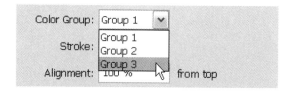

Color group setting.

Subtitle duration can be adjusted by hovering over the head or tail of the subtitle on the subtitle track. When the red icon becomes visible, click and drag to adjust the duration.

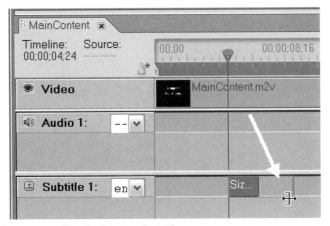

Red bracket cursor allows you to adjust the duration of subtitles.

You can also use the trim tools on the bottom left side of the Monitor window. Simply position the CTI marker in the timeline and press to trim the in or out point of the subtitle.

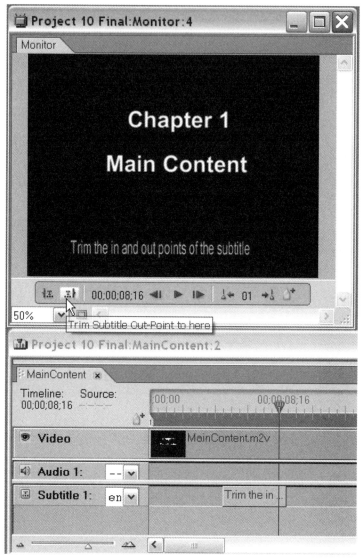

Monitor trimming.

Default subtitle duration can be adjusted by choosing Edit>Preferences. After adjusting the default duration, it will apply to all subsequently created subtitles.

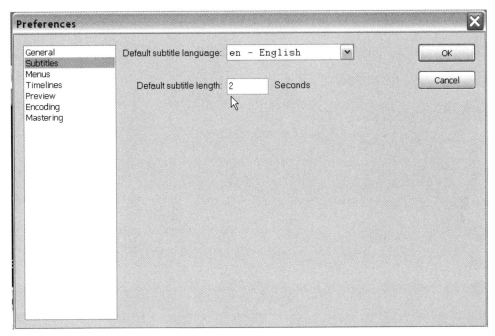

Subtitle preferences.

In my opinion, Encore's subtitle toolset still needs a little more refinement before it can be totally relied upon for full scale subtitle creation. Render times are very slow and typing subtitles in the monitor directly is not the perfect solution for large projects that contain a large amount of subtitles. Direct input in Encore is fine for creating a few subtitles, but for more extensive subtitle work, many authors have found Subtitle Workshop to be a better solution (http://www.redox. si/viplay/english/pages/home.htm). This stand-alone application is available at no cost and offers many great features including broad support for a wide variety of formats. For more information on using this program and how to export a format that Encore can accept, check the Adobe Encore Users Forum (http://www.adobe.com/support/forums/main.html). The Users Forum is also a great place to keep track of new events, patches, and newly released tools that will continue to improve subtitle creation inside Encore.

16:9 Considerations

Most NTSC televisions on the market today display 720×480 pixels representing a 4:3 aspect ratio. *(See Chapter 5 for more information on aspect ratios.)* The 16:9 aspect ratio used for HDTV, plasma, and widescreen displays will soon replace the bulky, bubble-type televisions that exist in most homes today. 16:9 is getting increasingly popular by the day. More and more displays support 16:9 content and many future standards are based on this aspect ratio.

The DVD specification supports both 4:3 and 16:9 video. Determining whether content for a DVD is 4:3 or widescreen is up to the author and will vary depending on the project. Fortunately, whether the source content is 4:3 or 16:9, Encore provides the ability create DVDs that will playback on both 16:9 widescreen and regular 4:3 displays. It's even possible to create DVDs that offer both 4:3 and 16:9 content.

When importing NTSC video into Encore, all files must be 720×480, 720×486, or 704×480 pixels per frame. With PAL, all files must be 720×576 or 704×576. This restriction applies to both 4:3 and 16:9 content. Widescreen NTSC source content is typically sourced with a frame size of 854×480. (PAL is 1024×576.) So this begs the question, How do I get 854×480 pixels out of a DVD when the maximum frame size I can get into Encore is 720×480 pixels (or 720×576 for PAL)? The answer is anamorphic video.

FYI: The DVD spec also supports half frame rate, 352×240 MPEG-2 as well as MPEG-1 video. At this time, Encore does not.

Let's assume we're working with NTSC for the moment.

The pixels in a widescreen 854×480 pixel frame can be compressed horizontally to fit on a 720×480 pixel frame. During this anamorphic conversion, the original image is compressed horizontally to fit within the 720×480 pixel limitation. This conversion takes place during the encoding process and can be "undone" when played back in a DVD player. It's a simple process of squeezing more information into a 720×480 pixel image.

When the image is encoded and the pixels are compressed anamorphically, a flag is added to the video stream that tells the player to expect anamorphic content. When the player sees this flag, it knows it is anamorphic and several different playback options are available from which to choose. The DVD player itself provides menu options to determine how the player outputs the video to a variety of displays.

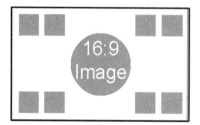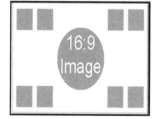

Figure 7.2 *Picture of anamorphic vs regular 854×480 frame.*

Figure 7.2 depicts a frame exported from Premiere. The source file was 854×480 widescreen footage, compressed anamorphically with MPEG-2 flags added to the video stream. Notice the output file is compressed horizontally.

To a DVD player, all video on the disc is actually encoded as 4:3 content. When encoded properly, the MPEG-2 flag added to the video stream tells the player that the content has been squeezed horizontally. This allows the player to re-stretch and create a larger frame from the smaller source content. In this situation, let's think of the player as creating a 854×480 pixel image by stretching the source content. If this footage is output to a progressive 16:9 display, it will display an 854×480 pixel frame. But what if this widescreen video is to be played on a regular 4:3 display? It's too big, it won't fit, right?

The following can be specified in the settings menu of the player.

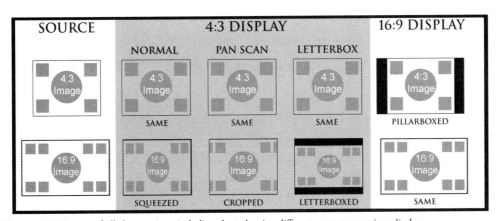

Figure 7.3 *Pictures of all three options, including chart showing different content on various displays.*

Normal 4:3

This is chosen for disc with 4:3 content to be played back on a standard 4:3 television.

Normal 16:9

This setting is for 16:9 content that is to be displayed on a 16:9 display.

Pan and Scan

Pan and scan reframes the picture to conform to a different aspect ratio. When working with NTSC, this is accomplished by cropping sections of the original 16:9 content (854×480) to create a new 4:3 picture (720×480). Correct resolution for a 4:3 display is achieved by chopping 67 pixels off of each side of the 854×480 pixel 16:9 image.

> TIP: Encore only supports 4:3, 16:9, and 16:9 letterboxed video. Pan and scan is not supported. Although pan and scan can be selected in the DVD player's menu, discs encoded with 16:9 content will revert to a letterboxed display.

Letterbox

Letterboxing displays the entire widescreen image on a screen that uses a 4:3 aspect ratio. First, consider that it is impossible to reproduce 854 horizontal pixels on a television that can only display 720. Letterboxing rescales the original widescreen image, essentially shrinking the widescreen source enough that it can fit inside a 4:3 frame. Horizontal resolution is reduced from 854 pixels to 720, and the vertical resolution is resized accordingly. This reduces the original 16:9 stream from 854×480 pixels to 720×404 and preserves the original aspect ratio. One side effect of this method is that to preserve the 16:9 aspect ratio, certain portions of the frame are not used in the 4:3 display device. This creates the effect of black bars at the top and bottom of the screen.

Creating 16:9 Menus

When designing graphics for motion menus, the source documents should use the following resolutions:

NTSC 854×480
PAL 1024×576

Once imported into Encore, widescreen menus will display in the Menu Editor using a 16:9 aspect ratio. The Preview window can also be set to display widescreen content letterboxed, or true 16:9.

When importing 16:9 menus, Encore automatically recognizes the aspect ratio. This setting can be toggled manually by selecting the menu and choosing Aspect Ratio in the menu's Properties palette.

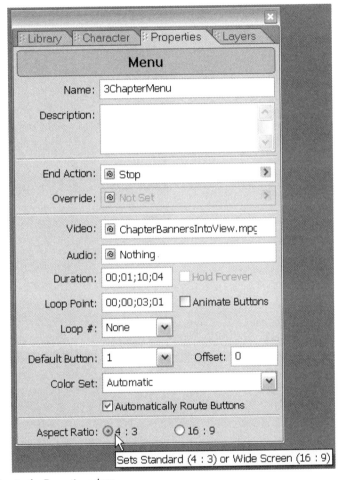

Aspect ratio selection in the Properties palette.

TIP: When a timeline is selected, the aspect ratio is indicated at the bottom of the Properties window. This setting simply indicates what type of footage Encore detects. This setting cannot be adjusted for a timeline.

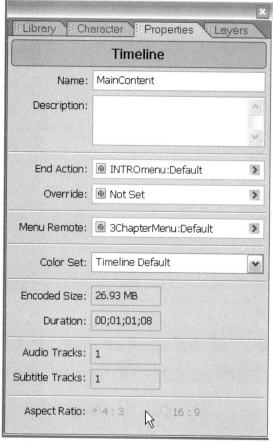

Timeline aspect ratio cannot be selected—only detected—by Encore.

In the past, several DVD applications have struggled when it comes to providing subpicture highlights for widescreen menus. This is because the original video can be played back at different sizes and offsets. The same menu could be played on a 4:3 device letterboxed, or as true 16:9 on a widescreen display. Some applications have had problems providing correct subpicture highlight information in order to accommodate multiple aspect ratios and playback scenarios. Fortunately, Encore takes care of these issues automatically and will play the subpicture highlights properly regardless of display device and aspect ratio.

23.976p Support (NTSC)

Many professional Hollywood DVDs provide the ability to output both progressive and interlaced content. Quite often, this is accomplished by encoding a 23.976p project that includes additional data, or flags, that when read by the player produce a regular interlaced 29.97 fps NTSC stream. This process, referred to as pulldown, is supported by the DVD spec, so rest assured that these types of projects will enjoy great compatibility with existing DVD players.

> TIP: 29.97 fps progressive video also supports progressive as well as interlaced playback.

This can be a huge benefit to an author as this provides the ability to create an "adaptive" video stream that can be output to numerous displays.

Encore DVD 1.0 and Premiere Pro do not produce these 23.976p, DVD-compliant MPEG-2 streams, so it's important to use an application that can encode these streams and add pulldown flags. The good news is that if you have other software or equipment that produces 23.976p, DVD-compliant MPEG-2 streams, you're in luck. Encore does allow you to import these streams and burn them to DVD.

> TIP: MainConcept offers a stand-alone encoder that exports these 23.976p streams.

This process will allow you to offer non-interlaced content and provide 20% more disc capacity when compared to regular 29.97 fps footage. This allows the content on the disc to play back non-interlaced on devices such as a plasma display or a computer monitor, and at the same time reconstructs an NTSC-legal interlaced stream for playback on regular television sets. It's a very efficient and versatile format. More people should acquaint themselves with this capability as 23.976p is only going to increase in popularity. Expect this feature to become more widely supported as newer programs are released/updated.

Now that all the hard work is done, it's time to preview the project. We need to make sure that our project is trouble free and ready for delivery.

Chapter 8

Final Output and Delivery

Okay, what kind of Encore DVD book would this be if we didn't actually talk about burning a disc? That's right, it's time to smooth out the kinks and put your disc together. Do you have to waste a DVD-R/+R on any of these or earlier projects? Of course not!

The DVD included with this book has everything you need. It was created with Encore and has used nearly all the features. If you haven't taken a look at the DVD-Video content on the disc, you should definitely watch it before you burn your own disc. It has many projects and tutorials that explore concepts best seen in action.

In this final chapter, we are going to look at button routing, which gives you more control over how complicated menus are navigated. We will also give the Preview window another whirl, and see what your projects are really doing when they output.

We will also consider other disc-related factors such as dual-layer, dual-sided discs; region codes; and copy protection.

Then, just before you burn, don't forget to check your links. We will see what this feature does and how it can keep you from saying "Duh" when your disc has that one tiny problem. And did you know you could "burn" your DVD project to your hard disc? Most DVD software can play this as if it was a disc. (Just make sure you have the disk space!)

Sending it to a replication house for stamping? DLT is the way to go. We'll give a once-over to the various formats and considerations.

So without any more flourish, let's get started. (Or should we say "let's get finished"?)

- Button routing
- Project preview window
- Working with dual-layer and dual-sided discs
- Disc tab
- Adding DVD-ROM content
- Project settings
- Region codes
- Copy protection
- Checking links
- Building a project
- More export options
- Outputting to DLT (DLT formats)

Button Routing

Encore offers a tremendous amount of control over how the end user interacts with the menus; however, Encore, by default, takes much of that control out of your hands by automatically routing buttons for menus. These automatic settings expect certain arrangement patterns such as rows or columns, and a pattern that strays from this may provide unexpected results. It's generally not a great idea to rely solely on these automatic settings for every project. At the very least, make sure to double check the button routing before burning a disc.

TIP: Encore offers a little control over how it automatically routes buttons. In the Menu Preferences dialog, you can choose a total of six different options for automatic routing. This is nice, but we'll see in this next project how sometimes even that's not quite enough.

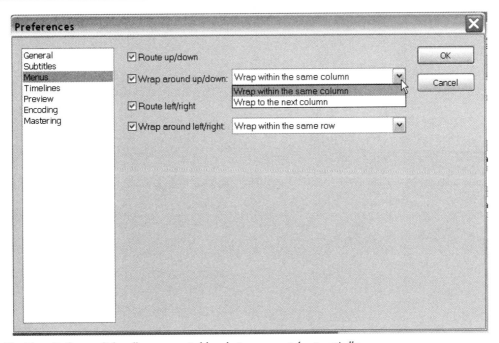

The Menu Preferences dialog allows you control how buttons are routed automatically.

Disabling the Automatic Button Routing allows easy access and direct control over button routing. In order to modify button routing behaviors, the menu must be selected and automatic button routing must be turned off in the Properties palette. This is accomplished by selecting the desired menu and toggling the "Automatically Route Buttons" option in the Menu Properties. The next step is to click the button routing icon in the Menu Editor. This will bring different icons into view that can display button numbers as well as routing information. To change these settings, use the navigation indicators in conjunction with the Pickwhip. Simply click and drag between buttons to determine the direction and behavior of the button routing. To change button numbers, select the button and make changes in the Properties palette.

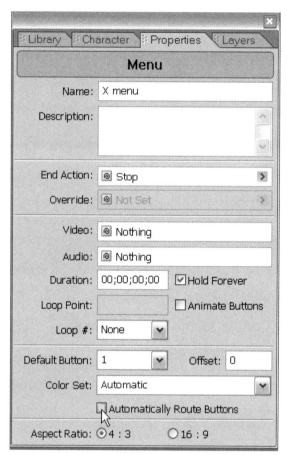

Disabling automatic button routing.

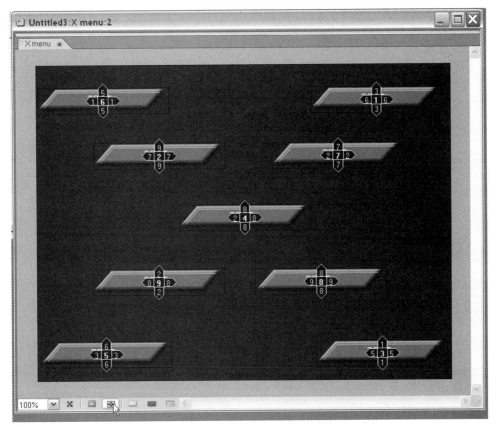

Button routing in the Menu Editor.

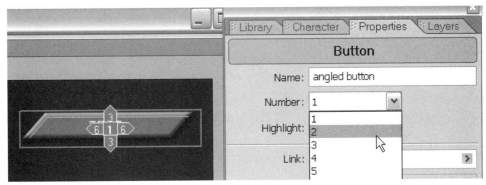

Button number selection in the Properties palette.

PROJECT 15

Let's take a look at a menu that navigates poorly with the automatic button routing.

1. File>Open Project.
2. In the Projects folder find the Project15.ncor file and click Open.
3. Click on the Menu tab and view the menu in the Menu Editor.

As you can see, the buttons are staggered.

4. Right click inside the Menu Editor and select Preview From Here.
5. Using just the Navigation buttons, navigate the buttons.

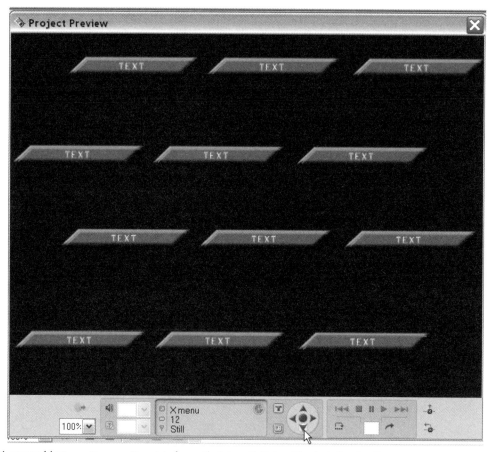

A staggered button pattern sometimes interferes with Automatic Button Routing's functionality.

Because the buttons are staggered off center, the navigation skips rows. This type of problem runs the risk of ruining navigation in the menu.

6 Close the Preview menu and open the Menu Editor.

7. Click on the Button Routing icon.

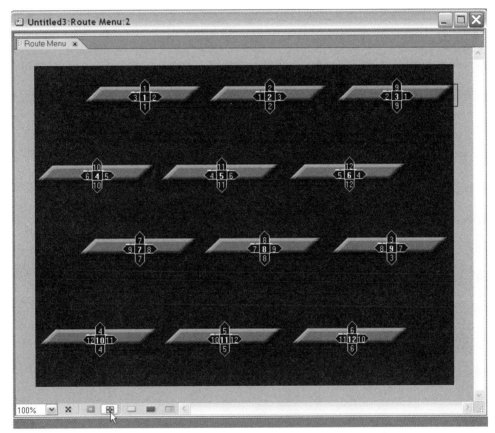

Revealing the button routing reveals the cause of the problem navigation.

You will notice that the numbered crosses appear on each button. However, if you attempt to manually route these buttons, Encore will not allow it.

8. Open the Properties palette for the menu.

9. Uncheck the Automatically Route Buttons box.

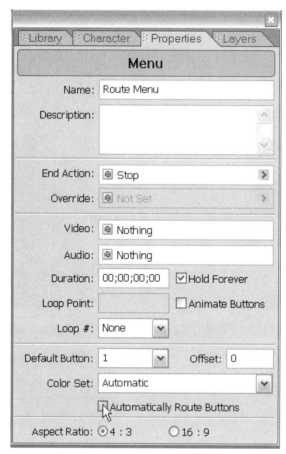

You must uncheck the Automatically Route Buttons box to manually route the buttons.

10. Return to the Menu Editor and route the buttons.

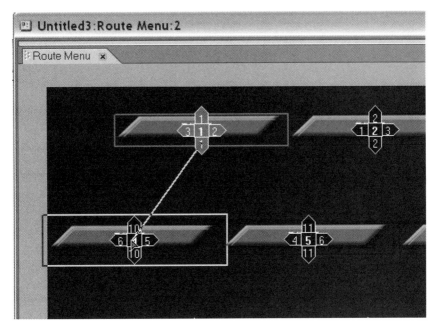

Drag the directional corner of a button to the button you wish to route to.

The route buttons interface uses a Pickwhip feature, allowing you to click and drag a line from a button compass point to another button. In this case, route the down arrow on button number 1 to button number 4 below it. Repeat this process on all buttons that have improper routing.

11. Open the Preview window and check your navigation.

Finally, use the Properties palette to make sure that all buttons are numbered properly.

Use the Menu Editor to see the selection area of your buttons. Click the layer set of a button to view the bounding box that defines the related layers. This bounding box shows the selection area for combined elements of the button.

When played back on a computer, this selection area defines what areas of the menu can be clicked on with a mouse to activate the button.

All layers within the button layer set are combined to define the overall selection area.

If additional text layers are accidentally added to a button's set, this can increase the selection area. Overlapping selection areas between buttons will usually ruin the navigation functionality of a menu.

You can also simply turn off button routing in the Menu Properties and select the different buttons in the Menu Editor. Once selected, the selection areas will become visible. Remember to take a few minutes to double check these settings on every project. A little foresight in the beginning will eliminate huge headaches down the road.

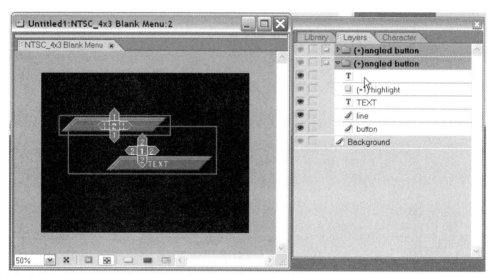

Notice how just one extra text layer made such a huge difference the selection area. Check your Layers palette for blank text layers often.

Project Preview Window

The Project Preview window allows for complex navigation of your project by simulating the interface of a DVD player. It goes without saying that this feature can save you time and money by providing a fully functional preview before burning the project to disc.

Throughout the book we have used the Preview window to check our menus and see our timelines, but it has much more to offer as a disc simulator. You can change your audio tracks and subtitles as you watch the preview.

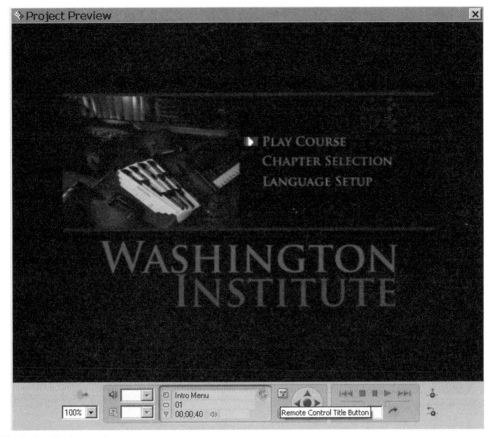

The Project Preview window.

PROJECT 16

1. Locate project16.ncor in the sample files folder.
2. Open the project.

This opens a preassembled project.

3. Select INTROmenu, then open the Menu Editor.

By looking at the Menu Editor, you can see this is much like the project we built in Chapter 6.

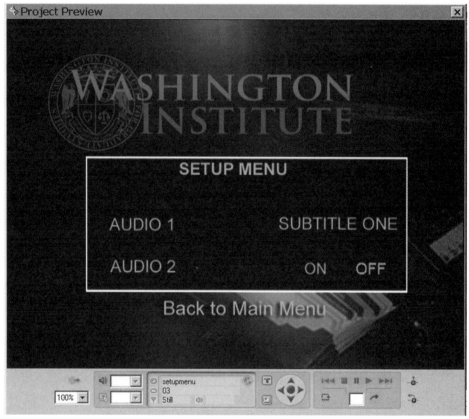

The INTROmenu in the Menu Editor.

If you look at the Project window you can see there are a few additions. We've included two additional audio tracks and another menu. In the Timeline window for the MainContent clip, there is now a subtitle track.

Next, let's open up the Project Preview window.

4.   Go to File>Preview.

Open the window from the File Menu to preview the disc from First Play.

As before, the BeginningSequence clip runs in the INTROmenu background. And we are left with our grey buttons. Now there is a third button for Language Setup.

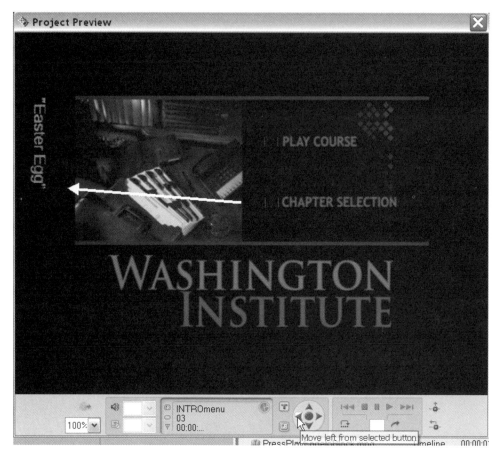

5. Use the center navigation key to select the Language Setup.
6. This opens the Audio and Subtitles menu.

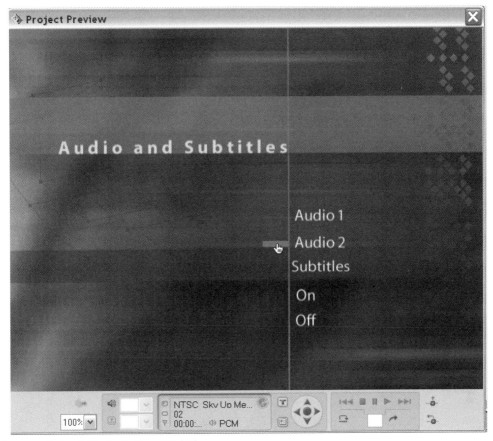

Languages button led to the Audio and Subtitles menu.

Here we have the two audio options and the subtitle option. Selecting any of these buttons takes you back to the main menu.

7. Select Audio 2.

8. Upon returning to the main menu, select Play All.

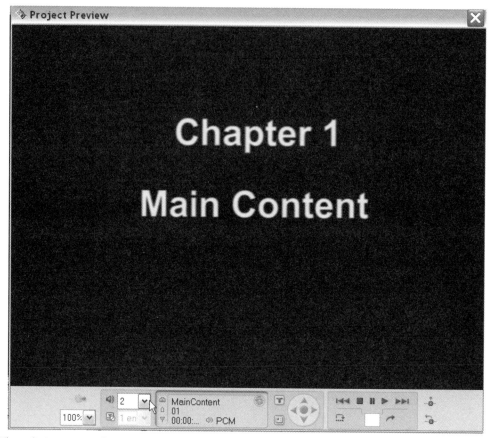

The audio is now on track 2. This can be switched back nearly instantly using the pulldown.

Notice that the audio track is different. To return it to the previous audio track, use the audio pull-down menu in the Preview window. You can also turn on and off the subtitle track from here.

9. As the Tutorials timeline plays through, click on the Remote Control Title button.

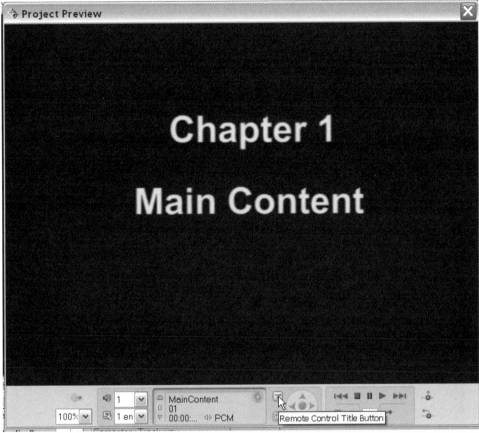

The Remote Control Title button. Press it to return to the default disc menu/timeline.

The Title Menu button brought you back to the INTROmenu. The INTROmenu is the default title menu for this project. It doesn't matter where you are in the disc when you press the Remote Control Title button—it takes you back here. With one exception....

10. Click the Remote Control Title button again.

Notice that the Title button now brings you back to your last place in the timeline.

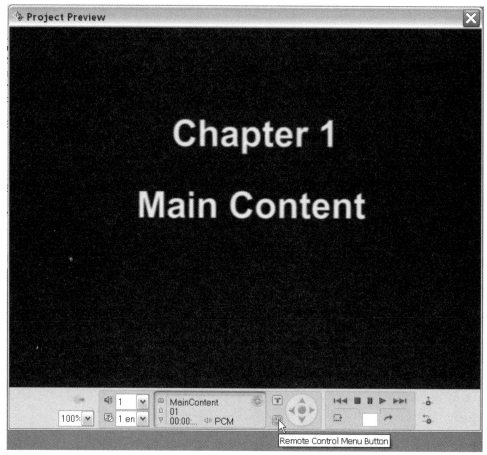

The Remote Control Menu button. Press it to return to the menu/timeline specified in the Properties palette of the current timeline.

11. Click on the Menu button.

Notice that this takes you to the 3chaptermenu. The location that the Remote Control Menu button takes the viewer is specified within the Properties palette *for that timeline.*

TIP: Do not confuse the Menu Remote button for the Title Remote button. The Title Remote button is a global setting, whereas the Menu Remote button is specific for each timeline or menu.

12. Click on Menu Remote button again, and it will take you back to your last place in the MainContent timeline.

In other words, the Title and Menu Remote buttons "pause" the video and return to their designated menus/timelines. But when you hit them again, they return to the video—a very convenient feature.

One of the best features of the Preview window is the Execute End Action button.

13. While playing in the MainContent timeline, click Execute End Action.

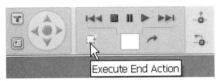

Instead of watching a timeline to the end, or waiting for the menu to complete a large series of loops, this allows you to go to the end and check the end action.

Execute End Action button. This takes you automatically to the end of the timeline/menu.

The Preview window gives you a perspective on how the final DVD will play on a set top or computer DVD player. Take the time in your own projects to check the links and make sure the menus stay on the screen long enough for the audience to make a selection. This is a great time to check the ease of navigation and the final look of your project.

Working with Dual-Layer and Dual-Sided Discs

Most authors will be creating single-sided, single-layer DVD-5 projects. However, Encore also supports dual-layer, single-sided and dual-layer, dual-sided projects. DVD-9 is a format that uses two different layers on a single-sided disc, effectively doubling capacity. This is a professional format that can only be produced by replication houses and is commonly used for Hollywood-style films. Encore also supports many other DVD physical formats such as DVD-5, DVD-9, DVD-10, DVD-14, and DVD-18.

Have you ever been viewing a movie on DVD and noticed a slight pause during playback? Many Hollywood titles are produced on dual-layer discs. The video is encoded on both layers of the disc and will require a slight pause when transitioning between layers. The transition point between layers is known as a layer break. This is very normal and is noticeable on many Hollywood titles.

In the Disc Properties palette, a project settings tab is used to specify the intended format. When creating a dual-layer DVD-9 project, two different DLT tapes are used, each representing one layer of the project. When designing dual-sided discs, a project must be created for each side of the disc, effectively creating two projects that will each produce two DLT tapes. *See Project Settings in Disc Properties Palette section.*

When building a dual-layer project, Encore can create this layer break point automatically. Encore looks for a break between timelines or menus that corresponds closely with the end of the first disc layer. If no such break exists, Encore will prompt the author to specify a chapter point that can be used to determine the layer break.

As an author, it can be a good idea to plan ahead, trying to find the perfect section of source video, then place a chapter point manually. When building the project, simply choose that chapter point and your layer break will be set properly.

Disc Tab

The Disc tab is definitely one of the more versatile windows inside Encore. It provides a lot of options that are typically specified when applying the final touches to a DVD project.

This tab can be used to view the available capacity of a project, and can also be used to specify a name for the disc. It's used to specify copy protection options, region codes, and additional DVD-ROM content.

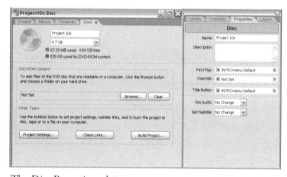

The Disc Properties palette.

Finally, we can use this window to check links, making sure our project doesn't have hidden issues, and export the project.

In the middle of the window, several other options are provided.

Once the Disc tab is selected, the Properties palette can be opened to display even more properties. The Title button can be specified as well as default audio and subtitle tracks.

Adding DVD-ROM Content

There will be times when authors may want to include content that is not intended for set top players. This DVD-ROM content is also referred to as PC content. Common uses for the DVD-ROM content are screensavers or small games or programs. This allows the author to cater the DVD to users that have access to DVD-ROM drives in personal computers.

Encore makes adding PC content relatively easy. All you need to do is access the Disc Properties palette and specify the folder with your content.

DVD-ROM content is added in the Disc Properties tab.

Select a folder containing content meant for a computer.

Disc Information Settings

Toward the top, the author can specify the media and project type. Use this setting to specify disc size as well as the number of sides and layers in the project.

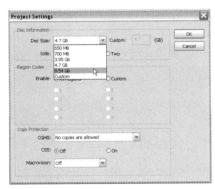

Specify media and project type with the disc information settings.

Typically region codes are most applicable to larger, Hollywood-style movies. They help the entertainment industry maximize profits by maintaining different pricing structures in different parts of the world. Many discs won't require this feature, but if you plan on using Encore in a professional environment, this feature can certainly come in handy.

You'll notice that after specifying the files Encore will immediately update the remaining capacity of the disc. It's very important when planning a DVD project to account for issues such as PC content in the beginning, before video and audio assets are encoded.

Project Settings

Press this button to access copy protection option, region codes, and disc information settings.

Select Project Settings inside the Disc tab.

Region Codes

DVD-Video players are manufactured with a specific region code. When a disc is inserted, the player checks to ensure that it is "authorized" to play the disc.

Region codes determine which regions worldwide that the disc will play in. Several regions are divided across the world....

You can specify regional codes by selecting Custom.

TIP: For projects that contain region codes, CSS copy protection must be specified and the project must be output via DLT tape. Many players will recognize region codes on a burned DVD. This might make a nice tidbit for the adventurous, but if you are serious about region encoding, it must be enforced with CSS and replicated.

Copy protection options.

Copy Protection

Copy protection can be added to projects to help limit or prevent unauthorized duplication of your work.

Multiple forms of copy protection are available.

CGMS (Copy Guard Management System) is a copy control system for DVD recorders that either prevents copies or controls the number of copies that can be made. Inside Encore, CGMS must be set to either "one copy is allowed" or "no copies are allowed" in order to access CSS and Macrovision options.

The Content Scrambling System (CSS) is used to scramble video data on a DVD-Video disc. Content is scrambled using a unique key stored on the disc in encrypted form. In the player, original "master" keys are stored and used to descramble protected content. If unauthorized copies are made, the decryption keys are not included in the duplicated content and playback is not possible. The keys used should be unique for every disc title and are encrypted by the CSS Licensing Authority. This is done at a replication house. CSS is mainly used to prevent digital to digital copies of DVDs using a personal computer.

The **Macrovision Analogue Copy Protection (ACP)** offers analogue copy protection that can supplement CSS encryption. Macrovision modifies a video signal so that it appears distorted when played back from a taped recording of the original. The interference is produced through an interaction between the Macrovision signal and the circuits of the videocassette recorder. Macrovision is typically used to help prevent copying between devices such as DVD players and VCR, DVD recorders, or personal video recorders.

Macrovision utilizes two separate technologies to provide copy protection for the disc.

- **AGC.** AGC is virtually identical to VHS copy protection. This process adds bipolar pulse pairs to the output signal, causing the recording device to record a weak, noisy, and unstable signal.
- **Colorstripe.** Colorstripe has been implemented in digital set top boxes since 1994. This process modulates the phase of colorburst signal, causing annoying horizontal stripes in the picture.

These two processes correspond to three individual settings inside Encore.

- Macrovision Type 1 specifies AGC-only copy protection.
- Macrovision Type 2 specifies AGC + 2 line Colorstripe.
- Macrovision Type 3 specifies AGC + 4 line Colorstripe (more aggressive version of Type 2).

Current model PAL DVD players only output AGC-only (Type 1) copy protection, regardless of which setting is chosen inside Encore.

Reminder: Copy protection options only work when a project is exported to DLT and delivered to a professional replication house. Additional charges will apply. Contact your local replication house for more details.

Checking Links

In the course of a DVD project, many different situations can arise in which content is replaced, deleted, or simply forgotten about. For this reason, Encore provides the Check Links option to help avoid missing links, orphan timelines, or orphan menus.

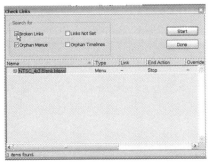

Check Links option locates unlinked, or unused, assets, menus, and timelines.

Orphan menus are menus that are not used in the project; of course, this is the same situation with orphan timelines.

Using the Check Links option, it's possible to search the project for potentially troublesome issues.

Choose between the different parameters to determine if links are not set, or if links are broken. Use the orphan menu and orphan timeline checkboxes to search the project for menus and timelines that are not required for the DVD disc.

Building a Project

Once you have successfully dotted all of your *i*'s and crossed all of your *t*'s, it's time to create a DVD-compliant file that is ready to be burned or output via DLT for professional replication. At this point, make sure you have previewed the project in the Disc Simulation window, and make sure you have explored all of the settings in the Disc Properties window. Make sure your project has a name specified, make sure the transcode settings are set, make sure the disc parameters are specified (single- or dual-layer, etc.), then use the Check Links box to make sure that everything is up to snuff.

Access the DVD Export options in the File Menu.

Make DVD Image

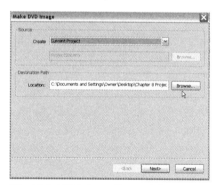

The Make DVD Image Export dialog.

After all that is done, it's time to output the project.

The File Menu offers several options for building a project:

Make DVD Disc

This option burns the project directly to disc (i.e., DVD-R, −RW, +R, +RW, etc.). When building a project intended for local duplication, it's a good idea to build a disc image on a local drive first. See below.

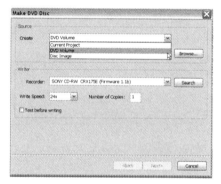

The Make DVD Export dialog.

Encore includes the ability to build a completed project to a hard drive as a disc image. Disc images can be stored on a hard drive for convenient access and local duplication. Creating images is simple and easy, provides another backup of the project, and makes creating subsequent copies a breeze.

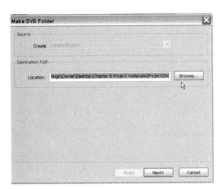

The Make DVD Folder Export dialog.

Make DVD Folder

This option stores the project on a hard drive using a DVD directory structure that includes the Video_TS and Audio_TS folders. These are the same folders that are visible if you view the contents of a DVD-ROM on a computer. This option creates an actual disc volume on a local hard drive allowing you to play the project back using a software DVD player. The player sees the DVD directory exactly as if it were a disc in a DVD-ROM drive. This allows the author another method of previewing, testing, and storing the finished project.

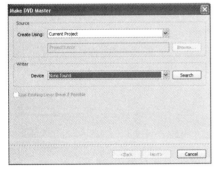

The Make DVD Master Export dialog.

Make DVD Master

This option is for exporting out to DLT. This option requires a DLT drive connected to your computer. See next section.

After choosing one of these options, the Make DVD Disc dialog appears. This window varies depending on your build choice and provides the following options.

More Export Options

Create Using

This setting allows you to specify a project or file to export. The default setting is to export the current project; however, this can be changed to allow exporting disc images or disc folders that have previously been written to a hard drive.

Location

When creating disc images or disc folders, use this setting to specify where the project is written.

Recorder

This specifies which burner the project is sent to. If only one DVD burner is available on your system, this will be visible in this window. If multiple burners are available, use the Browse button to specify the desired device.

Device

This setting is used to specify the DLT drive.

Write Speed

This determines the write speed of the DVD burner. Encore sets the maximum speed by default; however, if a lower setting is desired, this can be easily modified. Some authors report higher compatibility using lower write speeds.

Number of Copies

Use this setting if you wish to burn more than one copy to disc. Encore will automate this process, asking you to change discs as necessary.

Test Before Writing

This setting determines whether Encore simulates the build process before burning to disc. If there are problems, Encore will display the error; if not, the project will continue on and write to disc.

Outputting to DLT (DLT Formats)

DLT, or digital linear tape, is a mass storage format that can be used to deliver DVD projects to a professional replication house. If you plan to utilize copyright protection and region codes, your project must be written to DLT and sent to a replication house. Although it is possible to burn these projects to a regular DVD-R in Encore, the copy protection and region codes will not be included. It's also recommended to check with your local replication house to see if they have any special requirements for submitting a project.

> TIP: DLT Types III and IV are the common DLT formats used by most replication houses. Type III DLT uses a 10/20 gigabyte tape, while Type IV uses 20/40. How do you choose between the two? Type III is the most common. It's also cheaper and provides plenty of capacity.

> TIP: Earlier, it was mentioned that every project should be burned to disc in order to check final links and navigation in a set top player. With DVD-9 this gets more difficult as there are limited ways to burn these projects to a DVD-5 disc. One way of getting around this is to duplicate the project (save the original project in a safe place) and re-encode the major MPEG-2 files to a lower bitrate. After replacing the original MPEG-2 files with highly compressed, smaller versions, you can then burn the project to disc and proceed with checking the disc and navigation in a set top player. The image quality won't be up to par, but if everything works, you can return to your original project and write to DLT knowing that your project works properly.

Appendices

APPENDIX A: KEYBOARD SHORTCUTS

Menu Keyboard Shortcuts

Bring Forward	**Control ·] (right bracket)**
Bring To Front	**Control · Shift ·] (right bracket)**
Constrain aspect ratio on scale	**Shift · Drag**
Constrain movement to 45 degrees	**Shift · Drag**
Convert To Button	**Control · B**
Convert To Object	**Control · Shift · B**
Create Subpicture	**Control · Alt · B**
Drop Shadow	**Control · Shift · O**
Duplicate	**Alt · Drag**
Edit In Photoshop	**Control · Shift · M**
New Menu	**Control · M**
Nudge selection 1 pixel down	**Down Arrow**
Nudge selection 1 pixel to the left	**Left Arrow**
Nudge selection 1 pixel to the right	**Right Arrow**
Nudge selection 1 pixel up	**Up Arrow**
Nudge selection 10 pixels down	**Shift · Down Arrow**
Nudge selection 10 pixels to the left	**Shift · Left Arrow**
Nudge selection 10 pixels to the right	**Shift · Right Arrow**
Nudge selection 10 pixels up	**Shift · Up Arrow**
Open menu from button	**Double-click**
Open timeline from chapter point	**Double-click**
Paste As Subpicture	**Shift · Control · V**
Replace object in menu	**Alt · Drag**
Scale from center point	**Alt · Drag**
Send Backward	**Control · [(left bracket)**
Send To Back	**Control · Shift · [(left bracket)**
Set audio background for motion menu	**Drag**
Set video background for motion menu	**Alt · Drag**
Show Button Routing	**Control · 7**
Show Safe Area	**Control · 6**
	Control · Shift ·] (right bracket)
Show Normal Subpicture	**Control · 3**
Show Selected Subpicture	**Control · 4**
Show Activated Subpicture	**Control · 5**

Windows Keyboard Shortcuts

Add/remove multiple objects from current selection	**Shift · Drag**

Add/remove range of objects from current selection	**Shift · Click**
Add/remove single objects from current selection	**Shift · Click**
Clear	**Delete (del)**
Copy	**Control · C**
Cut	**Control · X**
Cycle through active windows	**Control · Tab**
Cycle through active windows	**Control · F6**
Delete	**Backspace/Delete**
Paste	**Control · V**
Selects current button	**Return/Enter**
Selects current button or controller	**Space Bar**

Text Keyboard Shortcuts

Add to selection by line	**Triple-click · Drag**
Add to selection by paragraph	**Quadruple-click · Drag**
Add to selection by word	**Double-click · Drag**
Enter inline text mode	**Double-click**
Exit inline text edit mode	**Esc**
Increase selection 1 character to the left	**Shift · Left Arrow**
Increase selection 1 character to the right	**Shift · Right Arrow**
Increase selection 1 word left	**Control · Shift · Left Arrow**
Increase selection 1 word right	**Control · Shift · Right Arrow**
Increase selection of text	**Shift · Click**
Increase selection to beginning of line	**Shift · Home**
Increase selection to beginning of text	**Control · Shift · Home**
Increase selection to end of line	**Shift · End**
Increase selection to end of text	**Control · Shift · End**
Increase selection to next paragraph	**Control · Shift · Down Arrow**
Increase selection to previous paragraph	**Control · Shift · Up Arrow**
Move insertion point 1 word left	**Control · Left Arrow**
Move insertion point 1 word right	**Control · Right Arrow**
Move insertion point to beginning of line	**Home**
Move insertion point to beginning of text	**Control · Home**
Move insertion point to end of line	**End**
Move insertion point to end of text	**Control · End**
Move insertion point to next paragraph	**Control · Down Arrow**
Move insertion point to previous paragraph	**Control · Up Arrow**
Move text object	**Control · Drag**

Select line	**Triple-click**
Select paragraph	**Quadruple-click**
Select word	**Double-click**

Project Window Keyboard Shortcuts

Adobe Encore Help	**F1**
Close	**Control · W**
Close Project	**Shift · Control · W**
Close selected folder	**Left Arrow**
Deselect All	**Control · Shift · A**
Disc tab	**F12**
Duplicate	**Control · D**
Exit	**Control · Q**
Exit	**Alt · F4**
Menus tab	**F10**
New Folder	**Shift · Control · N**
New Project	**Control · N**
Open menu or timeline	**Double-click**
Open menu or timeline in new window	**Alt**
Open Project	**Control · O**
Open selected folder	**Right Arrow**
Open/close folders	**Double-click**
Project tab	**F9**
Redo	**Shift · Control · Z**
Rename	**Control · Shift · R**
Save	**Control · S**
Save As	**Control · Shift · S**
Select All	**Control · A**
Select object above the current selection	**Up Arrow**
Select object below the current selection	**Down Arrow**
Timelines tab	**F11**
Undo	**Control · Z**

Timeline Window Keyboard Shortcuts

Add Chapter Point	*** (asterisk)**
Bring Tracks Into View	**Control · Alt · T**
Move CTI one tic mark	**Left Arrow**
Move CTI one tic mark	**Right Arrow**
Move CTI to beginning	**Home**
Move CTI to beginning	**Up Arrow**
Move CTI to end of timeline	**End**

Move CTI to end of timeline	**Down Arrow**
New Timeline	**Control · T**
Play Timeline	**Control · Space Bar**
Play Timeline	**Space Bar**
Save Frame As File	**Shift · Control · F**
Set Poster Frame	**Shift · Control · F1**
Set Poster Frame	**Shift · ★ (asterisk)**
Fit In Window	**Control · 0**
Zoom In	**Control · = (equal)**
Zoom Out	**Control · – (hyphen)**

Miscellaneous Keyboard Shortcuts

Open Character palette	**F6**
Open Layers palette	**F7**
Open Libraries palette	**F8**
Open Properties palette	**F9**
Open Preview mode	**Alt · Control · Space Bar**
Edit Original	**Control · E**
Locate Asset	**Shift · Control · H**
Replace Asset	**Control · H**
Import As Asset	**Control · I**
Import As Asset	**Double-click**
Import As Menu	**Control · Shift · I**
Import As Menu	**Double-click**
Import As Menu	**Alt · Drag**
Toolbar—Switch between Horizontal and Vert Text tools	**T**
Toolbar—Switch to Direct Selection tool	**A (Tap)**
Toolbar—Switch to Direct Selection tool temporarily	**A (Hold)**
Toolbar—Switch to Selection tool	**V (Tap)**
Toolbar—Switch to Selection tool temporarily	**V (Hold)**
Toolbar—Switch to Text tool	**T (Tap)**
Toolbar—Switch to Text tool temporarily	**T (Hold)**
Toolbar—Switch to Vertical Text tool	**Y (Tap)**
Toolbar—Switch to Vertical Text tool temporarily	**Y (Hold)**
Toolbar—Switch to Zoom tool	**Z (Tap)**
Toolbar—Switch to Zoom tool temporarily	**Z (Hold)**
Check Links	**Control · Shift · L**
Link To	**Control · L**

APPENDIX B: RESOURCES

DVD Resources

General DVD information
DVD Forum
www.dvdforum.org

DVD Specification and Logo licensing
DVD Format / Logo Licensing Corp
http://www.dvdfllc.co.jp/

Macrovision
http://www.macrovision.com/
Learn everything you need to know about analog copy protection.

Dolby Labs
www.dolbylabs.com
Loads of great information regarding AC-3 / Dolby Digital compression, tips, tricks, and settings.

Internet Resources

DMNforums / Digital Media Net Communities
http://www.dmnforums.com/
World's largest on-line DV community. Come visit me on the Encore or Premiere Pro forums!

Wes Howell
weshowell@weshowell.com
Feel free to drop me a line with comments or questions on the book.

Video Tutorials online
http://www.weshowell.com/
Updated on a regular basis.

Recommended Books

DVD Authoring and Production – Ralph LaBarge – CMP Books
DVD Demystified – *Jim Taylor* – McGraw Hill

APPENDIX C: MPEG-2 GOP STRUCTURE

GOPs are the smallest increments of MPEG-2 video streams displayed in Encore. Multiple GOPs are combined to create the different sections of your MPEG-2 video stream. When encoded content is imported into Encore, white tic marks in the timeline display the placement of the GOP header, the first frame of every GOP.

The GOP size is referred to inside Encore as the N value, the number of frames between I-frames. The maximum GOP size is 18 frames; the most common is 15 for NTSC and 12 for PAL or Progressive content.

Encore also lists the M value in the encoder settings. The M value is the number of B frames between consecutive I and P frames. The N frame must be a multiple of the M frame value.

GOPs consist of 3 different picture types.

I-frame or Intra Frame

An I-frame, or I-picture, is the first frame of a GOP, also referred to as a reference frame. The I-frame is compressed independently and spatially using an algorithm similar to JPEG. An I-frame can reconstruct the entire source video frame and does not utilize temporal compression. The functionality of an I-frame can be compared to a keyframe in other compression schemes. It's generally best to use only one I-frame per GOP.

P-frame or Predicted Frame

P-frames are based on previous I- and P-frames. A P-frame uses motion vectors to calculate the difference between itself and the frame before it. A P-frame only contains information about how the frame has changed from the previous frame, essentially increasing efficiency by re-using portions of the previous frame that have not changed over time.

B-frame or Bidirectional Predicted Frame

B-frames are somewhat similar to P-frames, differentiating themselves with the ability to use bidirectional motion vectors. B-frames analyze information from (adjacent) previous and next I- and P-frames.

Index